THE SNAITH SCHOOL

PRESENTED . TO . STUART . NORFOLK

FOR . EFFORT . AND . ACHIEVEMENT .

1992-93 . . . .

. . . .

THE WORLD'S
ARMIES

THE W✜RLD'S
ARMIES

An illustrated review of the armies of the world

MILITARY PRESS
New York

A Salamander Book

This 1991 edition published by Military Press, distributed by Outlet Book Company, Inc., a Random House Company, 225 Park Avenue South, New York, New York 10003.

All correspondence concerning the content of this volume should be addressed to Salamander Books Ltd., 129-137 York Way, London N7 9LG, United Kingdom.

Filmset by The Old Mill, London

Designed by Tony Truscott Designs and Paul Johnson

Color Reproduction by Scantrans PTE Ltd, Singapore

Printed and bound in Spain

ISBN 0-517-05240-7

8 7 6 5 4 3 2 1

Photo Credits

The publishers would like to thank all the embassies, defence attaches, and manufacturers who assisted with photographs and information. The efforts of Virginia Ezell in Washington also contributed much to the completion of this book.

Jacket: (front) Associated Press, (back, top left) UKLF, (rest) US DoD, **Endpapers:** US DoD, **Page 1:** Italian Embassy, 2/3: USAF, 4/5: Swiss Armeefotodienst, 6/7: Royal Netherlands Embassy, 8: US Army, 10/11: Canadian Forces, 12/13: US Army, 14/15: US Army, 16: (bottom) US DoD, (rest) US Army, 17: US Army, 18: US Army, 19: (top) US Army, (bottom) McDonnell Douglas, 20: Boeing-Vertol, 21: US Army, 22: USAF, 24: Thyssen Henschel, 25: US Army, 26: ENGESA, 27: Julio A. Montes, 28: (left) USAF, (right) US Army, 29: Frank Spooner/Gamma, 30: US Army, 31: Steyr Defence Products, 32: (left) Julio A. Montes, (right) USAF, 33: (top) USAF, (bottom) Julio A. Montes, 34: (left) US DoD/IRSAIS, (right) USAF, 35: Jamaican DoD, 36/37: Rex Features/SIPA, 38: US Navy, 39: (top) US DoD/IRSAIS, (bottom) US DoD, 40: David Browne, 41: Frank Spooner/Gamma, 42: Singapore MoD, 44: Salamander, 45: HMS *Tamar*, 46: Rex Features/SIPA, 47: Salamander, 48: Salamander, 49: (top left) Salamander, (rest) IRSAIS, 50: (top) Ed Besch, (bottom) Rex Features/SIPA, 51: Steyr Defence Products, 52: US Army, 53: USAF, 54/55: US Army, 56: David Browne, 57: Rex Features/SIPA, 58: Rex Features/SIPA, 59: USAF, 60/61: Singapore MoD, 62: (top) Frank Spooner/Gamma, (bottom) USAF, 63: USAF, 64: Rex Features/SIPA, 65: (left) US Navy, (right) USAF, 66: Australian Defence Photo, 68: Australian Defence Photo, 69: (top) Australian Defence Photo, (bottom) Steyr Defence Products, 70: (top) US Army, (bottom) New Zealand MoD, 71: New Zealand MoD, 72: Polish Embassy, 74/75: Steyr Defence Products, 76/77: Belgian Embassy, 78: Salamander, 79: IRSAIS, 80: Royal Danish Embassy, 81: Finnish Embassy, 82: (top) Rex Features/SIPA, (centre) Thomson-CSF, (bottom) Aerospatiale, 83: (left) Matra, (right) Aerospatiale, 84: (left) US DoD, (right) IRSAIS, 85: Krauss-Maffei, 86: Olympic Hellas S.A., 87: Patrick Walshe, 88: Stato Maggiore Dell'Esercito, 89: (top) Stato Maggiore Dell'Esercito, (bottom) IRSAIS, 90: Royal Netherlands Embassy, 91: Norwegian MoD, 92: Polish Embassy, 93: IRSAIS, 94: Spanish Embassy, 95: (top) Santa Barbara, (rest) Spanish Embassy, 96/97: Swedish MoD, 98/99: Swiss Armeefotodienst, 100/101: IRSAIS, 102/103: Salamander, 104/105:

Contents

Salamander, **106/107:** (top left) Associated Press, (rest) UKLF, **108:** UKLF, **109:** Salamander, **110:** USAF, **112:** (top) US DoD, (bottom) Rex Features/SIPA, **113:** (top) US DoD (bottom) Embassy of Bahrain, **114/115:** USAF, **116:** Frank Spooner/Gamma, **117:** Rex Features/SIPA, **118/119:** Sam Katz/IDF, **120:** (top) USAF, (bottom) Rex Features/SIPA, **121:** Rex Features/SIPA, **122:** Rex Features/SIPA, **123:** (top) Rex Features/SIPA, (bottom) IRSAIS, **124:** (top) US Army, (bottom) Rex Features/SIPA, **125:** USAF, **126/127:** Frank Spooner/Gamma, **128:** USMC, **131:** Embassy of Cameroun, **133:** Rex Features/SIPA, **134:** (top) Rex Features/SIPA, (bottom) David Browne, **136:** David Browne, **137:** USAF, **138:** ARMSCOR, **139:** (top left) Rex Features/SIPA, (rest) ARMSCOR, **140:** Frank Spooner/Gamma, **141:** Rex Features/SIPA,

Endpapers: US Army M113
Page 1: Italian paratrooper
2/3: US Army UH-60A Black Hawks
4/5: Swiss mountain troops
6/7: Dutch YPR 765 (Armoured IFV)

INTRODUCTION

Whether Israeli or Indian, American or Australian, the professional soldier shares many things in common with fellow soldiers around the world, yet he operates as part of a distinctly national unit with its own history, traditions and values; a unit that by its nature must be aware of this fact and of what makes it different — makes it better than the others even — because the occasion may arise when the soldier is called upon to confront another army in war.

There are thought to be 20 million regular soldiers in the world today and 30 or more separate wars raging which are affecting tens of millions of people. An army is considered to be so vital to national survival that there are almost no states that do not have one, and even these exceptions invariably receive protection from larger nations.

Two recent developments have been most significant: the end of the Cold War and the occurrence of the Gulf War. The thaw in the Cold War finally brings to a close the stand-off between two power blocs produced by the end of WWII. The most obvious results of this are the reunification of Germany and its restoration as the power of central Europe, and the re-emergence of sovereign independent nations in the east. These events will have enormous repercussions militarily; already in the Balkans region there are nationalistic rivalries resurfacing which have been frozen for 50 years within totalitarian states, meaning the new armies will perhaps be faced with internal trouble rather than conventional war. It has also removed the raison d'etre for the large armies which formed part of both superpower alliances, and, crucially, it forces the US to review the position of its large forces in Europe. NATO is coping with this by forming plans for a multinational rapid reaction force deployable to trouble spots as required.

The speed of the allies' success in the Gulf War has shown the destructive power of the weaponry possessed by the US and her allies, and how it can decimate an opposing army. Yet the Gulf War has also shown the difference between well-trained, well-motivated professional forces operating with a highly-sophisticated communications and logistics network, and a body of poorly-supplied, badly-motivated conscripts fighting with a broad mixture of ill-matched equipment.

The Gulf War revealed starkly the technological chasm that now exists between rich countries' armies and those of the relatively poor. Although the circumstances were crucially different, the US-led coalition army achieved in weeks what could not be done by fiercely motivated Iranians in nearly a decade.

The very existence of that coalition army was also important, for it showed that with good leadership and a sense of moral purpose armies and countries could be brought together that might otherwise be in confrontation.

As the world changes, so too will its armies. Developments in Europe and their effect on North America has been mentioned, but around the world other changes will be more widely felt. In Latin America there is every chance that several guerrilla wars may ease. The civil war in Nicaragua appears over and the army is scaling down as a result; meanwhile in neighbouring El Salvador the government and left-wing insurgents (FMLN) have indulged in serious and protracted talks aimed at ending a decade of bitter strife. In Asia the tensions over Korea have eased due to the three-way Sino-Soviet-American detente, though elsewhere wars continue to rage unabated in Afghanistan and Cambodia. Throughout south-east Asia and in India there are a variety of ongoing insurgencies. In the Middle East the repercussions of the Gulf War are not yet clear, but the civil war in Iraq goes on, peace in Israel remains distant and victorious participants from the Gulf Cooperation Council are looking to re-equip their armies. In sub-Saharan Africa a number of long running civil wars in Ethiopia and Angola have reached crucial stages and the largest country, South Africa, appears close to fratricidal civil war in many places.

At this crucial stage of history a knowledge of the world's military forces is important. *The World's Armies* is the most informative and highly illustrated guide to the situation today.

List of abbreviations

AAA — Anti-Aircraft Artillery
AAG — Anti-Aircraft Gun
ACE — Allied Command Europe (NATO)
ACR — Advanced Combat Rifle
ADA — Air-Defence Artillery
AFP — Armed Forces of the Philippines
AFV — Armoured Fighting Vehicle
ANP — Armee Nationale Populaire (Algeria)
ANZUS — Australia — New Zealand — United States (defence treaty)
APC — Armoured Personnel Carrier
ARMSCOR — Armaments Corporation of South Africa
ARVN — Army of the Republic of Vietnam (South Vietnam)
ASEAN — Association of South East Asian Nations
ATG — Anti-Tank Gun
ATGM — Anti-Tank Guided Missile
ATGW — Anti-Tank Guided Weapon
BAOR — British Army of the Rhine
CAF — Canadian Armed Forces
CAFGU — Citizens Armed Forces Geographical Units (Philippines)
CENTAG — Central Army Group NATO
CETME — Centro de Estudios Tecnios y Materiales Especiales (Spain)
CF — Citizen Force (South Africa)
CFE — Conventional Forces Europe
CFV — Cavalry Fighting Vehicle
CIST — Chungshan Institute of Science and Technology (Taiwan)
CMBG — Canadian Mechanized Brigade Group
COIN — Counter-Insurgency
CONUS — Continental United States
CPSU — Communist Party of the Soviet Union
CW — Chemical Warfare
DIO — Defence Industries Organization (Iran)
DMZ — De-Militarized Zone
DSP — Special Presidential Division (Zaire)
EAF — Egyptian Armed Forces
EPLF — Eritrean People's Liberation Front (Ethiopia)
ETC — Electro-Thermal-Chemical gun
FAR — Force d'Action Rapide (France)
FAR — Force Armees Royales (Morocco)
FCA — An Forsa Cosanta Aitiuil (Irish Army Reserve)
FDT — Territorial Defence Force (France)
FIBUA — Fighting in Built Up Areas
FIP — Force Improvement Programme (ROK)
FMLN — Farabundo Marti Frente de Liberacion Nacional (El Salvador)
FN — Fabrique Nationale (Belgium)
FNL — Funf Neue Lander (Germany)
FORSCOM — US Army HQ Forces Command
FPDA — Five-Power Defence Alliance
FPM — Free Papua Movement
FRG — Federal Republic of Germany
FROG — Free-Rocket-Over-Ground
GCC — Gulf Cooperation Council
GDP — Gross Domestic Product
GDR — German Democratic Republic
GIAT — Groupement Industriel des Armaments Terrestres (France)
GPMG — General Purpose Machine Gun

GSDF — Ground Self Defence Force (Japan)
H — Howitzer
HEAT — High Explosive Anti-Tank
HMMWV — High Mobility Multipurpose Wheeled Vehicle
ICI — Imperial Chemical Industries (UK)
IDF — Israel Defence Force
IFV — Infantry Fighting Vehicle
IMI — Israel Military Industries
INDPFL — Independent National Democratic Patriotic Front of Liberia
IPKF — Indian Peace-Keeping Force (Sri Lanka)
IRA — Irish Republican Army
IRIGF — Islamic Republic of Iran Ground Force
JDF — Jamaica Defence Force
KDP — Kurdish Democratic Party
KHAD — Ministry of State Security (Afghanistan)
KOPASSUS — Indonesian Special Forces
KOSTRAD — Indonesian Strategic Reserve
KPA — Korean People's Army (North Korea)
LAW — Light Anti-tank Weapon
LPA — Lao People's Army
LTTE — Liberation Tigers of Tamil Eelam (Sri Lanka)
MBT — Main Battle Tank
MFO — Multinational Force and Observers (Sinai)
MILAN — Missile d'Infanterie Leger Anti-char
MLRS — Multiple Launch Rocket System
MOUT — Military Operations on Urbanized Terrain
MPLA — Movement for the Popular Liberation of Angola
MRL — Multiple Rocket Launcher
MSE — Mobile Subscriber Equipment
NATO — North Atlantic Treaty Organization
NBC — Nuclear, Biological, Chemical
NCO — Non-Commissioned Officer
NDF — Namibian Defence Force
NDPFL — National Democratic Patriotic Front of Liberia
NMF — National Maneuvre Force (Philippines)
NPA — New People's Army (Philippines)
NRA — National Resistance Army (Uganda)
NSM — National Service Members
NVA — Nationalen Volks Armee (East Germany)
ODP — People's Defence Organization (Angola)
ONUCA — Observadore de la Unidos Naciones Central America
ORBAT — Order of Battle
OSGAP — Observers Special Group Afghanistan and Pakistan
PACOM — Pacific Command (US Army)
PAP — People's Armed Police (PRC)
PAVN — People's Army of Vietnam
PF — Permanent Force (South Africa)
PLA — People's Liberation Army (PRC)
PNG — Papua New Guinea
POLISARIO — Frente Popular para la Liberacion de Saguia el Hamra y Rio de Oro (Morocco)
PRC — People's Republic of China
RAAWS — Ranger Anti-Armor/Anti-Personnel Weapon System
RAP — Rocket Assisted Projectile
RBA — Royal Bhutan Army
RBAF — Royal Brunei Armed Forces
RCL — Recoilless Rifle
RENAMO — National Resistance of Mozambique
RG — Revolutionary Guard (Iran)
RGFC — Revolutionary Guard Forces Command (Iran)

RL — Rocket Launcher
ROK — Republic of Korea (South Korea)
RPG — Rocket Propelled Grenade
RVN — Republic of Vietnam (South)
SAA — South African Army
SAAF — South African Air Force
SADF — South African Defence Force
SAF — Singapore Armed Forces
SAF — Standing Alert Force (Austria)
SALF — Saudi Arabian Land Force
SAM — Surface-to-Air Missile
SAMS — South African Medical Service
SAN — South African Navy
SANG — Saudi Arabian National Guard
SAS — Special Air Service (UK and Australia)
SAW — Squad Automatic Weapon
SEAD — Suppression of Enemy Air Defences
SF — Special Forces
SFU — Standing Field Units (Austria)
SLA — South Lebanese Army
SOLF — Sultan of Oman's Land Force
SM — Securite Militaire (Algeria)
SNM — Somali National Movement
SPAAG — Self-Propelled Anti-Aircraft Gun
SPAF — Sudanese People's Armed Forces
SPC — Special Purpose Corps (ROK)
SPH — Self-Propelled Howitzer
SPLM — Sudanese People's Liberation Movement
SSF — Special Services Force (Canada)
SSM — Surface-to-Surface Missile
SSO — State Security Organisation (Sudan)
ST — Singapore Technology
SWAPO — South West African People's Organization
TAM — Tanque Argentino Mediano
TDF — Tonga Defence Force
TDF — Transkei Defence Force
TOC — Tactical Operations Commands (Myanmar)
TOW — Tube-launched Optically-tracked Wire-guided
TPDF — Tanzanian People's Defence force
TPLF — Tigrean People's Liberation Front (Ethiopia)
TT — Territorial Troops (Angola)
UAE — United Arab Emirates
UKLF — United Kingdom Land Forces
UKMF — United Kingdom Mobile Forces
UN — United Nations
UNAVM — United Nations Angola Verification Mission
UNDOF — United Nations Disengagement Observer Force (Golan)
UNFICYP — United Nations Force in Cyprus
UNIFIL — United Nations Interim Force in Lebanon
UNIIMOG — United Nations Iran-Iraq Military Observer Group
UNITA — National Union for the Total Liberation of Angola
UNTSO — United Nations Truce Supervision Organization (Jerusalem)
USAF — United States Air Force
USC — United Somali Congress
USDF — Umbufto Swaziland Defence Force
USSR — Union of Soviet Socialist Republics
VDF — Venda Defence Force
VSEL — Vickers Ship and Engineering Limited
YPA — Yugoslav People's Army
ZNA — Zimbabwe National Army

NORTH AMERICA

David Miller

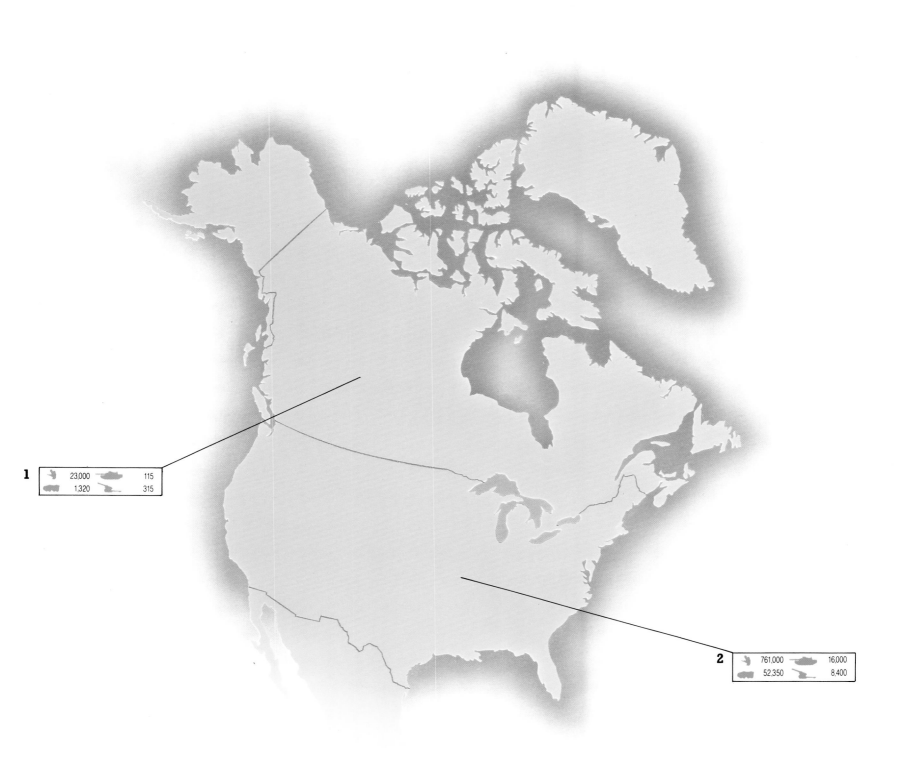

1

	23,000		115
	1,320		315

2

	761,000		16,000
	52,350		8,400

	Men		**Tanks**
	AFVs		**Artillery**

CANADA

CANADA provided very large contingents to assist British forces in both world wars, and since then Canada has managed to maintain full membership of NATO while simultaneously establishing a reputation as an independently-minded country able to play a part in most United Nations' peacekeeping and monitoring operations.

In the 1960s Canada's armed forces were unified and reorganized into five functional commands (Mobile, Maritime, Air, Communication and Training). After a long period, with sometimes painful experiences, the unified Canadian Armed Forces (CAF) now seem to have reached a stage of organizational maturity with three distinct elements recognizable as a navy, army (''Mobile'') and air force, and a fourth element providing such combined support as communications and logistics. All elements are manned by volunteers, and the army has a strength of 23,000 with a reserve of almost 20,000.

A key element in Canadian defence planning has been the retention of land and air forces in western Europe. These are based at Lahr in southern Germany; the 4,000 strong land component is the Canadian Mechanized Brigade Group (CMBG), and is assigned to NATO's Central Army Group (CENTAG). In wartime this would be joined by a brigade from Canada (previously committed to Norway) to form 1st Canadian Division. The Canadian battalion assigned to NATO's ACE Mobile Force is also earmarked for deployment to Norway.

Maintained in Canada itself are a further

Above: The vast spaces of the Canadian north offer ideal conditions and training areas for winter warfare. These men are members of the airborne regiment on an exercise in Ontario. Note that they are carrying snowshoes. Skies require far less effort to use and they are much faster, but they make heavy demands in terms of training time. The SSF does, however, have some of the best such ski troops there are. It contains one company speaking French, one English, one bi-lingual.

Left: The Bell CH-135 Twin Huey in use during an exercise.

Above: The Cougar is a wheeled fire-support vehicle produced in Canada under licence from the Swiss company MOWAG. It is armed with a 76mm gun and has now been joined in service by the LAV-25.

Below: A soldier of the Royal Canadian Regiment Battle School, Petawawa, aiming a 66mm M72 anti-tank weapon. This light, disposable weapon is now old and remains in service in small numbers only.

mechanized group, an infantry brigade group, and an air-defence regiment of four batteries. There is also the powerful Special Services Forces (SSF), composed of one air-borne, one infantry and one armoured regiment, together with full support elements (one artillery, and one engineer regiment). The SSF is essentially a Canadian rapid deployment force trained for action in a variety of climates, from winter weather to desert and jungle. (As a result of the unification all army air support is provided by the air force).

The Canadian land forces use a mixture of equipment. The Leopard 1 MBT has been bought from Germany, while most APCs currently in service are developments of Swiss MOWAG designs.

The CAF have a large commitment, for their size, to UN peace-keeping activities. Currently, these include a battalion in Cyprus (UNFICYP), 240 men in Syria/Israel (UNDOF), 176 men in Central America (ONUCA), 136 in Egypt (MFO), 22 elsewhere in the Middle East (UNTSO), 14 in Iran/Iraq (UNIIMOG) and one in Afghanistan (OSGAP). As with most western countries Canada is currently reviewing its future defence requirements, but it has already stated a firm intention to retain land and air forces in Europe.

EQUIPMENT

Armour:
Leopard C-1 MBT
Lynx & LAV-25 armoured cars
M113, Cougar & Grizzly APCs
Anti-Armour:
84mm Carl Gustav & 106mm M40A1 RCLs
TOW ATGW
Artillery:
155mm M109 SPH
105mm C1 & 155mm M114 Hs
Air-Defence:
35mm Oerlikon GDF-005 SPAAG
ADATS & Blowpipe SAMs

UNITED STATES

WITH A current active strength of some 761,100 men and women the United States Army is the largest of the country's four armed services, the others being the Navy (590,500), Air Force (571,000), and Marine Corps (195,300). However, to the strength of the active army must be added the 454,600 of the Army National Guard and 588,400 of the Army Reserve, for a total strength in the region of 1,794,000. As the war in the Gulf has shown, these can be mobilized and deployed rapidly, efficiently, and in various combinations to meet any operational requirement.

The US Army emerged from WWII with a high reputation, having been extremely successful in the land campaigns in North Africa, Italy, northern Europe, and in the Pacific. As is usual in a democracy, there was a very rapid post-war rundown in strength and capability from 1946 onwards, but this had to be reversed when war broke out unexpectedly in Korea in 1950. That conflict ended with an armistice in 1953, but has required a large US force to remain in the country to this day, with no end to the conflict in sight.

That war had scarcely wound-down, however, when US involvement began to increase in the nearby countries of Vietnam, Laos and Cambodia, then known collectively as French Indochina and where the French had been effectively defeated by the forces of the Communist movement in North Vietnam (the Vietminh), led by General Vo Nguyen Giap. What had been envisaged as a relatively minor commitment in support of the government of the Republic of Vietnam in the south (RVN), turned into a major war, which at its peak involved no less than 539,000 US servicemen inside Vietnam supported by many more outside. Despite all their efforts the Vietnam War ended in a United States' withdrawal in 1973, followed by the defeat of the RVN forces in 1975. It was a humiliation which was to weigh heavily upon the US military, and public opinion, for many years.

The first major combat deployment by the US Army after the Vietnam War was the invasion of Grenada in 1983, a limited action which was completed quickly enough but also revealed some limitations in the US war machine, especially in the crucial area of inter-service cooperation. A second major operation went better, when, in December 1989, the Republic of Panama was taken over in order to oust President Noriega.

Since the end of WWII massive US forces have been deployed in western Europe as part of NATO's answer to the Soviet threat. In early 1990 there were some 211,200, but with the Cold War effectively coming to an end in 1988/89 the US Defense Department, like most of the ministries of defence who took part in it, started to plan deep cuts. The first of these were about to be implemented when Iraqi forces invaded Kuwait and the "Gulf crisis" erupted.

The extremely quick and easy Iraqi victory over Kuwait indicated a major threat not only to the other small Gulf states (Bahrain, Qatar, the United Arab Emirates and Oman), but also to the much larger Saudi Arabia. So, US ground, air and naval forces were deployed rapidly to the area, supported by contingents from many other nations, of which the strongest were those from Saudi Arabia, the UK, France, Syria and Egypt. The initial US forces were followed by even larger numbers of men and women, both regular and reserve, and huge quantities of equipment and supplies — most from the USA — in one of the most massive military deployments ever undertaken. However, one of Saddam Hussein's many miscalculations was to overlook the fact that, with the end of the Cold War in Europe, the threat from the Warsaw Pact had receded to such a low level that large United States' forces could be taken from Germany as well, without affecting the inregrity of NATO forces in central Europe. In Saudi Arabia the entire US Army

Below: Army Rangers moving out from Point Salines airfield during the invasion of Grenada. They made several classic air assaults during the campaign, all were successful.

Above: Specialist skills such as skiing, when needed, can be learned abroad in German or Italian Alpine schools.

Above: Arctic and mountain warfare needs are demanding; US Army Rangers and Special Forces are both prepared for it.

contingent was headed by a unified Central Command under the commander-in-chief, General Norman Schwarzkopf.

The actual scale and complexity of the American logistical moves only became clear after the war when the order of battle (ORBAT) of the US Army forces involved in Operation "*Desert Storm*" was revealed. A list of the major combat formations and their peacetime bases illustrate the scale and complexity of the move, as well as the capability of the USA to concentrate huge military forces anywhere in the world: There were two corps headquarters, VII Corps from Stuttgart in Germany, and XVIII Airborne Corps from Fort Bragg, USA. Each consisted of a number of divisions; VII Corps had 1st Infantry (Fort Riley, Kansas), 1st Armored (Ansbach, Germany), 2nd Armored (Fort Hood, Texas), 3rd Armored (Frankfurt, Germany), 2nd Armored Cavalry Regiment (Nürnberg, Germany), 11th Combat Aviation Brigade (Illesheim, Germany), and the corps' artillery from Augsburg, Germany; XVIII Corps had 24th Infantry (Fort Stewart, Georgia), 82nd Airborne (Fort Bragg, North Carolina), 101st Airborne/Air Assault (Fort Campbell, Kentucky), 1st Cavalry (Fort Hood), 3rd Armored Cavalry Regiment (Fort Bliss, Texas), 12th Combat Aviation Brigade (Wiesbaden, Germany), III Corps Artillery (Fort Sill, Oklahoma), and the XVIII Corps Artillery (Fort Bragg).

Directly under Central Command were a number of other units: 11th Air Defense Artillery Brigade (Fort Bliss, Texas), and two from the reserves, 41th Engineer Brigade (Brooklyn, New York), and 416th Engineer Command (Chicago, Illinois). There was

Below: The Rangers' mission is to strike deep in enemy areas. This means tough training to create quick reactions.

also the Special Forces Command which contained an unspecified number of special operations units among them Delta Force, Rangers, and a number of psychological operations groups.

The US Army is spread across the world to fulfil its country's international obligations and to further its national interests. There are, of course, small groups and individuals in many countries, and there is constant movement due to exercises. A further factor is that the overseas deployments, particularly in the NATO area, are being reviewed in the light of the dramatic end of the Cold War; however, no definite moves have yet been announced.

The largest single permanent peacetime deployment has been to western Europe, and particularly to Germany where there are some 203,000 men and women. The principal formations here are V (US) Corps and VII (US) Corps, both of which are fully committed to NATO as part of the Central Army Group (CENTAG). There are also smaller numbers of army personnel in most other western European countries: Belgium (1,500), Greece (400), Italy (1,400), Netherlands (900), Turkey (1,200) and the United Kingdom (300).

In addition to these, however, there are extensive preparations to move reinforcements from the continental United States (CONUS) to Europe in times of tension or war. Thus, many of the US Army forces committed to NATO remain in the USA in peacetime, but maintain large depots full of equipment (known as POMCUS) and small forward planning HQs in Europe. (Thus, for example, Headquarters III (US) Corps, which has a major role in NATO's war plans, is located in peacetime at Fort Hood in Texas, but maintains its forward headquarters at Maastricht in The Netherlands.) All such formations and units practice their wartime deployments regularly in peacetime in a series of exercises known as "*Reforger*"

Pacific Command (PACOM) is a unified HQ located at Hawaii. Army formations in the theatre include two light-infantry divisions in the US states of Alaska (6th Division)

and Hawaii (25th Division), and there is a heavy-infantry division (2nd Division) in South Korea. There is also an infantry brigade based in Panama.

The bulk of the US Army is in CONUS, where the army formations are grouped under HQ Forces Command (FORSCOM). This command has five subordinate army headquarters and three corps headquarters, and is responsible for the preparation for war of nine active and ten Army National Guard combat divisions, as well as six active and twenty National Guard brigades.

The basic principles of current US operational thought are contained in a doctrine known as the "Air-Land Battle 2000". This has been developed over the past 15 years as a new military theory, basically for use in Europe against a Warsaw Pact attack, although the new doctrine was eventually given a proper test in Operation "Desert Storm". The central idea is a strategic defence by aggressive tactics, which include immediate, sustained and simultaneous attacks, both along the line of contact and in depth (although in the war against Iraq it was modified into a strategic offensive).

The essential element of this doctrine is to attack the enemy throughout the depth of his formations, using air, artillery and electronic means, and by employing a high degree of manoeuvrability. The intention is to cause the enemy to fight in several directions at once, thus not only forcing him to dissipate his resources, but also to confuse him as to when and where the main thrust will be developed. All this involves attacks in great depth, penetrating as much as 200 miles (321km), and fully integrated between the air forces (hence the "air-land" title), artillery and deep-penetration ground units. The doctrine relies upon new technology, especially in command, control and communications systems (the so-called C³) and on the rapid collection, collation and dissemination of intelligence, if it is to achieve its full value.

All this was put to the test in the Gulf War and resulted in one of the most resounding victories of modern times, with the much-vaunted and supposedly battle-hardened Iraqi Army being totally defeated in precisely 100 hours. A series of subterfuges led the Iraqis to believe that there would be a massive amphibious assault by the US Marine Corps, whereas the actual main thrust came many miles inland with a huge US-French armoured attack which cut off the Iraqi Army from its escape routes homewards.

During the Vietnam War all the US armed forces, but particularly the army, devoted increasing attention and resources to special forces (SF). After that war a number of new units were formed, such as the Delta Force led by Col. Charlie Beckwith. The limitations of the approach of that period were shown only too clearly during Operation "Eagle Claw", the attempt to rescue the United States' hostages from Teheran in 1980. The operation fell apart in a series of minor disasters at a landing spot in southern Iran and had to be abandoned, resulting in a major political embarrassment for the United States. The lessons of that debacle, coupled with the pressure of increasing activity by international terrorists, led to US special forces being reorganized and given much greater resources.

Today, the unified Special Operations Command at Fort Bragg controls a large number of assets, of which the army produces the lion's share. The active army provides the 75th Ranger Regiment, based at Fort Benning, Georgia, and five special forces groups, an aviation group and a psychological operations group, together with some supporting units; a total of some 4,000 men and women. There are a further two SF groups and an SF aviation battalion in the Army National Guard, and two SF groups and three psychological operations groups in the Army Reserve.

The missions of these forces may include unconventional warfare, direct action, counter-terrorism, special recce, psychological operations, and civil affairs. Many of these missions are conducted in peacetime, but are also applicable in "hot

Bottom: "Freedom From Oppression" is the motto of 1st Special Forces Group which is worn as an insignia on the green beret.

Below, left: In the Gulf it was feared that gas might be used; an ability to fight in a mask and NBC suit is vital for a soldier's survival.

Below, right: Rangers wading quietly down a stream, practising the skills needed to stage ambushes behind enemy lines.

wars'' and army SF were deployed with considerable success in the Grenada, Panama and Kuwait operations.

The US Army relies for the majority of its equipment on the most efficient and capable industrial base in the world, although there are areas where weapons systems and equipment are bought from abroad. The most evocative symbol of military might is the M1 Abrams MBT, of which over 6,000 are now in service, with a current aim of producing a grand total of 7,789. The initial production version was the M1, armed with the British-designed 105mm main gun, of which 2,374 were produced until January 1985. These were followed by 894 Improved M1s (IPM1), which have enhanced survivability features and an upgraded suspension system; production of these lasted from early 1985 to May 1986. The main production version is the M1A1, of which 4,459 are planned, in which the 105mm main

Below: A line-up in Saudi Arabia of M60 tanks with reactive armour protection.

Above: M1A2 kicks up sand in the desert. The tank more than proved its worth in the heat of battle against Iraq's Soviet-supplied T-72s.

gun has been replaced by the German-developed Rheinmetall 120mm smoothbore main gun. There are also numerous other enhancements to the armoured protection and to the NBC protection system, with yet further improvements to the suspension and drive-train. The latest version is the M1A2, which features many technological enhancements, mainly in the electronic and data-handling areas. Current plans call for just 62 of this model (sufficient to equip only two battalions), but it seems likely that there will be a retrofit programme to bring previous models up to this standard.

The M1-series MBTs are among the most sophisticated MBTs in the world, but they have one feature that sets them apart from the others and that is the fact that they are powered by a gas-turbine engine. This has long been a controversial issue, with criticism being made of a variety of its

characteristics, including its noise, its heavy smoke emissions, its infra-red signature and its fuel consumption. However, the tanks deployed to the Gulf War seem to have performed satisfactorily, albeit against very weak opposition, and it will be of great interest to see what effect the fuel requirements of the somewhat thirsty engine had on the logistic support system.

Despite the fielding of so many M1/IPM1/M1A1/M1A2s, large numbers of 105mm-armed M60s and M48s will remain in US Army service for many years to come. All M60s are currently being upgraded to M60A3TTS standard, which combines all the improvements of the final production version (the M60A3) with the AN/VSG-2 tank thermal sight (TTS). About 1,000 M48A5s remain in the US inventory; most are in storage, but some Army Reserve and Army National Guard units are still equipped with the type.

Below: An M551 light tank with a TOW armed M998 HMMVW Hummer behind it.

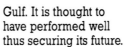

Above: The "Humvee" in the Gulf, armed with an M2 .50in (12.7mm) machine gun and capable of speeds of 70mph (113kmh).

Below: The Bradley IFV played its part in the fast land advance in the Gulf. It is thought to have performed well thus securing its future.

Above: A convoy of M113 APCs. Now quite old, many thouands serve around the world, reconfigured to suit the different local needs.

The development of the M551 Sheridan light tank was dogged by problems, especially in its 152mm combined gun/missile launcher. However, some 1,334 remain in service, and it is still the only light tank in the US inventory. A number were deployed to Saudi Arabia in Operation "Desert Storm".

There are about 30,000 armoured infantry fighting vehicles (AIFV) and armoured personnel carriers (APC) in service. The mainstay is the elderly M113, of which 14,203 are still around; it remains a very suitable vehicle for many tasks, being sturdy and, due to its aluminium construction, not too heavy. Over 80,000 M113 family vehicles have been produced in various factories around the world and the type will remain in service with the US and other armies well into the next century.

US Army fighting units are, however, being re-equipped with the much more advanced M2 Bradley IFV. This vehicle is designed for mounted combat, with a two-man turret equipped with a 25mm "chain-gun", a 7.62mm machine-gun and two TOW anti-tank missile launchers, for which a total of seven rounds is carried. It can carry a nine-man infantry section for whom firing ports exist fitted with special versions of the M16A1 rifle. A total of 6,724 M2 IFVs are currently planned. Closely related to the M2 is the M3 Bradley Cavalry Fighting Vehicle (CFV), which is externally indistinguishable from the M2 IFV and has the same armament and performance. The main difference is that the CFV carries only a five-man section, the extra space being used to carry double the number of rounds for the "chain-gun" and an extra three TOW missiles. There are no firing ports. Some 3,300 M3s are planned.

Fire support is provided by two basic families of self-propelled (SP) artillery pieces. Largest in calibre is the M110A2, consisting of an extended range 203mm (8in) tube mounted on a tracked, non-amphibious chassis. With a maximum range for its rocket-assisted projectiles (RAP) of 32,808yd (30,000m), the M110A2

Below: The M110A2 carries five of its crew of 13. The rest travel in the M548 tracked carrier. Note the hydraulic spade which is lowered prior to the weapon's firing.

can fire a variety of rounds, including high-explosive, chemical and nuclear. Some 1,029 M110A2 are in service.

The other SP weapon is the 155mm M109 with a maximum RAP range of 25,700yd (23,500m). About 2,500 M109s are in service, most of them of the M109A2 and M109A3 sub-types, but most will be upgraded to M109A4 status, with improved reliability and availability, and possibly later to -A5 stan-

dard, with a new tube and re-designed mount to give yet further increases in range. There are also numerous 105mm and 155mm towed guns in service, intended for use in less demanding environments or where air-mobility is required.

Revolutionary techniques are now under development and US artillery could well be of a quite different nature in the next century. Various technologies are being tested,

Left: The M109 serves with many countries. The US Army has the most modern types and allocates over 50 per armoured division.

Below: There are 500 towed 105mm M102s. It is the standard light howitzer for airborne and air-mobile US Army divisions.

including electro-magnetic railguns, electro-magnetic coil guns, and electro-thermal-chemical (ETC) guns. All utilize electrical pulse power, with the ETC guns using electrical energy to initiate and control chemical reactions in the propellant.

The move towards artillery missiles has become more rapid in the past 20 years and in the Gulf War two different US systems were able to prove their value in a most remarkable and public manner. The Multiple-Launch Rocket System (MLRS) has

recently entered service, with some 400 launchers with the US Army (and numerous others in allied armies). The tracked launch vehicle mounts twelve 9in (23cm) rockets, which can be fired either singly or in ripple to a maximum range of some 32,000yd (30km). Designed to use "shoot-and-scoot" tactics, MLRS can deliver a variety of warheads, including high-explosives and-scatterable mines. Other warheads using so-called "smart" munitions are under development.

The other missile to have achieved instant fame in the Gulf was the Patriot surface-to-air missile (SAM). Designed to intercept aircraft at medium- and high-altitudes, it proved to be capable of intercepting incoming Scud missiles at relatively low levels. Its nightly appearances on television protecting Saudi and Israeli targets were dramatic proof of its new capabilities, which were the result of a recently-fielded modification package designed to provide Patriot battery bases with a self-protection capability against Soviet SS-21 and SS-23 tactical missiles used in the counter-battery role.

One of the more tangible signs of decreased tensions in Europe are the arms reductions, as a result of which the US Army's Pershing II surface-to-surface nuclear missiles have been withdrawn from

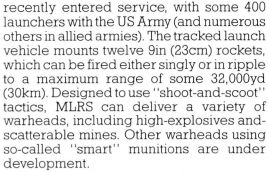

Left: The MLRS gives the US Army awesome firepower. It works under all weather and terrain conditions.

Below: The OH-58D operates as a forward scout helicopter in partnership with the AH-64A Apache.

Europe and are being destroyed. The Lance battlefield missile, however, remains in service with five battalions in Europe and two in CONUS, with an independent battery in South Korea. Production, however, has ceased and plans for a replacement missile have been shelved for the moment.

The US Army controls its own aviation arm, which operates some 700 fixed-wing aircraft and nearly 8,500 helicopters. By agreement with the USAF, the fixed-wing aircraft are light types, performing tasks which the air force is either unable or unwilling to do itself. Apart from liaison tasks, most are involved in electronic warfare duties for which they are fitted with a heavy load of electronic sensors. The most capable type is the Grumman OV-1D Mohawk, a twin turboprop, two-man aircraft which is deployed' in military intelligence battalions. Also involved in electronic intelligence duties is the Guardrail D-series of modified Beech KingAir and Super KingAir twin-engined light transports.

The smallest helicopter in service is the Hughes OH-6A, of which some 340 remain in service with the Army National Guard and Army Reserve, but the numbers are decreasing rapidly. Meanwhile, the Bell OH-58D Kiowa Warrior Scout is the latest development of the long-lived OH-58, with a new drive-train, mast-head sight, laser-designator and improved electronics. Some 151 were in service by March 1990, with an eventual total of 243 expected to be reached by mid-1992.

The largest single component of the huge helicopter fleet are some 3,200 UH-1 Hueys, of which many will serve well beyond 2000. This will give the type in excess of 40 years service with the US Army. However, increasing numbers of UH-60 Black Hawk combat helicopters are taking over in most combat tasks, offering many significant improvements including greater speed, improved reliability and survivability, as well as the ability to carry a full infantry section of 11 soldiers compared to the UH-1's maximum load of eight.

The attack helicopter fleet consists of 1,041 Bell AH-1S HueyCobras and some 534 of the newer McDonnell-Douglas AH-64 Apache. The AH-1S was developed from the UH-1 and is currently being replaced in front-line units by the AH-64, but is being modernized and re-issued to other units, such as the Army National Guard. Meanwhile, increasing numbers of AH-64s are in service and the type acquitted itself with great distinction in the Gulf War — its first major combat deployment.

The US Army also operates some larger transport helicopters. There are 102 of the older models of the CH-47 Chinook and 270 of the latest and much improved -D model, with most of the earlier types being earmarked for eventual upgrading to -D standard. Some 70 or so of the older but still very effective CH-54 Tarhe flying cranes also remain in service. Helicopters are also of great value to special forces and both the Sikorsky MH-60K Black Hawk and Boeing MH-47E Chinook have been specially developed for such use with upgraded engines, increased range (including in-

Above: Troops in the Gulf mount their UH-60 Black Hawks and head for the action.

Below: A sight to fear, an AH-64 Apache hovering menacingly with bad intentions.

flight refuelling), and enhanced electronics and navigation systems.

Nothing affects the individual soldier more than his personal weapon. The US Army's current service rifle is the 5.56mm M16A2, an improved version of the M16A1 from which it differs in having a slightly longer and heavier barrel which is capable of much more accurate fire. There are numerous other minor improvements, such as a new foresight, a spent-cartridge case deflector and a three-round burst control device. The M16A2 will be replaced at the turn of the century by the Advanced Combat Rifle (ACR), which will include many

new features. Among the technologies being investigated are caseless rounds; high-velocity, low-impulse projectiles, and multiple projectiles.

Also currently being fielded is the M24 7.62mm sniper rifle. A six-shot, bolt-action, repeating weapon, firing special 7.62mm rounds. It is being issued to SF units as well as to conventional infantry battalions. The M1911A1 0.45in (11.4mm) pistol entered service with the US Army in 1926 and is only now being replaced by a new weapon: the Beretta 9mm M9. No less than 315,930 are currently on order for all the US military services, with an estimated completion date of 1994; many more are likely to be purchased. Finally, the 5.56mm M249 Squad Automatic Weapon (SAW) is the new basic

infantry general-purpose machine-gun, weighing 15.5lb (7.03kg) empty compared to the 23lb (10.84kg) of the 7.62mm M60 it is replacing.

It is sometimes alleged that the USA fails to make use of foreign military equipment, preferring instead to use its industrial and military strength to persuade other armies to buy US equipment. It is certainly true that a great deal of American equipment is sold abroad, but it is equally true that the US Army uses a lot of foreign equipment. For example, the new 9mm pistol is an Italian Beretta design, the Squad Automatic Weapon (SAW) comes from FN of Belgium, the Ranger Anti-Armor/Anti-Personnel Weapon System (RAAWS) is based on the Swedish Carl Gustav recoilless rifle, the

Below: The US Army has 700 Chinooks. It can carry a load of 28,000lb (12,700kg).

81mm mortar is a British Royal Ordnance design, and the new 120mm mortar comes from Soltam in Israel. The standard 105mm towed howitzer is the British L118 Light Gun, while on the MBT the British 105mm rifled gun is being superseded by the German 120mm smoothbore. Finally, in this by no means comprehensive list, mention must be made of the Mobile Subscriber Equipment (MSE) the new tactical communications system which is based directly on the French RITA system.

The US Army performed well in the Vietnam War, despite the grave disadvantage of intense opposition to the war from many civilian elements at home. Since that time the army has gone onto an all-regular basis and has been gradually but surely

rebuilding its self-confidence. The operation in Grenada contributed to that process, as did the overrunning of Panama, but these were very minor in size and influence compared to the desert war and the re-taking of Kuwait in early 1991. In this latest war the US Army showed its ability at the operational and tactical levels, as well as demonstrating the soundness of the all-regular concept. Doubtless there will be many detailed, post-war examinations of the performance of the US Army — including its doctrine and equipment — with a view to improving effectiveness even further. One thing is, however, clear: that, while it is by no means the largest, the US Army is almost certainly the most efficient and best equipped army in the world today.

EQUIPMENT

Armour:
M1/M1A1 MBTs
M6OA1/M6OA3 MBTs
M48 medium tank
M551 Sheridan light tank
M2/M3 Bradley IFVs
M577 & M113 APCS

Anti-Armour:
90mm & 106mm RCLs
TOW & Dragon ATGWs

Artillery:
155mm M109A1/A2 SPH
203mm M11OA1/A2 SPH
105mm M101, M102 & M119 Hs
155mm M114 & M198 Hs
227mm MLRS

Air-Defence:
20mm M167 Vulcan & M163 SPAAGs
40mm M42 SPAAG
Patriot, Improved Hawk, Chapparal, Avenger, Stinger & Redeye SAMs

Aircraft:
Beechcraft U-8/RU-8D Seminole
Beechcraft C-12D, RC-12D/G/H, RU-21J
Beechcraft T-42 Cochise
Cessna U-3A/B
Cessna T-41B Mescalero
De Havilland Canada UV-18A Twin Otter
Grumman OV-1C/RV1D Mohawk
Helio U-10A Courier
Shorts C-23 SD3-30 Sherpa 3
Bell UH-1, EH-1H Iroquois (Huey)
Bell AH-1S HueyCobra
Bell OH-58A/C Kiowa & OH-58D Kiowa Warrior Scout
Boeing-Vertol CH-47A/B/C/D Chinook
McDonnell-Douglas OH-6A Cayuse
McDonnell-Douglas AH-64A Apache
Sikorsky CH-54A Tarhe
Sikorsky UH/MH-60A EH-60 Black Hawk

Left: A paratrooper cradles his M60E3 during a desert patrol. The M60 has mostly been replaced by FN's 5.56mm SAW.

Below: Shaded by a Saudi palm tree, an 82nd Airborne soldier holds an M16A2 rifle. It has an effective range of 875yds (800m).

CENTRAL AND SOUTH AMERICA

Adrian English

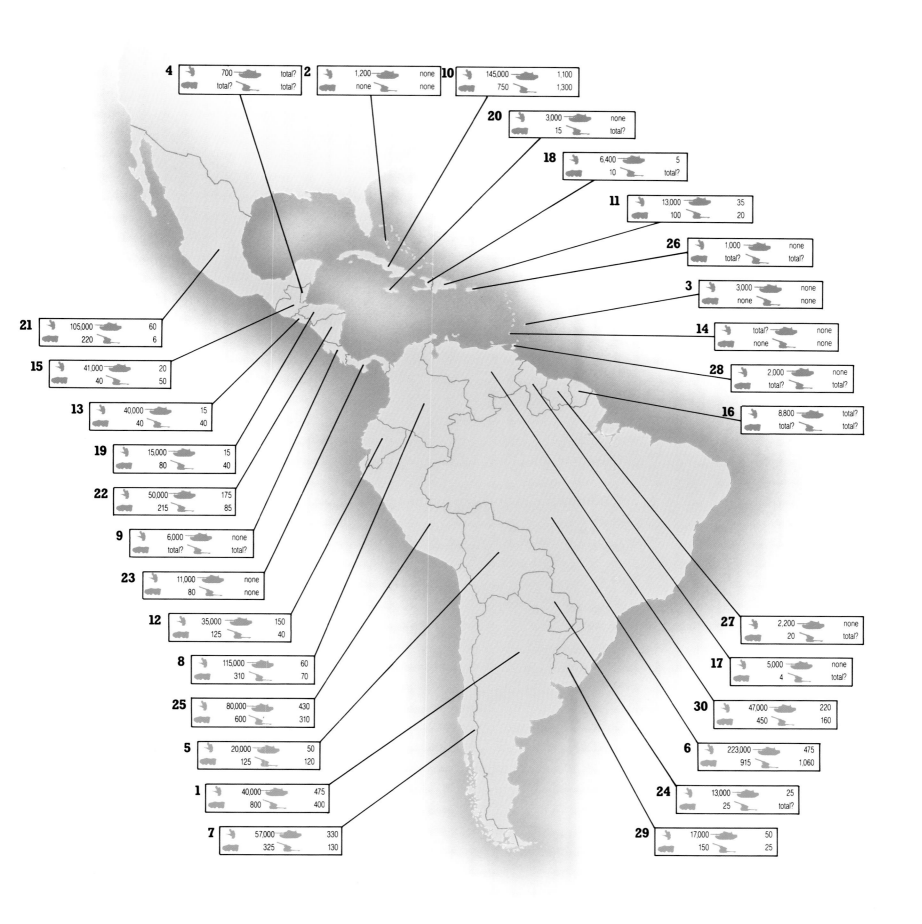

4 700 / total? / total? / total?

2 1,200 / none / none / none

10 145,000 / 1,100 / 750 / 1,300

20 3,000 / none / 15 / total?

18 6,400 / 5 / 10 / total?

11 13,000 / 35 / 100 / 20

26 1,000 / none / total? / total?

3 3,000 / none / none / none

14 total? / none / none / none

28 2,000 / none / total? / total?

21 105,000 / 60 / 220 / 6

16 8,800 / total? / total? / total?

15 41,000 / 20 / 40 / 50

13 40,000 / 15 / 40 / 40

19 15,000 / 15 / 80 / 40

22 50,000 / 175 / 215 / 85

9 6,000 / none / total? / total?

23 11,000 / none / 80 / none

12 35,000 / 150 / 125 / 40

27 2,200 / none / 20 / total?

8 115,000 / 60 / 310 / 70

17 5,000 / none / 4 / total?

25 80,000 / 430 / 600 / 310

30 47,000 / 220 / 450 / 160

5 20,000 / 50 / 125 / 120

6 223,000 / 475 / 915 / 1,060

1 40,000 / 475 / 800 / 400

24 13,000 / 25 / 25 / total?

7 57,000 / 330 / 325 / 130

29 17,000 / 50 / 150 / 25

Men — Tanks
AFVs — Artillery

ARGENTINA

Above: Developed in Germany the Tanque Argentino Mediano (TAM) was purpose-built for South American bridges and roads which it was felt would not be strong enough for 40 and 50 ton. Also, the chassis could be used for an infantry fighting vehicle. Some 350 are in service and it is reputed to have good mobility and firepower with its 105mm gun.

A FRONTIER dispute with Chile almost led to war in the early 1900s and again during the late 1970s but it was not until the 1982 Falklands War with Britain that Argentina indulged in a major external military engagement. Despite their defeat, the acquisition of the Falkland Islands remains a cornerstone of Argentine foreign policy.

Before the Falklands War the Argentine Army was regarded as one of the best in Latin America. From the 1930s onwards it had been adopting an increasingly political orientation and despite a successful anti-guerrilla campaign during the late 1970s the Anglo-Argentine conflict exposed many defects of leadership, training and organization. Since the return to civilian government it has suffered from curtailed budgets and reduced manpower, leading to a number of minor military uprisings.

The country is divided into five military regions: the first covers Buenos Aires and most of the centre of the country, the second the north-east, the third the north-west, the fourth the west and the fifth the south.

Up to and including the Falklands War the army was organized in five corps — one per military region — comprising a total of two armoured, three mechanized, one airborne, two infantry, three mountain and one jungle brigades, with no intermediate divisional organization. The politically-motivated disbanding of I Corps, with headquarters (HQ) at Buenos Aires was one of the first acts of the Alfonsín civilian administration when it took office in 1984. The 7th Jungle Brigade was also suppressed, its constituent units being divided between the 8th Mountain and 12th Infantry Brigades. Both the 3rd Infantry and 8th Mountain Brigades were reduced and a force based on an establishment strength of over 100,000 is now manned by little over 40,000

The Argentine Army currently comprises II Corps (HQ Rosario) with the 2nd Armoured Brigade at Paraná and the 3rd and 12th Infantry Brigades at Curuzú-Cuatiá and Posadas, respectively; III Corps (HQ Córdoba) with the 4th Airborne Brigade at Córdoba and the 8th Mountain Brigade at Mendoza; IV Corps (HQ Tucumán) consisting of only the 5th Mountain Brigade at Tucumán; and V Corps (HQ Bahia Blanca) with the 1st Armoured Brigade at Tandil, the 6th Mountain Brigade at Neuquén and the 9th and 11th Mechanized Brigades at Comodoro Rivadavia and Rio Gallegos. The 10th Mechanized Brigade, at La Plata, is directly subordinate to army headquarters, as are the "Granaderos a Caballo" Cavalry and the 1st "Patricios" Motorized Infantry Regiments, both of which perform ceremonial duties in Buenos Aires.

Each brigade consists of three regiments (battalions) of the main arm, plus a recce squadron, a battalion-sized group of artillery, a logistic support battalion and companies of engineers and signals. Each corps also has a battalion-sized armoured recce unit, a group of medium artillery, an air-defence artillery group, and engineer, signals, logistic and ordnance battalions; these support units being numbered 121 in the case of II Corps, 141 in that of III, 161 in that of IV and 181 in the case of the V Corps. II Corps also incorporates some units numbered in the 101 series which formerly belonged to the defunct I Corps. In addition, at HQ level, there are a number of engineer, signals, logistic, medical and veterinary units numbered in the 601 series, together with the 601st Commando Company, the 601st Aviation Battalion and the 601st Aviation Maintenance and Support Company.

The contemporary Argentine Army lacks a military police corps, the military police battalions which existed at army and corps level having been disbanded, together with the brigade military police companies, due to the heavy involvement of the military police in the so-called "dirty war" against terrorists from 1975 to 1983.

A project aimed at maximizing the effectiveness of the limited available resources is being considered at present. This involves the abandonment of the present system of selective compulsory military service in favour of an all-professional army which would be reduced to five or six brigades, all of which would be equipped and manned to full war establishment. The creation of a Rapid Deployment Force is also being discussed

Recruits receive their basic training in the units to which they are assigned. Further specialist training is received at the Escuelas de Aplicación of the various arms and services, most of which are located at Campo de Mayo outside Buenos Aires. The Airborne Forces School is at Córdoba, and the Mountain and Jungle Warfare Schools are at Mendoza and Corrientes respectively. Regular NCOs are trained at the Escuela de Suboficiales "Sargento Cabral".

EQUIPMENT

Armour:
TAM medium tank
AMX-13 light tank
Kurassier tank destroyer
Panhard AML-90 armoured car
TAM & AMX IFVs
M113 & MOWAG Grenadier APCs
Anti-Armour:
90mm M67 RCL
SS-11, SS-12, Cobra & Mathogo ATGWs
Artillery:
105mm M56 & M101 Hs
155mm M2 & MM L33 Hs
155mm F3 SPH
105mm SLAM Pampero MRL
127mm SAPBA-1 MRL
Air-Defence Weapons:
20mm Rheinmetall Rh-202, 35mm
Oerlikon K63 & 40mm Bofors L/60 AAGs
Tigercat, Roland & Blowpipe SAMs
Aircraft:
Agusta A.109
Bell 47, & UH-1H Iroquois
Aerospatiale SA.315 Alouette II, SA.330J
& SA.332B
Boeing-Vertol CH-47 Chinook

BAHAMAS

THE BAHAMAS maintains no armed forces although its 1,200 strong police force is a paramilitary organization equipped with modern small arms and trained to offer some military resistance in the event of invasion.

BARBADOS

BARBADOS has a single-battalion part-time army, expanding to 3,000 on mobilization. Most equipment is of British origins and training assistance is also provided by Britain. It provided troops for the Caribbean force in Grenada.

BELIZE

THE ENTIRE territory of Belize is claimed by Guatemala, the pretensions of which have been so far restrained by the presence of a token British military force consisting of a single infantry battalion, a troop of Scorpion tanks, a field battery, an air-defence battery, an engineer squadron, and a flight each of Harrier fighters, Puma and Gazelle helicopters.

A tri-service Belizean Defence Force, with a target strength of 3,000, is in the process of being formed. Its 700-man ground element is made up of a single infantry battalion with three reserve rifle companies.

Although other ranks receive their basic training in the country, officers, senior NCOs and specialists are trained either in the United Kingdom, Canada or the United States.

Their weaponry is a mixture of small arms, including M16A1s and L7 Brens.

Right: Paratroopers from the battalion attached to 7th Division line up ready to board their C-130 transporter. The unit was formed in the 1960s and took part in the COIN effort against Che Guevara's guerrillas. The Jump Commando badge, an advanced award, is visible on the left sleeves of a number of soldiers. US instructor personnel are often involved in these exercises.

BOLIVIA

BOLIVIA HAS suffered losses of territory to almost all of its neighbours in a series of disastrous wars, the most recent of which was against Paraguay in 1932/35. Although relations with the latter country are relatively cordial, resentment against Chile continues for having deprived Bolivia of its sea coast as a result of the Pacific War of 1879/83. Bolivia is also a centre of illicit narcotics production and the United States is assisting the Bolivian Government in a campaign against traffickers.

The country is divided into six military regions. The first (HQ La Paz) covers the capital and the western part of the country, the second (HQ Sucre) the centre, the third (HQ Tarija) the south-east, the fourth (HQ Potosi) the south-west, the fifth (HQ Trinidad) the east and the sixth (HQ Cobija) the north-western part of the country.

The 20,000-man Bolivian Army is organized in ten divisions, the composition of which is highly variable. Military service is theoretically compulsory but in practice it is enforced on a selective basis.

The 1st Division (HQ Viacha) comprises three ordinary and one mechanized infantry regiments, a mechanized cavalry regiment, an armoured battalion, a tank battalion, an artillery regiment, an air-defence group and a military police battalion. The 2nd Division (HQ Oruro) consists of two infantry, two Andean and one Ranger regiments, an armoured battalion, an artillery regiment and an air-defence group. The 3rd and 4th Divisions (HQs Villamontes and Camiri, respectively) each consist of three infantry, one cavalry and one artillery regiments, plus an engineer battalion. The 5th Division (HQ Roboré) has four regiments of infantry, one each of cavalry and artillery and an engineer battalion.

The 6th Division (HQ Trinidad) comprises three infantry, one cavalry and one artillery regiments, plus two engineer battalions. The 7th Division (HQ Cochabamba) comprises one infantry, one mechanized infantry and one Andean regiments, a paratroop battalion, a tank battalion and an artillery regiment. The 8th Division (HQ Santa Cruz) has one ordinary infantry, one mechanized infantry, one Ranger, one cavalry and one artillery regiments, an air-defence group and an engineer battalion. The 9th Division (HQ Apolo) contains three infantry, one Andean and one cavalry regiments, plus an engineer battalion. Finally, the 10th Division (HQ Tupiza) has only two infantry regiments, a cavalry regiment, an artillery regiment and part of an engineer battalion which it shares with the 4th Division.

Conscripts receive their training mainly in the units to which they are assigned. The Paratroop School is at Cochabamba, the Special Forces School at Santa Cruz, the Mountain Warfare School at Coraguara de Carangás, the Jungle Warfare School at Riberalta, the Armoured Forces School at Viacha and the Artillery School at Cochabamba.

EQUIPMENT

Armour:
Kurassier tank destroyer
EE-9 Cascavel & V-150 Commando armoured cars
EE-11 Urutu, MOWAG Roland Steyr 4K7FA & M113 APCs
Anti-Armour:
106mm M40A1 RCL
Artillery:
75mm M116 H
105mm M101 H
Air-Defence:
20mm single & twin Oerlikon AAGs

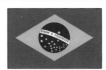

BRAZIL

BRAZIL supported the Allies actively in both world wars and aspires to spread its influence throughout Africa and the Middle East. It has no real or potential enemies among its immediate neighbours.

The Brazilian Army, numbering 223,000 and scheduled to increase to 296,000 by 1993, is organized into both garrison and manoeuvre elements. There are twelve military regions divided between seven geographical commands and comprising eight divisions. These eight are further divided into one armoured cavalry and four mechanized cavalry brigades, three armoured infantry and 10 motorized infantry brigades, and four infantry, one paratroop, two jungle and one mixed brigades.

Eastern Military Command (HQ Rio) embraces the First and Fourth Military Regions and contains the 1st Division (HQ Rio), consisting of the 1st Motorized Infantry and the 2nd Infantry Brigades (HQs Petrópolis and Niterói, respectively), and the 4th Division (HQ Belo Horizonte) consisting only of the 4th Infantry Brigade. This command also contains the independent 9th Motorized Infantry Training Brigade and the Paratroop Brigade, both based at Rio.

South Eastern Military Command (HQ Sao Paulo) coincides with the Second Military Region and contains the 2nd Division (HQ Sao Paulo) which is made up of the 11th Armoured Infantry and the 12th Infantry Brigades (HQs Campinas and Cacapava).

Western Military Command (HQ Campo Grande) coincides with the Ninth Military Region and contains the 9th Division (HQ Campo Grande) consisting only of the 13th Motorized Infantry Brigade (HQ Cuiaba). This command also houses the independent 2nd Mixed Brigade (HQ Corumbá).

Southern Military Command (HQ Porto Alegre) embraces the Third and Fifth Military Regions and contains the 3rd, 5th and 6th Divisions, plus the 1st, 2nd and 3rd Mechanized and the 5th Armoured Cavalry Brigades. The 3rd Division (HQ Santa Maria) consists of the 6th Armoured and the 16th Motorized Infantry Brigades (HQs Santa Maria and Santo Angelo, respectively) the 5th Division (HQ Curitiba) comprises the 5th Armoured and the 14th and 15th Motorized Infantry Brigades (HQs Ponta Grossa, Florianópolis and Cascavel); and the 6th Division (HQ Porto Alegre) contains only the 8th Motorized Infantry Brigade (HQ Pelotas). The HQs of the 1st, 2nd and 3rd Mechanized Cavalry Brigades are at Santiago, Uruguaiana and Bagé; that of the 5th Armoured Cavalry Brigade is at Santa Catarina.

North Eastern Military Command (HQ Recife) embraces the Sixth, Seventh and Tenth Military Regions and contains the 7th Division (HQ Recife) made up of the 7th and 10th Motorized Infantry Brigades (HQs Natal and Recife).

Planalto Military Command (HQ Brasilia) coincides with the Eleventh Military Region and contains the 3rd Motorized Infantry Brigade (HQ Goiania). Lastly, there is Amazonia Military Command (HQ Manáus) which embraces the Eighth and Twelfth Military Regions and contains the 17th Infantry and the 23rd Jungle Infantry Brigades (HQs Porto Velho and Marabá). Also under this command are the Amapá Frontier Command (HQ Macapa), the Southern Frontier Command (HQ Tabatinga) and the Roraima Frontier Command (HQ Boa Vista), each of which approximates to a weak brigade.

Each brigade usually consists of three battalions of infantry or three regiments of cavalry, a mechanized cavalry recce squadron, a group of artillery, an air-defence battery, a battalion or company of engineers and signals, and a logistic battalion. The divisions then add a group of medium artillery and a logistic battalion plus sometimes a mechanized cavalry regiment and a battalion of engineers or signals. The garrisons of the military regions vary enormously, consisting of from one to ten infantry battalions, a variable number of cavalry regiments, one or more field artillery groups, construction engineer, signals, logistic and military police units and up to five coastal and anti-aircraft artillery groups.

The first of a projected fourteen helicopter-equipped aviation battalions has been formed in Sao Paulo state. These will enable the projection of the army's power into previously inaccessible areas,often dense jungle and rainforest, in order, perhaps, to evict illegal squatters.

Military service is theoretically compulsory and approximately 140,000 conscripts are trained each year. However, over 50 per cent of the army's enlisted personnel are long-service volunteers who follow the same pattern of initial training to that of the conscripts but then continue in the specialist school of the arm or service to which they are assigned. There is a comprehensive selection of such specialist schools, most of them located in the vicinity of Rio de Janeiro, although the Jungle Warfare School is located at Manáus.

Aspiring officers may commence their military education at age 11 or 12 in one of the nine Colegios Militares. These

Below: The EE-T1 Osorio has not proceeded beyond the prototype stage, one of which was built with a Royal Ordnance 105mm rifled gun and another with the GIAT 120mm smoothbore; the latter is shown here.

impart a high-quality secondary education with a military flavour. On completion of their general education in the above establishments students pass automatically to the Escola Preparatoria de Cadetes do Exército at Campinas, 100km west of Rio de Janeiro. Here they complete a three-year course of pre-military education from which they pass directly to the Military Academy of Agulhas Negras, also at Campinas. Senior NCOs may also qualify to attend the academy by passing a course at their schools.

The basic course at the Military Academy is of four years duration, the first two of which are devoted to general subjects, the second two years being devoted to purely military subjects. The entire course is university-level standard. The summit of Brazil's very comprehensive military educational system is the joint-service Superior War College at Brasília.

EQUIPMENT

Armour:
EE-TI Osorio MBT
X1A, X1A2, M41 & M3A1 light tanks
EE-9 Cascavel & M8 armoured cars
EE-11 Urutu & M113 APCs
Anti-Armour:
106mm M40A1 RCL
Cobra & TOW ATGWs
Artillery:
105mm M101A1 & M2A1 Hs
105mm M108 & M7 SPHs
108mm SS-06 & 155mm M114A1 Hs
114mm SS-40 & 300mm SS-60 MRLs
Air-Defence:
12.7mm M55, 35mm Oerlikon GDF-002 & 40mm Bofors L/60 & L/70 AAGs
Roland SAM

CHILE

THE CHILEAN Armed Forces earned a reputation for efficiency in successful wars against an alliance of Peru and Bolivia in 1833-39 and again in 1879-83. They have also exerted considerable influence on the armed forces of many other countries of the region through their training missions, and Chilean military schools continue to attract students from many of the smaller Latin American countries.

Tension continues with both Bolivia and Peru, and there is also a perennial rivalry with Argentina which almost led to war in the early 1900s and again in the late 1970s, causing Chile to afford covert assistance to Britain in the Falklands War of 1982.

The 57,000 strong Chilean Army divides the country into six military areas, each of which is garrisoned by a division (plus an independent brigade in the case of the Fourth Area). A corps organization has recently been imposed on the existing divisional structure. The organization of I Corps (HQ Iquique) combines the existing 1st, 2nd and 6th Divisions, whereas II Corps (HQ Punta Arenas) groups together the 3rd, 4th and 5th Divisions with the 7th Brigade.

The 1st Division (HQ Antofagasta) covers the First Military Area with three motorized infantry regiments, a commando battalion, an armoured cavalry regiment, an artillery regiment, an independent ATGW company, an engineer regiment, a signals regiment and a logistic battalion.

The 2nd Division (HQ Santiago) covers the Second Military Area with two motorized and five mountain infantry regiments, a commando battalion, a motorcycle recce group, an armoured cavalry regiment, an artillery regiment and an engineer regiment, plus signals, supply and transport battalions.

The 3rd Division (HQ Concepción) covers the Third Military Area with two infantry and three mountain infantry regiments, a commando battalion, two armoured cavalry regiments, an artillery regiment, an engineer regiment and a signals regiment, plus a logistic battalion.

The 4th Division (HQ Valdivia), together with the 7th Brigade, covers the Fourth Military Area and is made up of two infantry and one mountain infantry regiments, a commando battalion, two armoured cavalry regiments, a tank battalion, an artillery regiment, an engineer regiment and a signals regiment, plus a logistic and a transport battalion. For its part, the 7th Brigade (HQ Coyhaique) comprises an infantry and a mountain infantry regiment, a commando company, a recce squadron, an artillery regiment, an aviation section, an engineer company and a logistic battalion.

The 5th Division (HQ Punta Arenas) covers the Fifth Military Area and comprises only two infantry regiments, two armoured cavalry regiments and an artillery regiment, an anti-tank battalion and engineer, signals and logistic battalions.

The 6th Division (HQ Arica) covers the Sixth Military Area with two infantry and one mountain infantry regiments, a commando battalion, two armoured cavalry regiments, an artillery regiment and an engineer regiment, plus a number of signals and logistic battalions.

Army troops include an army headquarters battalion, an aviation regiment, an engineer regiment, a signals regiment and a transport battalion. The infantry regiments each contain from one to four battalions, and eight of them — designated as "reinforced" — also have additional attached combat and logistic support elements.

The Escuela Militar "General Bernardo O'Higgins", the Staff College and the NCO School are all located at Santiago. Officer candidates must successfully complete the five-year course of the former before their commissioning and must complete an additional course at the Staff College to qualify for promotion to field rank or appointment to the General Staff.

EQUIPMENT

Armour:
AMX-30 MBT
AMX-13 & M41 light tank
EE-9 Cascavel armoured car
EE-11 Urutu, MOWAG Piranha & M113 APCs
Anti-Armour:
57mm M18 & 106mm M40A1 RCLs
MILAN & Mamba ATGWs
Artillery:
105mm LFH-18, M101 & M56 Hs
155mm F3 SPH
Air-Defence:
20mm Oerlikon K63 & HSS-639 AAGS
Blowpipe SAM
Aircraft:
Bell 206B & UH-1H Iroquois
Aerospatiale SA.315B Alouette II, AS.330 & AS.332S Super Puma

Below: This M3A1 was one of 50 surplus models received from the USA. Most have now been replaced by MOWAG Piranhas.

COLOMBIA

ALTHOUGH blessedly free from foreign war (apart from minor frontier incidents, the most serious of which was that with Peru in 1932), Colombia has been almost continuously racked by internal conflict since independence. Nevertheless, it was the only Latin American country to participate actively in the Korean War where its troops won a high reputation.

Colombia has recently reorganized and reinforced its ground forces in order to try and tackle a series of problems: chronic rural guerrilla activity, sporadic outbreaks of urban terrorism, an epidemic of violent crime principally related to the activities of narcotics smugglers, and frontier tensions with Venezuela in 1988. The guerrilla threat began to recede in the early 1990s with an election for a new constitutional committee which returned many radicals.

The 115,000 strong Colombian Army has doubled its manpower during the past decade and has been expanded further recently by the establishment of two additional infantry brigades. It is now organized into four divisions and up to four more infantry brigades are reported to be forming.

The 1st Division (HQ Santa Marta) covers the Second and Fourth Military Regions, corresponding to the north-western part of the country, and is composed of the 2nd, 4th and 11th Brigades with their respective HQs at Barranquilla, Medellín and Turbo.

The 2nd Division (HQ Bucaramanga) covers the First, Fifth and Tenth Military Regions, encompassing the area around the capital and the north-eastern part of the country. It consists of 1st, 5th and 10th Brigades with their HQs at Tunja, Bucaramanga and Melgar respectively.

The 3rd Division (HQ Cali) covers the Third, Sixth and Eighth Military Regions in the south-western part of the country, and contains the 3rd, 6th and 8th Brigades, the HQs of which are at Cali, Ibagué and Armenia. The 4th Division (HQ Villavicen-

Above: A soldier with an M14 guards a USAF C-130 during "Fuerzas Unitas", a joint US-Colombian COIN exercise in 1985.

Above: A Colombian contingent of the UN observer force in Sinai in 1982 drill with their Heckler & Koch G3 assault rifles.

cio) covers the Seventh and Ninth Military Regions. Responsible for the south-eastern part of the country it is made up of 7th, 9th and 12th Brigades with their HQs at Villavicencio, Neiva and Florencia.

Apart from an artillery group attached to the 4th Division and military police battalions attached to both the 1st and 2nd Divisions, no divisional level units are known to exist. Every brigade, however, has a logistics support battalion; each of the three-battalion brigades (1st to 6th inclusive) also having a group of mechanized cavalry, an artillery battalion and an engineer battalion. (The remaining brigades consist of only two infantry battalions.)

Directly subordinate to Army HQ are the Presidential Guard Battalion, which has infantry, cavalry, artillery and engineer elements; the "Leticia" Mixed Jungle Battalion; the "San Jorge" Mechanized Cavalry Regiment; the "Nueva Granada" Anti-Aircraft Artillery Battalion and the 11th Military Police Battalion. The 13th Brigade (HQ Bogotá), and the "Lanceros" Ranger and "Voltigueros" Airborne Battalions are also army level formations. So too is the Logistic Support Brigade, which consists of the 11th Supply and Ordnance Battalions at Bogotá.

There is a two-year period of compulsory military service and because conscripts receive most of their training in the schools of application of their respective arms and services the level of potential efficiency of the line units is higher than in the case of armies where these also fulfil a subsidiary training function.

Officers receive their professional education at the Escuela Militar; located, like the majority of the army's training institutions, at Bogotá it offers a five-year course leading to a commission in the rank of second lieutenant. Specialist training is received in the schools of application of the various arms and services.

EQUIPMENT

Armour:
M3A1 light tank
EE-3 Jararaca EE-9 Cascavel & M8 armoured cars
EE-11 Urutu & M3 APCs
Anti-Armour:
75mm M20 & 106mm M40A1 RCLs
Artillery:
75mm M116 & 105mm M101 Hs
Air-Defence:
40mm Bofors L/60 AAG

COSTA RICA

FOLLOWING a civil war in 1948 the Costa Rican Armed Forces were abolished and replaced by a paramilitary Civil Guard which combined internal security and defence functions. The Civil Guard was originally intended to have a very limited military capacity but

there has been an increasing reversion towards a conventional military role.

It is organized on military lines and deploys a company in each of the seven provinces of the republic. About 40 per cent of its total effectives are located at San José, the capital. These include the Presidential Guard, which is an élite unit of near-battalion strength, and another battalion-sized unit composed of the 1st and 2nd Companies. The so-called "3rd Company", which functions both as a strategic reserve, a depot and a training unit, also approaches battalion strength. Problems on the frontier with Nicaragua, due to the presence of contra groups, recently have led to the

formation of a counter-insurgency unit named the "Relámpago" Immediate Reaction Battalion.

All personnel are trained at the National Police School and a high proportion have undergone training in the United States.

EQUIPMENT

Armour:
M3A1 armoured car
M113 APC
Anti-Armour:
90mm M67 RCL
Air-Defence:
20mm Breda AAG

CUBA

AS AMERICA'S first and (to date) only fully-fledged Communist state Cuba feels itself under constant threat of United States military intervention and is probably the world's most completely militarized country. The Cuban Armed Forces, which include a 145,000-man army, are the second most numerous in Latin America (after those of Brazil) and are certainly the best equipped in the region.

The island of Cuba itself is divided into three major geographical commands, each garrisoned by an "Army". The Isle of Youth (formerly the Isle of Pines) has the status of an autonomous military region and is thought to be garrisoned by the 71st Infantry Division (HQ Nueva Gerona).

Cuban security is obsessive and almost nothing is released regarding the composition or deployment of the Revolutionary Armed Forces. The Western Army (HQ Havana) is thought to consist of the 1st Armoured Division (HQ Managua), the 20th Mechanized Division (HQ Havana) and the Pinar del Rio Army Corps (HQ Pinar del Rio); which, in turn, is believed to be made up of the 11th, 12th and 24th Infantry Divisions with their HQs at Pinar del Rio, Guane and Mariel respectively.

The Central Army (HQ Matanzas) is believed to comprise the 40th Mechanized Division (HQ Matanzas) and the Las Villas Army Corps (HQ Santa Clara). This corps is thought to comprise the 42nd, 67th and 68th Infantry Divisions.

The Eastern Army (HQ Santiago de Cuba) is thought to consist of the 2nd Armoured Division (HQ Santiago de Cuba), the 30th and 50th Mechanized Divisions (HQs Guantánamo and Bayamo), the Guantánamo Frontier Brigade, and the Holguín and Camagüey Army Corps. The Holguín Corps is believed to be made up of the 37th and 38th Infantry Divisions (HQs Holguín and Las Tunas), and the Camagüey the 55th and 56th Infantry Divisions (HQs Camagüey and Ciego de Avila).

Each army and army corps includes an armoured recce battalion, an artillery regiment, an air-defence regiment and engineer, signals, logistic and medical battalions. Each division consists of three regiments of the main arm, a recce battalion, an artillery regiment and engineer, NBC warfare, signals, service, supply and medical units. Armoured and mechanized divisions add a mechanized infantry and an armoured regiment respectively; each also has armoured recce units and a maintenance battalion and they increase the size of their other support units from companies to battalions. Infantry divisions have only motorized recce units, mounted mainly on soft-skinned vehicles, and company-level support units. Each division has a transport battalion and is supposed to have an air-defence regiment. Each infantry division would also, theoretically, have an armoured regiment on mobilization.

At higher levels there are the Army HQ Security Battalion; a two-battalion Paratroop Brigade (HQ Havana); an Artillery Division (HQ La Cabaña Fortress, Havana) which is believed to be made up of three heavy artillery, one missile and one air-defence regiments; and headquarters, supply, maintenance and medical units. There are also eight mixed security regiments for local defence.

There are three levels of combat readiness and strength; the 1st Armoured Division, the four mechanized divisions and the infantry division on the Isle of Youth are thought to be at almost full strength, as are the paratroop and frontier brigades. The 2nd Armoured Division and one infantry division of each army corps are at 60 per cent of establishment, and the remaining divisions are only cadres at 30 per cent.

Above: A last parade before the first big departure of Cuban forces from Angola. With their Soviet style helmets these may be troops from the 50th Mechanized Division, their "international duty" over. Cuba has forces in a dozen foreign countries.

EQUIPMENT

Armour:
T-62 & T-54/55 MBTs
PT-76 light tank
SU-100 assault guns
BRDM-1 & -2 armoured cars
BTR-40, -60 and -152 APCs
Anti-Armour:
76mm ZIS-3 ATG
85mm D-44 & D-48 guns
AT-3 Sagger & AT-1 Snapper ATGWs
Artillery:
122mm M-30 & 152mm D-1 Hs
122mm, D-74, & 130mm M-46 guns
122mm BM-21 to 240mm BM-24 MRLs
Air-Defence:
14.5mm ZPU-1, -2 and -4 AAGs
23mm ZU-23, 57mm S-60, 85mm KS-12A, & 100mm KS-19 AAGs
14.5mm TR-152AZPU & 57mm ZSU-57-2 SPAAGs
SA-3 & SA-7 SAMs

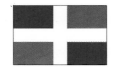

DOMINICAN REPUBLIC

DURING THE régime of the dictator Trujillo, who ruled the Dominican Republic from 1930 to 1961, its armed forces were unequalled by those of any other Caribbean state. Although it has been neglected during the last 30 years, the 13,000-man Dominican Army remains a highly-trained and professional force.

The country is divided into three defence zones garrisoned by four brigades. The 1st Brigade, with its HQ 25km north of Santo Domingo, garrisons the Southern Defence Zone (HQ Santo Domingo); the Northern Defence Zone (HQ Santiago) is garrisoned by the 2nd Brigade (HQ Santiago); and the Western Defence Zone (HQ San Juan de la Maguana) by the 3rd and 4th Brigades (HQs San Juan and Mao respectively).

The 1st and 2nd Brigades each have three infantry battalions, the 3rd and 4th Brigades have only two apiece. The 1st Brigade also includes a recce squadron, an artillery battalion and signals, supply, transport and medical companies; the 2nd 3rd and 4th Brigades having only a recce troop and a field battery as combat support troops. One of the infantry battalions of each of the reduced-strength brigades is concentrated in the headquarters town of the brigade, the other(s) being deployed at company level throughout the brigade area in order to enhance incident response time.

A Combat Support Command, with its HQ at Villa Mella to the north of Santo Domingo, controls an armoured battalion and an artillery battalion; a Support Service Command, with its HQ at Campamento Militar "Juan Pablo Duarte" in Santo Domingo, comprises engineer and signals battalions, an administrative company, a transport battalion, an ordnance maintenance battalion, a medical company and a military police company, all at Santo Domingo, and an armaments company at San Cristóbal. Other army troops include the Presidential Guard Battalion at Santo Domingo and the Mountain Ranger (Special Forces) Battalion, which has its HQ at Constanza and a detachment at Santiago.

Officers receive their professional training at the Escuela Militar at Haina, which offers a four year course. A Command and Staff School was established in 1984. Enlisted personnel are trained at the Centro de Entrenamiento de las Fuerzas Armadas at San Isidro. The special forces battalion trains troops in mountain and jungle warfare at Constanza.

EQUIPMENT

Armour:
AMX-13 & M41 light tanks
Landsverk & Lynx armoured cars
M3 APC
Anti-Armour:
106mm M40A1 RCL
Artillery:
75mm M02/33, 105mm Bofors L/22
& M10 Hs
Air-Defence:
40mm Bofors L/60 AAG

ECUADOR

ECUADOR HAS a bitter frontier dispute with Peru which annexed 55 per cent of its total territory following an invasion in 1941. Incidents occur frequently in the frontier zone and these erupted into full-scale hostilities in January/February 1981, all-out war being avoided only by the intervention of the Organization of American States.

The country is divided into four defence zones of which the first (HQ Quito) covers the capital and the northern part of the country, the second (HQ Guayaquil) the western coastal zone, the third (HQ Cuenca) the southern part of the country and the fourth (HQ Pastaza) the jungle-clad eastern most provinces.

The 35,000-man Ecuadorian Army is organized in six "divisions", comprising a total of five infantry, one armoured, one airborne and two jungle brigades. The First Zone is garrisoned by the 1st Division; the Second Zone by the 2nd Division; the Third Zone by the 3rd, 4th and 5th Divisions and the "Galápagos" Armoured Brigade; and the Fourth Zone by the 6th Division. In addition, each zone has two or three independent infantry companies for local defence, plus signals, military police and logistic support companies.

Right: The Colt M16A1 rifle being used by Ecuador's special forces. The choice of M16 is partly due to the relationship which exists with mobile US Special Forces teams who teach advanced warfare and weaponry skills to troops all over Latin America.

Below: The Ministerio de Defensa National bought the Steyr AUG in 1987. Its easy maintenance and integrated sight make it a good weapon for a conscript force.

The 1st, 2nd and 3rd Divisions (HQs Quito, Guayaquil and Cuenca) consist, respectively, of the "Pichincha", "Guayas" and "Azuay" Infantry Brigades, plus a mechanized cavalry group, a mixed artillery group and a combat engineer battalion. For their part, the 4th and 5th Divisions (HQs Machala and Loja) consist, respectively, of the "El Oro" and "Loja" Brigades plus only a cavalry group, while the 6th Division (HQ Pastaza) is made up of the "Napo" and "Zamora" Jungle Brigades and appears to have no division level combat support units.

Each division includes a signals and a logistic support unit. The brigades have only two battalions, except for the "Pichincha" and the two jungle brigades which have three each.

Both the "Galápagos" Armoured Brigade (HQ Riobamba) and the "Patria" Airborne Brigade (HQ Quito), which consists of one paratroop and one special forces battalion, are directly subordinate to Army HQ. So too are the "Granaderos de Tarquí" Presidential Escort Unit, the 1st Anti-Aircraft Artillery Group, the Army Aviation Group, the "Cotopaxi" Construction Engineer Battalion, the 1st Military Police Battalion, and the 1st Logistic Support Battalion.

Military service is, in theory, universal and compulsory, although in practice a system of selective service is employed. The period of compulsory training is two years.

Conscripts receive their basic training in the units to which they are assigned but there are specialist infantry, cavalry, armoured forces, artillery, engineer and signals schools. The Escuela de Perfeccionamiento at Quito offers specialist courses both for officers and potential

Above: These troops, with their specially trained tracking dogs, are paratroops from the "Patria" Airborne Brigade. They are leading experts in COIN warfare.

NCOs. There is a Paratroop and Special Forces School at Salinas and a Jungle Warfare School in the eastern part of the country.

Aspiring officers pursue a five-year course at the "Eloy Alfaro" Military Academy at Quito. The War College's two-year course must be completed successfully to qualify for promotion to senior rank or for appointment to the General Staff.

EQUIPMENT

Armour:
AMX-13 & M3 light tanks
AML 245 H-90 & EE-9 Cascavel
 armoured cars
AMX-VCI IFV
EE-11 Urutu & M113 APCs
Anti-Armour:
90mm M67 & 106mm M40A1 RCLs
Artillery:
105mm M101 & M56 Hs
155mm F3 SPH
Air-Defence:
20mm M168 Vulcan & M163 SPAAG
40mm Bofors L/60 & L/70 AAG
Chapparal & Blowpipe SAMs
Aircraft:
Aerospatiale SA.315 Lama & SA.316
 Alouette III

Left: These rapid-reaction troops are from the National Guard which bore the brunt of the civil war during the early years.

Above and right: A soldier awaits a UH-1 airlift. The FMLN has shown an increased ability to shoot these down.

EL SALVADOR

DESPITE various peace initiatives and the current climate of détente between East and West, the bitter civil war between the US-backed Government of El Salvador and the largely-Marxist guerrillas of the Farabundo Marti Frente de Liberación Nacional (FMLN) continues and is now entering its second decade. Although the army appears to have established an equilibrium with the guerrillas the latter can still mount major offensives, even in the vicinity of the national capital.

Until the brief, but victorious, war with Honduras in 1969 the Salvadorean Army — unlike those of its neighbours — was organized primarily for conventional warfare. Today, years of civil war have altered its orientation so that it is now almost exclusively devoted to the counter-insurgency role.

The 40,000-man army consists of six infantry and one artillery brigades. It also has nine detachments, comprising 24 anti-terrorist, 13 counter-guerrilla and five immediate-reaction infantry battalions, a two-battalion cavalry regiment, four artillery battalions, an anti-aircraft battalion and an engineer group.

The country is divided into four military zones: the Western Zone (HQ Santa Ana) is garrisoned by the 2nd Infantry Brigade (HQ Santa Ana) plus the 6th and 7th Detachments, at Sonsonate and Ahuachapán respectively; the Central Zone (HQ San Salvador) contains the 1st and 4th Infantry Brigades (HQs San Salvador and El Paraíso) plus the 1st and 5th Detachments at Chalatenango and Cojutepeque; the Paracentral Zone (HQ San Vicente) contains the 5th Infantry Brigade (HQ San Vicente), plus the 2nd Detachment at Sensuntepeque; and the Eastern Zone (HQ San Miguel) contains the 3rd and 6th Infantry Brigades (HQs San Miguel and Usulután), plus the 3rd and 4th Detachments at La Unión and San Francisco Gotera.

Each infantry brigade normally consists of three 600-man anti-terrorist battalions, and a combat-support company or battalion equipped with 105mm howitzers and/or 120mm mortars, plus a variable number of special forces and local security units — the exception being the 2nd Brigade which has three 400-man counter-guerrilla battalions, "Tecana", "Pipil" and "Tazumal". Apart from the 1st, 2nd and 4th Detachments, which have three battalions, each has two anti-terrorist or counter-guerrilla battalions and a variable number of special forces and local security units. The five 1,200-man immediate reaction battalions are deployed as occasion demands; these élite units are the "Atlacatl", "Atonal", "Belloso", "Arce" and "Bragamonte".

The single cavalry regiment has two APC battalions and an armoured squadron all based at San Andrés. The artillery brigade, based at Opico, has three battalions of 105mm howitzers and one of 120mm mortars plus an anti-aircraft battalion divided between Opico, Ilopango and San Miguel. The so-called "Military Engineer Detachment" at Zacatecoluca now appears primarily to be an infantry formation with two anti-terrorist battalions, a combat-support company, and security and replacement companies in addition to sundry minor engineering units.

All officers receive their basic training at the Escuela Militar "Capitán General Gerardo Barrios" at San Salvador. Specialist training for both officers and other ranks is provided by the Escuela de Armas y Servicios, also at San Salvador. The Special Forces School has been transferred from San Francisco Gotera to La Unión where there is also a basic training centre for recruits. Advanced officer training is provided by the Escuela de Comando y Estado Mayor "Manuel Enrique Araujo", at San Salvador.

EQUIPMENT

Armour:
AML 245 H-90 armoured car
Cashuat IFV
M113 & UR-416 APCs
Anti-Armour:
57mm M18A1, 75mm M20, 90mm M67 & 106mm M40A1 RCLs
94mm LAW
Artillery:
105mm M101, M102 & M56 Hs
Air-Defence:
20mm M55A2 SPAAG
Aircraft:
Bell UH-1 Iroquois

GRENADA

UNDER THE Marxist régime, nipped in the bud by the United States invasion of October 1983, Grenada was training a 2,200-man army. Currently, Grenada maintains no armed force of its own.

GUATEMALA

GUATEMALA, which is plagued by chronic internal insurgency, claims the entire territory of Belize and the Mexican state of Chiapas but it is unable to enforce either claim by military means. Indigenous Mayan Indians form the majority of the country's population and they have suffered the worst during the years of civil strife, with thousands dead.

The Guatemalan Armed Forces theoretically constitute a single institution with army, navy and air force elements. Each of the country's 22 departments constitutes a military zone.

The 41,000-man Guatemalan Army is organized largely as a counter-insurgency force. Each zone has a resident infantry battalion, in addition to which there are four brigades (each of three infantry battalions), a recce squadron, an artillery group and a logistic support company. Two of these, the "Mariscal Zavala" and "Guardia de Honor" Brigades, have their headquarters at Guatemala City; a third, the "General Manuel Lisandro Barrillas" Brigade, has its headquarters at Quetzaltenango; the fourth, "Capitán General Rafael Carrera" Brigade, has its headquarters at Zacapa.

Army level troops include the two-battalion Presidential Guard, which also includes a mounted escort squadron; one special forces and two paratroop battalions, collectively known as "Kaibiles"; an armoured battalion; an anti-aircraft artillery group; an engineer battalion; a military police battalion; an ordnance battalion and a medical battalion.

Above: The elite "Kaibiles" unit is at the forefront of a vicious civil war. Israel provides much assistance and this soldier carries a 5.56mm Galil rifle.

All male citizens between the ages of 18 and 50 are liable for military service, but most do not serve due to the employment of a selective draft system.

All officers are graduates of the four-year course of the Escuela Politécnica at San Juan Sacatépequez. Advanced level officer training is provided by the Centro para Estudios Militares at Guatemala City.

Recruits receive three months basic training at the "General Aguilar Santa Maria" training centre at Jutiapa. Specialist training for both officers and enlisted personnel is provided by the Escuela de Aplicación located at Guatemala City. There is a Paratroop School at Retalhuléu and a Special Forces School at El Infierno in the jungle department of El Petén.

EQUIPMENT

Armour:
M41A3 medium tank
M3A1 & M41 light tanks
M3A1, RBY-1, M8 &
  V-150 armoured cars
Armadillo & M113 APCs
Anti-Armour:
106mm M40A1 RCL
Artillery:
75mm M116, 105mm M101 & M56 Hs
75mm Le IG 18 infantry gun
Air-Defence:
20mm Oerlikon K63 AAG
40mm M1A1 AAG
Aircraft:
Bell UH-1 Iroquois

GUIANE

FRANCE divides three Foreign Legion and Marine battalions between its remaining Caribbean possessions, all of which have the status of overseas departments of France.

They are organized into four defence zones, one of which is based around Guiane. Covering the West Indies and Guiane these nearly 9,000 men are a formidable force in the region.

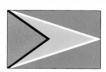

GUYANA

GUYANA HAS serious frontier disputes with Suriname, which claims some 6,000sq. miles of its territory, and Venezuela, which claims fully 60 per cent of it.

The 5,000-man land force element of the Guyana Defence Force consists of the Presidential Guard Battalion, which operates armoured vehicles; two infantry battalions; a special forces battalion; a mixed artillery battalion and an engineer company.

Immediately after independence the Guyana Defence Force was trained by British personnel but extensive Cuban training assistance has been received since the mid-1970s.

EQUIPMENT

Armour:
EE-9 Cascavel & Shorland armoured cars
EE-11 Urutu APC
Artillery:
130mm M1946 H
Air-Defence:
SA-7 SAM
Aircraft:
Bell 412

HAITI

THE HAITIAN Armed Forces, which combine the functions of national defence with those of internal security, form a single entity with distinct land, sea and air elements.

The country is divided into six regional military departments: North, North-West, Artibonite, West, Centre and South. There are a further three departments based on the capital, Port au Prince.

The only elements of the 6,400-man Haitan Army with any serious military potential are the Presidential Guard, the "Dessalines" Battalion and the "Leopards" special forces unit, all of which are located at the capital. There are no separate armoured or artillery units, the few AFVs and artillery pieces being operated by either the Presidential Guard or the "Dessalines" Battalion.

The other six military departments, which in some respects approximate to battalions as a level of command, contain a total of 21 companies operating principally as district police. Despite the severe poverty there exists no guerilla group on the island, the principal threat to order coming from the ex-dictator Duvalier's loyalists, the Tontons Macoutes.

Recruitment is entirely voluntary and is generally a life-long career, officers retiring at the age of 60 and enlisted men at 50.

Officers are trained at the Military Academy at Freres, which offers a three-year course.

EQUIPMENT

Armour:
M3A1 & M5A1 light tanks
V-150 armoured car
M2 APC
Anti-Armour:
57mm M18 & 106mm M40 RCLs
37mm M3A1 & 57mm M1 towed ATGs
Artillery:
75mm M116 & 105mm M2A1 Hs
Air-Defence:
20mm Ramta TCM-20, 40mm M1 AAGs

HONDURAS

HONDURAS was involved in a short but disastrous war with El Salvador in 1969 and relations between the two countries remained strained for many years afterwards. A peace treaty was finally signed in November 1980 and a further outbreak of hostilities seems highly unlikely in the forseeable future.

The country is divided into six military zones. The 15,000-man Honduran Army is organized in four three-battalion infantry brigades: the 101st (HQ Ojo de Agua, El Paraiso), 105th (HQ San Pedro Sula), 110th (HQ Choluteca) and 115th (HQ Juticalpa). In addition, there is the "Agrupación Táctica Especial" (HQ San Lorenzo), a brigade-type formation which combines the 1st Armoured Regiment with two infantry battalions and an artillery group.

Army troops include the Presidential Guard (HQ Las Tapias), which consist of an infantry battalion and a military police company; the 1st and 2nd Paratroop and the 1st Special Forces Battalions, collectively known as "Tesones"; the three-battalion Artillery Brigade (HQ Zambrano); and the 1st Engineer and Signals Battalions.

Although legislation provides for compulsory military service enlistment is entirely voluntary. Almost all officers are graduates of the Escuela Militar "General Francisco Morazán" at Tegucigalpa which offers a five-year course leading to a commission in the rank of second lieutenant. Most officers have also pursued some additional training abroad.

Above: Soldiers from the air-mobile 7th "Venceremos" Battalion armed with M16s await their helicopters during a COIN exercise.

Left: Blindfold re-assembly of an M60 GPMG. The camouflage pattern rather than olive fatigues suggest this is the work of an elite "Tesones" soldier but there is no insignia.

EQUIPMENT

Armour:
M24, Scorpion & Scimitar light tanks
M3A1, RBY-1, Staghound & Saladin armoured cars
M113 APC
Anti-Armour:
57mm M18 84mm Carl Gustav & 106mm M40A1 RCLs
94mm LAW
Artillery:
75mm M116, 105mm M101 & 155mm M198 Hs
Air-Defence:
20mm Breda, Madsen & M55A2 AAGs

JAMAICA

THE 3,000 strong land element of the tri-service Jamaica Defence Force consists principally of the 1st and 2nd Battalions of the Jamaica Regiment. There is also a support and service battalion which provides engineer and signals elements in addition to logistic support. The ground

force reserve is constituted by the 3rd Battalion of the Jamaica Regiment, manned by part-time volunteers.

Both officers and other ranks now receive their basic training at the JDF Depot, Kingston. All officers, however, continue to receive their advanced training abroad, either in Britain, the United States, Canada or Germany.

Left: V-150 Commando with the standard one man turret.

Below: A fast jeep carrying troops armed with L1A1s and L7A1s.

EQUIPMENT

Armour:
Ferret armoured car
V-150 Commando APC

MEXICO

ALTHOUGH the Mexican Armed Forces played a critical role in politics up to and during the revolution of 1910/20 they are now the least politicized in the region and their function has been reduced to that of an internal constabulary, with the country relying implicitly on the United States for its defence against external enemies.

The 105,000-man army is deployed between 39 military zones which correspond to the 31 states into which the country is divided, plus one for the Federal District, two each for the states of Chiapas and Guerrero, and three for that of Vera Cruz. Each zone is garrisoned by one or two infantry battalions, the majority also having at least one cavalry regiment and a variable complement of combat and logistic support units.

There are 70 independent infantry battalions; 20 mechanized, one armoured and two horsed cavalry regiments; six regiments and a number of independent battalions of artillery; and one combat and

a number of construction engineer battalions. Although plans exist for the superimposition of a brigade and corps structure on the army's combat units with no apparent intermediate divisional-level of command, the majority of these remain organized at battalion-level and the army-level units based at Mexico City provide the only effective tactical manoeuvre force.

This force consists of: the Presidential Guard with three infantry battalions, an assault battalion, an armoured recce battalion, an artillery battalion, a heavy mortar group and engineer, logistic and medical companies; the "José Maria Morelos y Pavón" Paratroop Fusiliers Brigade, which combines the army's 1st and 2nd Paratroop Fusilier Battalions with the air force's Paratroop Battalion; and the 1st and 2nd Infantry Brigades, each of which comprises two infantry battalions, an armoured recce squadron, an artillery battalion and engineer, logistic and medical companies.

Other army-level troops deployed at or in the vicinity of the capital include the 1st and 2nd Military Police Battalions, the 1st Construction Battalion and the 1st Transport Regiment.

Other troops deployed within the First Military Zone (HQ Mexico City) conform to the pattern throughout the remaining 38 military zones and include six infantry battalions, two horsed, one armoured and two motorized cavalry regiments.

All male citizens must undergo military training at the age of 18. In practice, the regular armed forces are recruited by voluntary enlistment with a large proportion of their personnel being long-service regulars.

All officers are trained at the Heróico Colegio Militar at Chapultepec Castle, Mexico City. They continue specialist, professional training at specific stages throughout their careers by attending the Centro de Aplicación para Oficiales de las Armas. There is also a system of specialist schools for other ranks, all such establishments being located at Mexico City.

EQUIPMENT

Armour:
M3 & M5 light tanks
Panhard ERC-90, M8 & MAC-1 armoured cars
Panhard VCR, M3, HWK-11, Sedena, DN-3, -4 & -5 APCs
Anti-Armour:
106mm M40A1 RCL
37mm M3 ATG
MILAN ATGW
Artillery:
75mm M116 & 105mm M101 Hs
75mm M8 SPH
Air-Defence:
12.7mm M55 AAG
20mm GIAT M693 SPAAG

NICARAGUA

ELECTIONS in February 1990 resulted in the surprise overthrow of the Sandinista Revolutionary Government and its replacement by a centre-right coalition. The new administration announced both the disbandment of the "Contra" guerrillas, which with U.S. military and financial support had been endeavouring to destabilize the Sandinista régime, and the reduction in strength of the Nicaraguan Armed Forces. However, large numbers of Contras have continued to resist such disbandment and although the Sandinista Revolutionary Army appears to have accepted the mandate of the new Government it remains essentially as before in its strength and organization.

The country is divided into seven military regions: First (HQ Estelí) covers the western part of the country, Second (HQ Chinandega) the south-west, Third (HQ Managua) the capital and its environs, Fourth (HQ Matagalpa) the central and eastern parts of the country, Fifth (HQ Puerto Cabezas) the north-east, Sixth (HQ Granada) the south coast and Seventh (HQ Bluefields) the south-east.

The 50,000-man Nicaraguan Army consists of seven infantry brigades, two mechanized brigades and one artillery brigade The infantry brigades consist of three infantry battalions without organic combat support units. The mechanized brigades comprise a single tank battalion and two APC infantry battalions with artillery support supplied by sub-units of the "General Omar Torrijos Herrera" Artillery Brigade on an ad hoc basis in accordance with operational requirements.

For operational purposes the military regions have been grouped into three "Zones": First Zone groups the First and Second Military Regions and contains the 1st and 21st Infantry Brigades; Second Zone combines the Third and Sixth Military Regions and contains the 30th and 32nd Mechanized and the 61st, 62nd and 66th Infantry Brigades; and Third Zone, which comprises the Fourth, Fifth and Seventh Military Regions, contains the 53rd and 54th Infantry Brigades.

There are also eleven counter-insurgency units, known as Irregular Warfare Infantry battalions, and six Light-Rifle battalions which also have a primary counter-insurgency orientation. Both types of unit are deployed in accordance with operational requirements and have been successful in taking the war to the Contras.

The irregular warfare battalions come under the control of army headquarters, as do the "Managua" Tank Battalion, the Artillery Brigade and the Engineer Battalion. Six Frontier Guard battalions, the current status of which is unknown, also came under army control during the recent emergency.

The external threats posed to the late Sandinista régime by active U.S. hostility resulted in the registration for military service of all men between the ages of 17 and 50 and all women between 18 and 40, conscripts serving for two years active service before passing to the reserve. Popular enthusiasm also resulted in widespread membership of the Sandinista People's Militia, which included at least 20 active brigades and approximately 100 battalions. These have probably been deactivated if not actually disbanded.

The major training establishments are the "Carlos Agüero Hechevarria" Officer Training School, the Centro de Estudios Militares "Comandante Hilario Sánchez Vázquez" which provides technical and specialized training for both officers and other ranks, and the Centro de Entrenamiento Militar "Eduardo Contreras" which is the basic conscript training school. All three institutions are located in the vicinity of Managua and named after Sandinista heroes and may therefore be renamed in the medium term.

Above: A Sandinista soldier, possibly from the People's Militia given his bare minimum of equipment, armed with the popular 7.62mm Soviet AKM assault rifle.

EQUIPMENT

Armour:
T-54 & T-55 MBTs
PT-76 light tanks
BRDM-2 armoured cars
BTR-60 & -152 APCs
Anti-Armour:
57mm ZIS-2 & 85mm ASU-85 ATGs
Artillery:
76mm M-1942 gun
122mm D-30, 152mm D-20 & M2A1 Hs
122mm BM-21 MRL
Air-Defence:
14.5mm ZPU-1, -2 & -4 AAGs
23mm ZU-23, 37mm M1939, 57mm S-60 AAGs
SA-7, -14 & -16 SAMs
Aircraft:
Mi-8 Hip
Mi-24 Hind

PANAMA

AT PRESENT the status of the Panamanian Army is uncertain. The existing Ground Defence Force, which at the time of the United States invasion of 1989 was in a state of transition from a paramilitary force to a national army, has been disbanded by the U.S. occupation forces.

PARAGUAY

PARAGUAY HAS the most uncompromisingly martial history of any South American country having fought a war against an alliance of Argentina, Brazil and Uruguay in 1865/70 which ended only when its population had been reduced from 525,000 to 221,000 of whom only 28,000 were males. This did not deter it from engaging in a bloody but victorious war against Bolivia in 1932/35.

The country is divided into six military regions of which the First (HQ Asunción) covers the capital and its environs, the Second (HQ Villarica) the south-east, the Third (HQ San Juan Bautista de las Misiones) the south-west, the Fourth (HQ Concepción) the north, the Fifth (HQ Puerto Presidente Stroessner) the north-east and the Sixth (HQ Mariscal Estigarribia) the Chaco which forms the western two-thirds of the country.

The 13,000-man Paraguayan Army provides the cadres of three corps which are in turn organized into eight infantry and one cavalry divisions.

The I Army Corps (HQ Asunción) cover the First and Third Military Regions with the 1st Infantry Division (HQ Asunción), which is based on two infantry regiments, the 3rd Infantry Division (HQ San Juan Bautista), also with two infantry regiments, and two frontier battalions.

II Army Corps (HQ Villarica) covers the Second, Fourth and Fifth Military Regions with the 2nd and 4th Infantry Divisions (HQs Villarica and Concepción respectively), each of which consists of a single infantry regiment, two frontier battalions and a cavalry detachment, and the 5th Infantry Division (HQ Curuguaty) which has only one infantry regiment and one frontier battalion.

The III Army Corps (HQ Mariscal Estigarribia) covers the Sixth Military Region which approximates to the theatre of operations of the Chaco War of 1932/35. It has the 6th Infantry Division (HQ Mariscal Estigarribia), which consists of one infantry regiment and two frontier battalions, and the 7th and 8th Infantry Divisions (HQs Campo Jurado and Capitán Lagerenza), each of which consists of a single infantry regiment and a frontier battalion.

Each peacetime infantry division includes a military police and a logistics company, but consists of three infantry regiments, a cavalry squadron, an engineer company and a logistic battalion on mobilization.

At army-level there is the 1st Cavalry Division (HQ Nú Guazú) which consists of four cavalry regiments, an armoured squadron and a field battery, plus logistic and military police companies. Also at army-level is the Presidential Escort Regiment which comprises an infantry battalion, a military police battalion, an armoured section and a field battery. Apart from the units attached to the Presidential Escort Regiment and the 1st Cavalry Division, artillery is centralized in the Army Artillery Command (HQ Paraguarí) which consists of four groups. There is also an Engineering Command (HQ Asunción) with one combat and four construction battalions and a Signals Command, also based in the capital Asunción, with one signals battalion.

Below: Troops armed with SIG and Madsen weapons march through Asuncion. In 1989 troops led by Gen. Rodriguez overthrew Alfredo Stroessner and amid fierce inter-army fighting some 300 died.

Military service is compulsory for all male citizens, who serve for two years (in practice reduced to 18 months) from the age of 18. Aspiring officers pursue the basic four-year course of the "Marshal Francisco Solano López" Military College at Asunción. Specialist training follows graduation and intermediate grade officers must successfully attend courses at the National War College in order to qualify for staff appointments or promotion to higher rank.

The Army maintains an NCO School and a series of specialist schools, all in the vicinity of Asunción, and an Artillery School at Paraguarí. Conscripts receive non-specialist military training in the units to which they are assigned.

EQUIPMENT

Armour:
M4 & Sherman Firefly medium tank
M3 light tank
EE-9 Cascavel & M8 armoured cars
EE-11 Urutu & M2 APCs
Anti-Armour:
75mm M20 RCL
Artillery:
75mm Schneider 1927
105mm M101 Hs
6in Vickers MkV gun
Air-Defence:
40mm Bofors L/60 AAG
Aircraft:
Bell UH-1B Iroquois

PERU

FEAR AND resentment of Chile, dating back to the Pacific War of 1879/83 and earlier, have conditioned Peruvian politico-military policies for over a century. Hostility against Ecuador predates even this rivalry and has manifested itself in sporadic conflict between the two countries, the most recent outbreak being in January/February 1981. Peru also has a long-standing border dispute with Colombia, which resulted in hostilities in 1932. The greatest actual threat, however, comes from internal guerrilla groups, principally by members of the neo-Maoist "Shining Path" movement whose activities the army has been able to contain only with much difficulty.

The country is divided into five military regions: First (HQ Piura) covers the northwestern coastal strip, Second (HQ Lima) the national capital and the central coastal strip, Third (HQ Arequipa) the south-western coastal strip, Fourth (HQ Cuzco) the central cordillera and Fifth (HQ Iquitos) the jungle-covered eastern part of the country.

The 80,000-man Peruvian Army consists of seven motorized infantry "divisions", an airborne "division", three armoured "divisions", a cavalry "division" and a jungle "division". Each so-called "division" averages only three units of infantry or cavalry and an artillery group, to which may be added an engineer battalion and/or an anti-aircraft unit. It therefore resembles a brigade rather than a division.

The First Military Region contains the 1st, 7th, 8th and 32nd Motorized Infantry Divisions (HQs Talara, Tumbés, Lambayeque and Trujillo respectively) and the 9th Cavalry Division (HQ Sullana). This region also accommodates a construction engineer group at Bagua and, supply and medical battalions, both at Piura.

The Second Military Region contains the 2nd and 31st Motorized Infantry Divisions (HQs Lima and Huancayo), the Airborne Division (HQ Callao) and the 18th Armoured Training Division (HQ Lima). The Third Military Region contains the 3rd and 6th Armoured Divisions (HQs Moqueguá and Tacna) and the Tacna Detachment which is an armoured brigade in all but name. It also contains a special forces group, a construction engineer group and a construction engineer battalion.

The Fourth Military Region contains only the 4th Motorized Infantry Division (HQ Cuzco) and the Santa Rosa Detachment which consists of an armoured cavalry regiment and a motorized infantry battalion, plus a construction engineer battalion. The Fifth Military Region contains the 5th Jungle Division (HQ Iquitos).

The military regions, each of which appears to approximate to an army corps as a level of command, would seem to include at least one battalion each of logistic support and medical troops, in addition to signals and military police units. Each "division" also appears to have at least a company each of signals, logistic support and medical troops.

Army-level troops, most of which are located within the Second Military Region, include the "Mariscal Nieto" Presidential Escort Regiment, the 1st Anti-Aircraft Artillery Group, the 501st Communications Battalion, the 511th and 512th Supply and Maintenance Battalions, the 511th Supply Battalion, the 511th Transport Battalion and the 512th Maintenance Battalion.

Military service is supposed to be universal and compulsory, but in practice it is selective with conscripts serving for two years. Officers receive their training at the Chorrillos Military Academy which offers a four-year course leading to a commission as a second lieutenant. Lieutenants must also successfully complete at least two specialized courses before promotion to captain. A further two-year course at the Escuela Superior de Guerra must be completed before promotion to field rank. There is a comprehensive system of specialized schools, almost all of which are located in the environs of Lima. There is a Jungle Warfare School at Iquitos.

EQUIPMENT

Armour:
T-54/55 MBT
M4 medium tank
AMX-13 light tank
Fiat 6616 & SPz-12-3 armoured cars
M113, MOWAG Roland & V-150
   Commando APCs
Anti-Armour:
106mm M40A1 RCL
Cobra ATGW
Artillery:
105mm M101 & M56 Hs
122mm M-46 & 155mm M114 Hs
Mk F.3 SPH
Air-Defence:
40mm Bofors L/60 & 76mm M1938 AAGs
23mm ZSU-23-4 SPAAG
SA-3 & -7 SAMs
Aircraft:
Aerospatiale SA.313 Alouette II
Mi-6 Hook
Mi-8 Hip

Left: A special warfare unit marching past reviewers in Lima. They are armed with FN FAL rifles. Their war is against an elusive enemy in the form of Sendero Luminoso guerrilas who are at their strongest in the mountainous and tough Andean terrain where many Indians live who lend them support.

PUERTO RICO

ALTHOUGH a U.S. dependency, the Commonwealth of Puerto Rico enjoys an ambiguous relationship with the United States of which it is technically neither a state, a federal territory nor a colonial possession.

The Armed Forces of the Commonwealth consist of the Puerto Rican National Guard, a part-time organization which is nevertheless equipped on the scale of the regular US armed forces and which furnishes the 92nd Infantry Brigade of the US Army on mobilization.

The United States maintains large military bases in Puerto Rico but does not normally deploy major units of its armed forces within the boundaries of the Puerto Rican Commonwealth.

SURINAME

SURINAME has frontier disputes with both Guyana and Guiane.

The 2,200-man land force element of the tri-service Suriname Armed Forces consists of a Guards battalion, a single reinforced infantry battalion and a military police battalion. Most of the potential effec-

Above: A Surinamese soldier conducting a search armed with an elderly M1 carbine.

tiveness of this force is concentrated in the vicinity of the capital.

Recruitment for the armed forces is entirely voluntary. Officers are trained in the Netherlands, the former colonial power, although a recent defence agreement was concluded with Brazil.

More modern weapons such as FN FALs and Soviet AKMs are also thought to be used.

EQUIPMENT

Armour:
EE-9 Cascavel armoured car
EE-11 Urutu & DAF YP-408 APCs
Anti-Armour:
106mm M40 RCL

TRINIDAD & TOBAGO

THE 2,000-man ground force element of the Trinidad and Tobago Defence Force consists of the 1st Battalion of the Trinidad and Tobago Regiment which also has a volunteer reserve battalion and supporting units. Recruitment is entirely voluntary, most officers continuing to be trained in Great Britain.

EQUIPMENT

Anti-Armour:
82mm B-300 RL

Left: Troops from the Caribbean peace-keeping force on the island of Grenada following the US invasion. Men from Jamaica, Trinidad & Tobago, Barbados, Antigua and Barbuda all took part.

URUGUAY

ALTHOUGH it is traditionally the least politicized in South America, the Uruguayan Army seized power from 1973 to 1984 in response to an outbreak of guerrilla and terrorist activity. They successfully suppressed this and the country has now returned to civilian rule. Although it owes its existence to its geographical position as a buffer state between Argentina and Brazil, Uruguay has no immediate external threat and enjoys amicable relations with both its powerful neighbours.

The country is divided into four military regions: First (HQ Montevideo) covers the national capital and its environs, Second (HQ San José) encompasses the southwestern part of the country, Third (HQ Paso de los Toros) the north-west and Fourth (HQ Treinta y Tres) the eastern and south-eastern regions.

The army currently numbers approximately 17,000 and each of the four military regions is garrisoned by a nominal division of identical numerical designation. Each division has one engineer battalion, one signals company, logistic support units, and one field artillery group attached to it; the exception is 1st Division which has an extra field artillery group.

The 1st Division (HQ Montevideo) consists of the 1st Infantry and 3rd Cavalry Brigades, plus an Artillery Command comprising two field and one anti-aircraft artillery groups. The 2nd Division (HQ San José) consists of the 2nd Infantry Brigade (HQ Colonia) and a single armoured cavalry regiment.

The 3rd Division is composed of the 3rd Infantry Brigade (HQ Salto) and the 1st Cavalry Brigade (HQ Rivera); the 4th Division (HQ Minas) comprises the 4th Infantry Brigade (HQ Minas) and the 2nd Cavalry Brigade (HQ Melo). All the infantry brigades and the 3rd Cavalry Brigade consist of three battalions or regiments, the other brigades having only two sub-units.

Army troops, almost all of which are deployed at or in the vicinity of Montevideo, include the 1st "Blandengues de Artigas" Cavalry Regiment (which performs ceremonial duty in the capital), the 5th Infantry Brigade which is actually an administrative rather than a tactical or operational formation comprising an armoured, an airborne and a motorized infantry battalion, and the 1st Engineer and Signals Brigades.

The Uruguayan Army remains one of the very few in Latin America to rely on voluntary enlistment and the rank and file are largely long-service professionals, which helps improve the force's quality.

Officers are trained at the Military Academy which offers a four-year course leading to a commission in the rank of second lieutenant. Both junior officers and other ranks receive specialist training in the School of Arms and Services. The Command and Staff School provides postgraduate training for officers at mid-career, leading to promotion to field rank or to staff appointments.

EQUIPMENT

Armour:
M41A1, M24 & M3A1 light tanks
M3A1, EE-3 Jararaca, FN-4-RM-63 & EE-9
    Cascavel armoured cars
M113, M2 & Condor APCs
Anti-Armour:
57mm M18 & 106mm M40A1 RCLs
57mm M1 ATG
Artillery:
75mm M1935 gun
105mm M101 & 155mm M114 Hs
Air-Defence:
40mm Bofors L/60 AAG
20mm Vulcan M167 SPAAG

VENEZUELA

VENEZUELA claims most of the territory of Guyana and has a long-standing frontier dispute with Colombia which almost led to hostilities in 1988.

The country and its 47,000 strong army is divided into six military areas of which Area One (HQ San Cristóbal) covers the southwest of the country, Area Two (HQ Maracaibo) the north-west, Area Three (HQ Barquisimeto) the northern and central regions, Area Four (HQ Maracay) the federal capital and its environs, Area Five (HQ Maturín) the north-east and, lastly, Area Six (HQ Ciudad Bolívar) the south and south-east.

Under the Plan Carabobo adopted in 1975 the ground forces were to be divided into a Territorial Defence Force consisting of the 1st, 2nd and 4th Infantry Divisions, the 5th Jungle Division, the 1st Mechanized Cavalry Division, and an Immediate Intervention Force consisting of the Armoured Brigade (HQ Valencia), the Airborne Brigade (HQ Maracay) and the Ranger Brigade (HQ Maturín). This has now been superseded by the Plan Ejército 2000 under which all the above formations will be grouped under six divisional headquarters.

The existing 1st Infantry Division (HQ Maracaibo), which consists of the 2nd and 3rd Infantry Brigades (HQs Maracaibo and Barquisimeto respectively) plus a frontier detachment and a group of self-propelled missile artillery, will remain essentially unchanged except that its component brigades will forthwith be renumbered 11th and 12th respectively.

The 2nd Infantry Division (HQ San Cristóbal), which is made up of the 1st and 7th Infantry Brigades (HQs San Cristóbal and Mérida) plus a group of medium artillery and a heavy mortar battery, will also remain essentially unchanged apart from the renumbering of its component brigades as the 21st and 22nd.

The 4th Infantry Division (HQ Maracay), which consists only of the 4th Infantry Brigade (HQ Caracas) plus a medium artillery group and a combat engineer battalion, will cede the 4th Brigade, which will be renumbered 31st, to a new 3rd Division (HQ Caracas) which will cover the capital and the Fifth Military Area together with the Ranger brigade, which will be renumbered 32nd. The 4th Division will acquire the existing armoured and airborne brigades which will be numbered 41st and 42nd respectively.

The 5th Jungle Division (HQ Ciudad Bolívar), which comprises the 5th and 6th Jungle Infantry Brigades (HQs Caicará del Orinoco and Upata) plus a combat engineer battalion, will be unchanged apart from the renumbering of its brigades as 51st and 52nd. Finally, the existing 1st Mechanized Cavalry Division (HQ San Juan de Los Moros), which has as its major elements the 9th and 10th Mechanized Cavalry Brigades (HQs San Juan de Los Moros and San Fernando) plus an artillery group, will become the 6th Division, its component brigades being renumbered 61st and 62nd.

Each brigade (apart from the six-battalion 32nd, and the 41st which has three armoured and one armoured infantry battalions) consists of three battalion-sized units of the basic arm, a battalion or company-sized recce unit, an artillery group and a company or battalion of engineers, in addition to signals and logistic support units, and

Below: A member of the UN force sent to Nicaragua following a civil war ceasefire.

Above: A mission to interdict drugs along the Colombian border. It is likely these are Rangers from the "Hunter" battalions.

may or may not have an attached air-defence battery. Each division also includes a signals company and a military police company, plus — optionally — a group of divisional artillery and/or an engineer battalion.

The independent anti-aircraft elements, which are apparently unaffected by the organizational changes, consist of the 1st and 3rd Air-Defence Artillery Groups at Caracas and the hydro-electric complex of El Gury respectively, plus the 2nd and 4th Groups forming at the important oil port of Maracaibo and at the military-industrial complex at Maracay.

Army troops comprise an Army HQ battalion; construction engineer and combat communications regiments and a military police regiment, each of three battalions; a logistic support regiment composed of ordnance, administration, supply and transport battalions; and an army air regiment.

Military service is theoretically obligatory for all male citizens although in practice a selective draft system is employed with conscripts serving for two years from the age of 18. The Military Academy at El Valle offers a four-year course for officer cadets who may pursue a degree at one of the civilian universities, or at the Universiadad Politécnica de las Fuerzas Armadas, after commissioning in the rank of second lieutenant.

The Escuela Superior de Guerra "Libertador Simón Bolívar" is at Chorrillos and aspirants to promotion beyond the rank of lieutenant colonel must successfully complete either its command and staff course or a course at a recognized foreign military establishment of equivalent category. The NCO School and the various arms and services schools are all located at Maracay which is the principal military centre in the country. Conscripts receive their non-specialist training in the units to which they are assigned on induction.

EQUIPMENT

Armour:
AMX-30 MBT
AMX-13 & Scorpion light tanks
V-150 Commando & Dragoon 300
  armoured cars
AMX-VCI IFV

Anti-Armour:
106mm M40A1 RCL
SS-11 ATGW

Artillery:
105mm M101, M56 & 155mm M114 Hs
155mm F3 SPH
160mm IMI LAR MRL

Air-Defence:
20mm Vulcan M167, GIAT M693 &
  Panhard AML S.530 SPAAGs
40mm Bofors L/60 & L/70 AAGs
Roland SAM

Aircraft:
Bell UH-1H Iroquois
Aerospatiale SA.316/319 Alouette III
Agusta A.109
Bell 205 A-1

ASIA AND FAR EAST

Edwin W. Besch

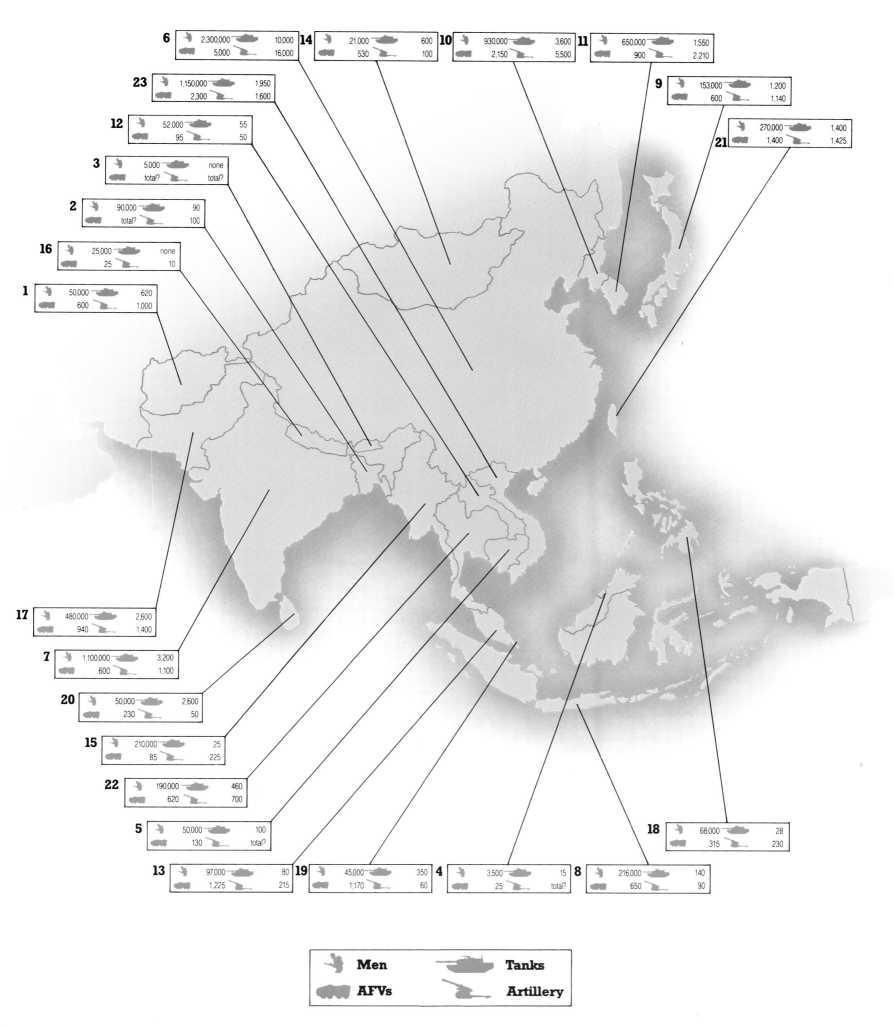

6 🧍 2,300,000 🚗 10,000
🚙 5,000 🔫 16,000

14 🧍 21,000 🚗 600
🚙 530 🔫 100

10 🧍 930,000 🚗 3,600
🚙 2,150 🔫 5,500

11 🧍 650,000 🚗 1,550
🚙 900 🔫 2,210

23 🧍 1,150,000 🚗 1,950
🚙 2,300 🔫 1,600

9 🧍 153,000 🚗 1,200
🚙 600 🔫 1,140

12 🧍 52,000 🚗 55
🚙 95 🔫 50

21 🧍 270,000 🚗 1,400
🚙 1,400 🔫 1,425

3 🧍 5,000 🚗 none
🚙 total? 🔫 total?

2 🧍 90,000 🚗 90
🚙 total? 🔫 100

16 🧍 25,000 🚗 none
🚙 25 🔫 10

1 🧍 50,000 🚗 620
🚙 600 🔫 1,000

17 🧍 480,000 🚗 2,600
🚙 940 🔫 1,400

7 🧍 1,100,000 🚗 3,200
🚙 600 🔫 1,100

20 🧍 50,000 🚗 2,600
🚙 230 🔫 50

15 🧍 210,000 🚗 25
🚙 85 🔫 225

22 🧍 190,000 🚗 460
🚙 620 🔫 700

5 🧍 50,000 🚗 100
🚙 130 🔫 total?

13 🧍 97,000 🚗 80
🚙 1,225 🔫 215

19 🧍 45,000 🚗 350
🚙 1,170 🔫 60

4 🧍 3,500 🚗 15
🚙 25 🔫 total?

8 🧍 216,000 🚗 140
🚙 650 🔫 90

18 🧍 68,000 🚗 28
🚙 315 🔫 230

🧍 **Men**   🚗 **Tanks**
🚙 **AFVs**   🔫 **Artillery**

AFGHANISTAN

DUE TO ITS central location, Afghanistan has been invaded numerous times in its history. Coups and counter-coups have plagued the country during this century, and in response to one such incident the Soviet Union intervened in December 1979 and installed Babrak Karmal as President. In turn, he was deposed in 1986 by Sayid Mohammed Najibullah, the former head of KHAD, the Afghan intelligence service.

Internal strife with Muslim insurgents increased as a result of the Soviet invasion and eventually they were forced to commit some 120,000 men. They secured the capital, Kabul, and several provincial cities and attempted to seal off the borders with Pakistan and Iran in order to stop the exodus of refugees and the flow of munitions being

provided by China, the United States, Egypt, and Pakistan to the guerrillas known as the Mujahideen. After a decade of military stalemate and failed negotiations, Soviet troops withdrew in February 1989.

Afghan government forces retain tenuous control over limited areas of Afghanistan, but they have unexpectedly strengthened control in some places due to lack of cooperation among the Mujahideen and their evident inability, despite their numbers, to fight decisive conventional pitched battles with government forces.

The Afghan Army has received advice, training, and equipment from the Soviet Union since 1956, but it remains organized on British lines. It has been wholly committed to counter-insurgency and internal security operations since 1979. Its strength is estimated to be 50,000 (down from 110,000 in 1979), and mostly conscripts. It suffers serious losses from desertions, as well as battle attrition, and all units are seriously under-strength — some may only be at 25 per cent. All the equipment is of Soviet origin.

The army has four corps headquarters which control three armoured brigades, 16 infantry divisions, one mechanized infantry brigade, a Special Guard division and three independent brigades, an artillery brigade of three regiments, five commando

brigades and an air-defence brigade. The army has no identifiable reserves, but it is backed by numerous paramilitary forces: a Border Guard of 7,000 (under Army control); KHAD (Ministry of State Security) with 70,000, some 27,000 of them in combat units; and 100,000-plus in a host of regional militias, among them Defence of the Revolution, Pioneers, Afghan Communist Party Guards, Khalqi Youth, National Fatherland Front and a variety of tribal brigades.

EQUIPMENT

Armour:
T-34, T-54/55 & T-62 MBTs
PT-76 light tank
BMP-1 & -2 IFVs
BTR-40, -50, -60, & -152 APCs
Anti-Armour:
73mm SPG-9 & 82mm B-10 RCLs
AT-3 Sagger & AT-4 Spigot ATGWs
Artillery:
100mm M-1944, 76mm & 130mm M-46
  guns
85mm D-48, 122mm M-30 & D-30, &
  152mm D-1 Hs
122mm BM-21 & 132mm BM-13-6 MRLs
Air-Defence:
14.5mm ZPU-4 AAGs
23mm ZSU-23-4 SPAAG
SA-7 & -9 SAMs

Below: Afghan troops view Soviet armour. Fighting alone since early 1989 the Afghan Army seems unlikely to lose the civil war.

BANGLADESH

THE PEOPLE'S Republic of Bangladesh is bordered on three sides, by India, Myanmar, and the Bay of Bengal. Created in 1971 by declaring independence from Pakistan, the state was forged in war and assisted in it by Pakistan's enemy, India.

The army is actively engaged in combatting several insurgencies, one against Buddhist Chakma rebels along the Indian Border, the other against Shanti Bahini guerrillas in the Chittagons Hill Tracts region in the eastern tri-border area that has required commitment of an army division.

Periodic Bangladesh-India tensions are the only external threat and are offset by a Chinese defence committment which intimidates the Indians.

The Bangladesh Army is 90,000 strong. It has five infantry division headquarters and is organized into 13 infantry brigades (two battalions each), an armoured brigade of two regiments, six artillery regiments, and six engineer battalions. Paramilitary forces consist of the 30,000 strong Bangladesh Rifles, a border security force which has borne the brunt of counter-insurgency operations and also serves as a reserve; 20,000 Ansars security guards; and 5,000 armed police.

EQUIPMENT

Armour
T-54/55 & Type 62 MBTs
Anti-Armour:
106mm M40A1 RCL
Artillery:
105mm M101 & M56,
  & 122mm Type 54 Hs
6-pdr (57mm) & 25-pdr (88mm) guns

BHUTAN

THE KINGDOM of Bhutan lies in the Himalayas of central Asia, bordered by India and Chinese-occupied Tibet. The Royal Bhutan Army (RBA) is 5,000 strong and receives aid and training from India. It is answerable directly to the king and plays an important internal security role due to ethnic and social rivalries that are potential sources for disruption.

Military service is compulsory for males aged 18 to 50. The RBA is backed by a 15,000 strong militia which is both a reserve and security force. Its organizational structure, uniforms, and rank insignia are patterned after the Indian Army, which also maintains troops in Bhutan.

BRUNEI

NEGARA BRUNEI Darrisalam, or Sultanate of Brunei, is one of the wealthiest nations in the world on a GDP per capita basis, and it could afford to field well-equipped armed forces. However, with a relatively small population (372,000) and no economic imperative operating, the Royal Brunei Armed forces (RBAF) is a small 4,200 strong limited self-defence force.

Most of the senior officers are British-trained, the Sultan himself being a Sandhurst graduate. RBAF equipment is also mostly of British origin, reflecting its traditional relationship with the UK. The Sultan has supplemented the RBAF with British officers and technicians on loan or contract and by recruiting Gurkhas from British Army Gurkha units stationed in Hong Kong.

The volunteer army has 3,500 personnel who fill the ranks of two infantry battalions (a third battalion, including artillery, is planned), an armoured recce squadron, an air-defence battery armed with Rapier SAMs, and engineer and signals squadrons. The Royal Malay Brunei Regiment, composed of 900 reservists, rounds out the army. Paramilitary forces consist of a 900-plus Gurkha Reserve Unit and 1,750 Royal Brunei Policemen.

EQUIPMENT

Armour:
Scorpion light tank
Sultan armoured car
VAB & AT-104 APCs
Air-Defence:
Rapier SAM

Below: The Gurkhas are a warrior hill people that make excellent soldiers, supreme in jungle craft. Their record in the British Army is what makes them attractive to Brunei; in 1982 the Argentinians fled rather than fight such a brave and ferocious foe.

CAMBODIA

FORMERLY A French Protectorate, Cambodia proclaimed its independence in 1953. Eyed covetously by both of its more powerful neighbours, Thailand and Vietnam, Cambodia had to try and balance its internal political forces and maintain a foreign policy of neutrality and non-alignment. It failed to avoid destabilization, there was a military coup and in 1975 nationalist, ostensibly Communist, Khmer Rouge insurgents seized power.

Under their leader, Pol Pot, there began a period of genocidal upheaval in the newly-named Kampuchea. In just over three years more than a million Kampucheans died. It only ended when Vietnam invaded in 1978, overthrew Pol Pot and installed a pro-Vietnamese government known as the Cambodia National United Front for National Salvation. They named the country the People's Republic of Kampuchea.

The Khmer Rouge are not defeated. They have continued their guerrilla war in the countryside, gathering nationalist anti-Vietnamese sympathy, and await the day they believe they will return to power. In 1982 they were a principal component of the

forces which united under the name of the Coalition Government of Democratic Cambodia.

Facing this coalition is the government of Hun Sen supported by Vietnam. Again renamed Cambodia, its People's Armed Forces (PAF) relies on conscription and is considered to be badly trained and led. It is organized at the national level under a Ministry of Defence with three departments: political, operational, and logistical. It is then divided into national, provincial and district armies spread among four military regions. These probably total 160,000 with the National Army accounting for one-third; the armies are supplemented by 50,000 in village militias.

The National Army has six infantry divisions, three independent infantry brigades, an armoured regiment, and dozens of independent, artillery, air-defence, cavalry, and pioneer units. It tends to rely on better firepower and has little special warfare capability, operating in large units and failing to undertake the sort of missions which will disrupt opponents like the Khmer Rouge.

Below: A heavily camouflaged T-54. Its firepower is not enough on its own to defeat the Khmer Rouge guerrilla forces in the field.

EQUIPMENT

Armour:
T-54/55 MBT
PT-76 & Type 62 light tanks
V-150 Commando, M113 & BTR-40, -60, & -152 APCs
Anti-Armour:
82mm B-10 & 84mm Carl Gustav RCLs
Artillery:
76mm & 122mm guns
107mm Type 63, 122mm BM-21 & 140mm BM-14/16 MRL
Air-Defence:
37mm & 57mm AAGs
Aircraft:
Mi-8 Hip
Mi-24 Hind

CHINA

THE PEOPLE'S Republic of China (PRC) is the largest nation in Asia and the most populous state in the world. Militarily, the manpower available to China dwarfs anything offered by any other country in the world. The power of human-wave attacks was shown during the Korean War. As far as equipment is concerned, early post-war Soviet designs and technology modified by the Chinese remain the mainstay of the People's Liberation Army (PLA) equipment inventory even today.

China has developed an independent strategic nuclear force and has been active within its Asian sphere of influence, supporting with military hardware a number of war efforts, notably that of their traditional rivals Vietnam and, more recently, the Pol Pot-led

Khmer Rouge in Kampuchea. With tensions rising between the latter two, and given Vietnam's alignment with the USSR, the Chinese invaded northern Vietnam in 1979 and violent border clashes have continued ever since (as they did for many years between China and the USSR and India; the latter escalating to full-scale war).

Such clashes highlighted the PLA's need for new strategic and tactical doctrines, reorganization and re-equipment; it was especially deficient in command, control, communications, and logistics. Modernization; however, was deferred largely for economic reasons. It was not until the mid-1980s that major changes took place: veteran leaders, many political appointees, were retired and agreements concluded to import Western technology.

Sino-Soviet relations improved during the same period and more effort was devoted to regional arms control. The new generation of PLA leaders had begun to implement professionally-minded reforms in civil-military relations, organization, training, education, and operational methods — even to the extent of re-introducing rank insignia

and designing new PLA uniforms.

Mao's doctrine of "People's War", based on mass mobilization, luring an invader deep, and waging a protracted guerrilla conflict, was modified to a more modern, active defensive-strategy that emphasized use of minefields and counter-attacking armoured and mechanized infantry forces.

To obtain the foreign currency needed to purchase foreign military technology and to pay for indigenous production, China launched an extensive arms export programme during the arly 1980s. This was tied to China's foreign policy and military modernization goals rather than Communist ideology and supporting so-called wars of national liberation. The initial results were spectacular, with considerable quantities of relatively unsophisticated weaponry sold to a host of states. The Iran-Iraq War proved lucrative and sales of more sophisticated armaments, such as aircraft, tanks and missiles, led to China becoming one of the top arms exporters in the world. Indigenous design and manufacturing capabilities, via the state-run industry NORINCO, have increased markedly to the point where China is no longer a market for foreign military goods but joint-venture hopes remain unfulfilled.

The economy has delayed modernization, especially in the PLA ground forces, as has the lessening of Sino-Soviet border tensions. However, tension along the Sino-Indian border in 1987 resulted in deployment of Chinese forces and led to a strategic re-orientation to meet such southern threats. Then, in March 1988, conflict with Vietnam over the Spratley Islands resulted in another new strategic orientation and emphasis on light, offensive-orientated, rapid-deployment forces: airborne and Marine units, naval aviation, and helicopters, rather than massive ground forces. The strategy of rapid-reaction also furthered China's aspiration to be the dominant power in the Asia-Pacific region, and it fulfills China's stated desire to play a major world role.

Some Chinese defence planners propose a national emphasis on strategic deterrence. Others look to future contention over the world's oceans and in Space, requiring highly sophisticated offensive aerospace and naval capabilities — all difficult to attain under China's current economic and technological limitations.

The events in Beijing's Tiananmen Square in 1989 showed that the PLA could still be relied upon to supress ruthlessly any threats to the existing internal order. Militarily, it resulted in a temporary reduction of Western technology transfers and compounded the modernization problems.

The PLA has still not been properly reorganized and streamlined, although some progress has occured, with excess manpower cut, outdated tactical concepts discarded, training arranged to make the best use of available equipment, educational deficiencies reduced, and a professional officer and NCO corps established.

The huge PLA structure integrates all of China's active armed forces, reserves, and paramilitary forces, which, including the People's Armed Police now under the Ministry of Public Security, may together number as high as 15 to 16 million persons. The total active element of the PLA is, however, slightly smaller than that of the Soviet Union. The Chinese Army alone, at about 2.3 million, is the world's largest.

Government and Party control of the PLA is exercised through two military commissions, both chaired by Deng Xiaoping: the Central Military Commission of the National People's Congress and the Military Commission of the Chinese Communist Party Central Committee. These jointly control the PLA through the Ministry of National Defence of the State Council, a key administrative organization.

The PLA has three main directorates: General Staff; General Logistics, which is responsible for personnel and materiels; and General Political, which is responsible for maintaining ideological orientation and political perspective. The General Staff controls the PLA services and branches: air force, navy, artillery, armour, engineers, communications, chemical/nuclear/biological, and the Second Artillery Corps — China's strategic missile force. A fourth

Above: With more than one billion people China's PLA does not lack a recruit pool. These men will make resolute combatants.

Below: Cleaning a 130mm Type 63 rocket launcher. It has 19 tubes mounted on a NJ-230 truck, six of which make a battery.

Above: This Soviet RPG lookalike is the Type 56 anti-tank grenade launcher. It fires an accurate, effective 80mm HEAT warhead.

subordinate element of the Ministry of National Defence is the National Defence Science, Technology, and Industry Commission, which supervises weapons research and development and coordinates six hi-tech industries.

Seven military regions — condensed from 11 in 1985 — provide operational control over the ground forces and are subdivided into 28 military districts and three garrison commands. PLA operational forces consist of 24 group armies (each equivalent to a Western corps) which control 80 infantry divisions (including several mechanized); 10 armoured divisions; five or six field and air-defence artillery divisions; and numerous independent infantry, artillery, and air-defence regiments. Army reserves may provide another 12 or more infantry and combat support divisions, and are being reorganized on a provincial basis.

Other PLA ground combat and combat-support elements are part of the navy and air force. The Air Force includes 220,000 air-defence personnel in 16 AAA divisions equipped with 16,000 anti-aircraft guns, and 28 independent SAM regiments. It also controls an airborne corps of four divisions and support troops. There are 28,000 Marines organized under the Navy into nine regiments with four infantry, three tank, and three artillery battalions; support elements; and special recce units backed by sizable reserves who constitute eight divisions upon mobilization. Their missions are to conduct amphibious operations, defend islands, and protect against enemy landings. Navy coastal regional forces number another 27,000 personnel; they man 35 independent artillery and SSM regiments deployed in 25 coastal defence regions to

Right: This assault rifle is a wooden stock Type 56 fitted with a long bayonet.

Above: The 12.7mm Type 77 machine gun made by NORINCO is only one of a number of anti-aircraft weapons in use with the PLA.

Above: Ranges such as the Himalayas mean good mountain troops are needed. This man lies in wait with an LPO-50 flamethrower.

Below: The Type 67 light machine gun is 7.62mm calibre and belt-fed. It has been improved upon with the Types 74 and 81.

protect naval bases, islands, etc.

Paramilitary forces number an estimated 12 million. The Basic Militia is some 4.3 million strong, but is to be cut by 80 per cent. The leaner successor will train and maintain close relationships with the group armies with whom they will collaborate during wartime, including any operations behind an invader's front lines.

There is an armed militia composed of men and women 18-28 years old who annually serve 30-40 days with regular forces, and a Maritime Militia, with armed trawlers and air-defence units. Both are under the Ministry of Defence. The ordinary militia, about six million people aged 18-35, are generally not armed. The Ministry of Public Security controls the People's Armed Police (PAP), which has 1.8 million people who are organized into 29 divisions and 1,000 battalion-sized border, mountain, and internal security units.

EQUIPMENT

Armour:
Types 59, 69, 69II, 79 & 80 MBTs
Types 62 & 63 light tanks
WZ501, Types 63/531, 85, 77-1 & -2 APCs
Anti-Armour:
90mm Type 51 RL
57mm Type 36, 75mm Types 52, & 82mm
 Type 65 RCLs
HJ-8 & HJ-73 ATGWs
Artillery:
122mm Types 54 & 83 & 152mm
 Type 66 Hs
122mm Type 54-1 & 152mm
 Type 83 SPHs
107mm Type 81, 122mm Type 83, 130mm
 Type 63 & 320mm WS-1 MRLs
Air-Defence:
12.7mm Type 77, 14.5mm Type 80, 37mm
 Type 73, 57mm Type 80, 85mm Type
 56 & 100mm Type 59 AAGs
HN-5, -5A, & -5C SAMs
Aircraft:
Sikorsky S-70C-II
Aerospatiale SA.342L Gazelle
Z-9 Haitun

INDIA

INDIA dominates the South Asian subcontinent and the surrounding Indian Ocean because of its land mass, its large population, and its expanding economy and technological capabilities, which are reflected in the size and capabilities of its armed forces. India is a regional superpower and aspiring world power. It has nuclear weapons production capability and tactical and strategic surface-to-surface missile programmes.

Despite geographical advantages, India's recent history has been marked by invasion, conquest, border clashes, and internal conflict. Her soldiers fought for Britain in two world wars (and also against her in the second) and the Indian Army remains the dominant armed service. It has fought China and there have been several wars with Pakistan; within the past few years there have been fairly large clashes in the mountainous border passes between the two countries.

Internally, the army has been deployed to quell sectarian rioting and in the Punjab to suppress an armed uprising by militant Sikhs fortified in the Golden Temple. One major repercussion from this successful operation was the assassination of Indira Ghandi. Externally, India sent a 50,000 strong peace-keeping force, which included T-72 tanks, to Sri Lanka in 1987 in an unsuccessful attempt to contain a violent Tamil separatist movement. It also deployed a small airborne force to put down a coup attempt in the Maldives in 1988. Both forces are now withdrawn.

The army has five regional commands: Central, Eastern, Northern, Southern, and Western. The commander-in-chief controls both static formations (Areas, Independent Sub-Areas, and Sub-Areas) and corps, divisions, and brigade field units.

Indian recruitment practices are highly influenced by race and social position, with certain ethnic groups recruited for specific branches of services or regiments based upon social status or perceived proficiency in particular military occupations. India retains the "community" (same caste, linguistic, or territorial group) character in its fighting regiments as a hangover from British colonial days when the British favoured certain communities as "martial races." These were mainly the tribes, castes, and sects that had remained loyal to them during uprisings, such as the 1857 Sepoy Mutiny.

Officers are trained at three levels: precadet, cadet, and staff. Sainik schools at the state level prepare candidates academically and physically for entry as cadets into the tri-service, three-year National Defence Academy. Officers are further trained at service schools; staff officers are trained at the Staff College at Wellington; and senior

Above: India stresses self-reliance and the Arjun battle tank is one result. It has a 120mm rifled gun and will replace the Vickers-designed Vijiyanta. Entering service in the 1990s, 2,000 may be built eventually.

Below: The Indian Army's involvement in Sri Lanka as a peace-keeping force quickly turned sour and units found themselves at war with the Tamils. These men are armed with FALs, Brens and Sterling Mk4s.

officers are trained at the National Defence College at New Delhi. Army enlisted recruits are trained by training battalions of their regiment, starting at age 16.

The Indian Army has 1,100,000 regulars, 200,000 reservists, and 50,000 in the territorials. The army's five commands are equivalent to Field Armies, and there are 10 corps headquarters. Its major formations are: two armoured divisions, one mechanized infantry division, 19 infantry divisions (each having two to five infantry brigades and one artillery brigade; some have an armoured regiment), 11 mountain divisions (composed of three to four brigades and one or more artillery regiment each), 14 independent combat brigades (five armoured, seven infantry, one mountain, one parachute/commando), three artillery brigades, six air-defence brigades, and four engineer brigades.

The mountain divisions were created after the war with China in the Himalayas in 1963. It had revealed some deficiencies in the army regarding combat capability in such difficult terrain.

These formations are comprised of some 53 tank regiments (battalions), 19 mechanized and 332 infantry battalions, nine parachute/commando battalions, 164 artillery regiments, 39 mountain regiments, 29 air-defence regiments (including 10 SAM groups of three to five batteries each), seven squadrons and 25 aerial observation flights, and 10 helicopter squadrons.

Paramilitary forces are numerous in variety and size. They include the National Security Guard (a 5,000 strong anti-terrorism and contingency force composed of armed forces, Central Police, and Border Guard personnel), the Central Reserve Police Force (90,000 regulars and 250,000 reserves in 108 battalions armed with SLR and AK-47 rifles for internal security duties who serve as army first-line reserves), the Border Security Force (90,000 strong equipped with small arms, light artillery, transport/liaison aircraft), the Assam Rifles (40,000), the Ladakh Scouts (5,000), the Indo-Tibetan Border Police (14,000), the

Special Frontier Force (8,000), the Central Industrial Security Force (70,000), the Defence Security Force (30,000), the Railway Protection Forces (70,000) and the Provincial Armed Constabulary (250,000).

India has a large and increasingly sophisticated defence industry which is building the Soviet T-72M1 MBT and BMP-1 and -2 IFV and the Swedish Bofors FH-77 155mm howitzer under licence.

It is also developing the following: Arjun 60-tonne MBT to replace the Vijiyanta; Akash medium-range SAM; Trishul quick-reaction, low-level SAM; Prithvi 250km range tactical SSM; and Nag 3rd-generation fire-and-forget ATGM. Current 7.62mm small arms are to be replaced by a lighter and more efficient Indian-designed 5.56mm rifle, carbine, and machinegun now in the prototype stage. There also are advocates of establishing an Indian Marine corps, based on the US model but part of the army, to form the core of an expanded rapid-deployment force.

EQUIPMENT

Armour:
T-55, T-72/-M1, & Vijiyanta MBTs
PT-76 light tank
BRDM-2 armoured car
BMP-1 & Sarath IFVs
OT-62, OT-64 & BTR-60 APCs
Anti-Armour:
84mm Carl Gustav & 106mm M40A1 RCLs
MILAN & AT-4 Spigot ATGWs
Artillery:
105mm Abbot SPH
130mm M-46 gun
155mm FH-77B H
122mm BM-21 MRLs
Air-Defence:
40mm Bofors L40/60 & /70 AAGs
23mm ZSU-23-4 SPAAG
SA-6, -7, -8A, -8B, -9, & Tigercat SAMs
Aircraft:
Aerospatiale Chetak
Aerospatiale SA.315 Cheetah
Hindustan SA.316 Alouette III

INDONESIA

THE REPUBLIC of Indonesia has the largest population (190 million) in south-east Asia and it is expected to grow dramatically. It is also the largest debtor nation. Possible unrest due to overcrowding and poverty is the major internal security concern, while the major external threat is the potential for conflict in the South China Sea involving Indonesia's offshore oil platforms and Exclusive Economic Zone, which the air force and navy are deployed north to defend.

The Indonesian Army has created a rapid-deployment force to counter any insurgency and defend outlying territories. A joint Indonesian-Malaysian exercise in 1988 tested these capabilities when the Malaysian Army relieved a Jakarta garrison which had deployed on a counter-insurgency field exercise. Further combined exercises of this kind are planned.

Due to a constrained military budget Indonesia's armed forces must establish clear priorities and often make do by upgrading old equipment. For example, ageing Soviet PT-76 amphibious light tanks have been scheduled for modernization rather than replacement this will include re-arming with 90mm guns.

The Indonesian Army has an active component of 216,000 and plans for 800,000 reservists. The strategic reserve (KOSTRAD) consists of: two infantry division headquarters (a third is being organized), an armoured cavalry brigade, three infantry brigades with nine battalions, three airborne brigades with eight battalions, two field artillery regiments with six battalions, an air-defence artillery regiment with two battalions, and two engineer battalions.

The country is divided into ten commands which control 63 infantry battalions, four airborne battalions, eight field artillery battalions, nine air-defence battalions (six medium, three light), six engineer battalions, four special forces (KOPASSUS) groups, and composite aviation and helicopter squadrons. Airlift resources are, however, limited.

Indonesia also has very large paramilitary forces: 115,000 in the Department of Defence and Security; a 300,000 strong Militia whose members receive three weeks' annual training; and various maritime, police, customs units, local guards and auxiliaries including 12,000 well-armed men in the Police Mobile Brigade.

There are lightly-armed guerrillas operating against the army: the Fretilin (Revolutionary Front for an Independent East Timor) with 400 or so activists fighting the bloody annexation of their territory by Indonesia in 1975, and the Free Papua Movement (FPM) which has perhaps 600 activists.

Above: These men belong to the elite shock force known as the Mobile Brigade. Many are airborne and Ranger qualified.

EQUIPMENT

Armour:
AMX-13 & PT-76 light tanks
Saladin & Ferret armoured cars
AMX-VCI IFV
BTR-40 & -152, V-150
Commando & Saracen APCs
Anti-Armour:
90mm M67 & 106mm M40A1 RCLs
ENTAC ATGW
Artillery:
76mm M1938 gun
105mm M101 & FV Mk 61 Hs
Air-Defence:
20mm, 40mm M1 & 57mm S-60 AAGs
Rapier & RBS-70 SAMs
Aircraft:
MBB Bo-105
IPTN-Bell-412
Hughes 300C

JAPAN

MILITIARISTIC nationalism led an imperialistic Japan into WWII and subsequent defeat at the hands of the Allies. Following the war, and the imposition of a constitution which attempted to avert any resurgence of militarism, the Japanese Self-Defence Forces were formed in 1954 at the urging of the US which was then fighting in Korea (a traditional Japanese sphere of interest).

With Japan having become one of the world's most powerful economies and with memories in the region fresh with the atrocities committed during her aggressive years, resistance to expansion of the Japanese SDF is strong. The 1946 Constitution stresses the self-defence nature of the forces and specifically limits the level of military expenditure, but as this is a percentage of gross domestic product (GDP) it still permits a very large budget indeed. There are powerful forces in Japan who wish to ignore even these proscriptions, a pressure which will grow in the future.

The primary mission of the Ground Self-Defence Force (GSDF) is to repulse small-scale foreign attacks. The forthcoming defence budgets allow for modernization in order to concentrate on acquisition of long-range weapons, upgrading of air-defence capabilities, increased emphasis on helicopters, and improvements in command, control, and communications. The long-range weapons include the Type 88 ground-launched anti-ship missile, the multiple-launch rocket system (MLRS), and artillery to counter amphibious landings.

The prime minister exercises supreme civilian authority over Japan's SDF via the Japanese Defence Agency which is directly under his control. Defence policy is formulated by the National Defence Council which rarely meets, but key members usually decide policies. The parliament has a defence committee and holds financial control over SDF programmes.

Japan is organized into four army areas: Northern Army in Hokkaido, which has the largest concentration of forces because it is the most likely invasion area (situated opposite Soviet Sakkalin Island and the disputed Kurile islands); North-Eastern Army in central Honshu and Tokyo; Central Army in southern Honshu and on Shikoku; and Western Army in Kyushu.

The GSDF has a current manning level of 153,000 out of 180,000 authorized personnel, and 46,000 reservists. There are no paramilitary forces. The army headquarters control a total of 12 infantry divisions, one armoured division (the 7th Division which is committed to Hokkaido), two composite brigades, one airborne brigade, one artillery brigade, two artillery groups, one helicopter brigade with 24 squadrons and three platoons of attack

Above: A Mitsubishi light vehicle at Camp Fuji fitted with a 106mm recoilless rifle and ammunition trailer.

Below: A Type 74 MBT leading an exercise assault. Japan has about 800 of these 105mm gun tanks and an updated

replacement is now at prototype stage. It will become the Type 90 and has the 120mm smoothbore main gun.

Above: The Type SU 60 APC has a crew of four and can transport six infantrymen, fully armed, into battle.

helicopters, five engineer brigades, one signals brigade, two air-defence brigades with eight SAM groups, two SSM battalions, and three training brigades.

The GSDF is equipped with relatively modern weapons and vehicles produced in Japan. Its officers are trained in a tri-service academy near Tokyo; there is also a Staff College and a National Defence College in Tokyo. The volunteer recruits are placed in training brigades and then in their units.

EQUIPMENT

Armour:
Types 61, 74, & 90 MBTs
M41 light tank
Types 82 & 87 armoured cars
Types SU 60 & 73 APCs

Anti-Armour:
84mm Carl Gustav, 89mm M20, & 106mm
    Type 60 RCLs
Types 64, 79 Jyu-MAT, & 97 Chyu-MAT
    Medium ATGWs

Artillery:
105mm M101, 155mm M2, &
    203mm M115 Hs
105mm Type 74, 155mm Type 75, FH-70
    & 203mm M110 SPHs
130mm Type 75 MRLs

Air-Defence:
35mm, 37mm, 40mm, & 75mm AAGs
Improved Hawk, Type 81 Tan, & Stinger
    SAMs

Aircraft:
Bell UH-1B & -1H Iroquois
Bell AH-1S HueyCobra
Boeing-Vertol CH-47J Chinook

KOREA (NORTH)

PARTITIONED as a result of WWII, the division of Korea was solidified following the failed war of aggression in 1950 waged by Communist forces in the north to try and unite the country. The period since the ceasefire in 1953 has been one of heavily armed stand-off between the two separate states, punctuated by armed skirmishes along the border in which nearly 100 US servicemen alone have been killed. There are, however, increased contacts and talks to discuss re-unification.

The Korean Peoples' Army (KPA) encompasses all North Korean armed forces and, although its formal mission is to defend the southern border, it is offensively orientated. Nevertheless, despite annual expenditures of an estimated 25 per cent of GDP, the North is unlikely ever to overcome increasingly technologically superior Republic of Korea (ROK) armed forces and their rapid reserve mobilization capability. Indeed, the huge, dug-in armed forces on either side of the DMZ would be most limited by the terrain: attack corridors have become increasingly urbanized, there is much mountainous terrain, and the peninsula itself is very narrow.

The KPA is hampered by a heavily ideological bureaucracy. The Party's Military Affairs Committee controls the Ministry of National Defence, the formal government organ of control over the armed forces. The Party has political officers in each army, division, etc., down to company level, and Party committees in every corps, division, and regiment.

Operationally, the KPA is uniquely comprised of five branches under one general staff: the infantry, mechanized forces, artillery, air force, and navy. These are largely organized, politically administered, trained, equipped, and uniformed on the Soviet model, but they also retain unique North Korean characteristics. An unusual aspect, from a Western perspective, is the KPA's building of numerous tunnels, both defensive ones in the north and at least eighteen for infiltration under the DMZ into the south.

The army, or ground force of the KPA, has an estimated 930,000 active personnel and 500,000 reservists. Its ranks are filled by universal conscription of all able-bodied males of 20 years of age. Recruits join with rudimentary training having been obtained in youth corps of the Worker's and Peasants' Red Militia which trains for two hours per week. The term of service is for five years.

Officers are either regular or short-service and are selected from members of the Young Communist organization or the Socialist Working Youth League and from high schools and colleges. There are three main officer training schools: the one-year 1st Combined Officers Training School for

Above: The hostile look of this guard at the UN DMZ building befits a state that remains suspicious of the outside world.

short-service officers, the 1st Combined Military Academy with a two to three year course, and the Army War College which offers a two to three year mid-level staff course and a one-year course for seniors.

North Korea also has large paramilitary forces: there are 200,000 personnel in the Security Corps and Border Guards under the Ministry of the Interior, and perhaps three million in the Worker's and Peasant's Red Militia which is organized on a local basis but serves as a reserve for the regular army in defence of the homeland. There is also the Youth Red Guard.

The army is organized into 17 corps: one armoured, five mechanized, one infantry, eight combined-arms, and two artillery. They control 25 infantry divisions (three motorized), 15 armoured brigades, 30 mechanized/motorized infantry brigades, and four independent infantry brigades. In addition, there is a Special Purpose Corps (SPC), manned by 80,000 troops who constitute the worlds largest special operations force. They form 22 brigades, including three commando, four recce, three amphibious, and three airborne, plus a river-crossing regiment, 22 light-infantry and eight "Bureau of Reconnaissance" battalions.

The Artillery Corps consists of: eight heavy artillery and two mortar regiments, and six tactical surface-to-surface missile battalions at army level; four brigades of mixed 122mm and 152mm self-propelled artillery weapons and MRLs at corps-level; and air-defence artillery with two divisions and seven independent regiments.

The SPC would be used in conjunction with conventional forces attacking across the DMZ during wartime. They would be airlifted by the fleets of 250 An-2 Colt light transports and 87 Hughes Model 500D/E helicopters smuggled into North Korea dur-

ing 1983-85 or infiltrated by water craft into South Korea to attack critical points of communications, airfields, missile sites, etc. in order to disrupt ROK/US fighting and mobilization capabilities.

KPA equipment is increasingly designed and developed in North Korea as well as being produced there, often incorporating guns or other features developed in the USSR, China, or elsewhere in Europe. Export of North Korean weapons, ranging from small arms to tanks, APCs, heavy artillery, MRLs and perhaps even Scud-B missiles during the Iran-Iraq War, earns the country much-needed foreign currency. There are military advisers in 13 African countries.

EQUIPMENT

Armour:
T-54/55, Type 59, & T-62 MBTs
Types 62 & 63 light tanks
SU-76 & SU-100 assault guns
Type 63/531, & BTR-40, -50, -60,
  & -152 APCs

Anti-Armour:
75mm Type 52, RPG-7, 82mm B-10, &
  107mm B-11 RCLs
85mm D-48 & D-44 guns
AT-1 Snapper & AT-3 Sagger ATGWs

Artillery:
122mm D-30, 130mm D-74, & 152mm
  D-20Hs
122m M-1985 & 170mm M.1978 SPHs
122m BM-21 & 240mm BM-24 MRLs

Air-Defence:
14.5mm ZPU-4 & 23mm ZU-23 AAGs
57mm ZSU-57-2 SPAAG
HN-5A SAM

KOREA (SOUTH)

THE REPUBLIC of Korea (ROK) occupies the southern two-thirds of the Korean Peninsula. It owes its existence, independent of the Communist north, to the intervention of UN armed forces which saved it from being overrun in 1950. Today, a large force of US troops remains stationed in the country and attempts continue by the North to destabilize the South, including a bomb attack on a government delegation visiting Burma in 1983.

An authoritarian country, the ROK has been under a military junta for most of its 40 years. Economic growth and international acceptance, however, have led to growing self-confidence throughout the country, and nowhere more so than in the armed forces.

The prime security concern remains the North's stated ambition to re-unify the peninsula by force, if necessary, and its commitment of significant resources to achieve that ambition. Both countries have remained on a semi-wartime footing since the end of the

Above: A very well camouflaged M47 tank of the 31st Tank Battalion supports assaulting troops of 2nd Brigade, 25th Infantry Division during the annual ROK/US exercise named "Team Spirit". Joint training provides for a real war scenario.

Below: The 105mm KH-78 howitzer began production in 1984 and incorporates elements from both the British Light Gun and the German modified M101. It can fire a High Explosive round a maximum of 16,000yds (14,700m) and provides good fire support.

Above: These tough looking troops are members of a crack airborne brigade. The lead man carries a 5.56mm K1A1 machine gun, an indigenous weapon which embodies features from the Kalashnikov, M16 and others. It has three firing modes.

Below: ROK troops armed with M16A1s take cover behind an embankment. In Vietnam ROK soldiers earned a reputation for fearlessness. This, plus their active interrogation of captured Viet Cong, led to them being greatly feared.

Korean War in 1953. Important contributions to ROK security are the 1953 Mutual Defense Treaty with the United States and a similar commitment from 16 UN members to come to its aid if hostilities resume. The US retains large (40,000 strong) forces in the country, is integrated with the ROK forces, and undertakes annual combined maneouvres named "Team Spirit". In return, South Korea showed its goodwill by sending two army divisions — the elite 25th "Tiger" and 29th "White Horse" — and the Marine "Blue Dragon" Brigade to fight in the Vietnam war.

The ROK has a five-year Force Improvement Programme (FIP), which emphasizes the development of indigenous arms industries and the acquisition of sophisticated foreign technology. In addition to assembling/producing aircraft and helicopters, the ROK has developed the Type 88 MBT, which is comparable to the M1 Abrams, its own Korean infantry fighting vehicle (KIFV), plus a growing variety of artillery weapons, small arms, munitions, etc. The South's technological superiority increasingly offsets the North's numbers.

The ROK Army has 650,000 active personnel, and 1.4 million regular and 3.3 million reservists operationally grouped into three Homeland Defence Force armies: the First Army, about 10 divisions, guards the western half of the DMZ with North Korea; the Third Army, with about 8 divisions, guards the eastern half of the DMZ. The Second Army garrisons the interior, defends the coast, serves as the reserve, and performs the administrative functions: recruiting, training, and logistics.

Eight ROK Army corps headquarters control: two mechanized infantry divisions (each has three brigades, with three mechanized infantry, three motorized infantry, three tank, and one recce battalion per brigade, plus one field artillery brigade), 19 infantry divisions (each has three infantry, one tank, one recce, one engineer, and one artillery regiment), two independent infantry brigades, seven special warfare brigades, five airborne brigades; one army aviation brigade, two air-defence brigades, with three Hawk and two SAM brigades, two Nike Hercules battalions, and two SSM battalions. Reserves fill one army HQ and 23 infantry divisions.

Military recruitment is by conscription. The term of service for soldiers and Marines is 30 months. Army training is conducted initially at recruit training centres, and afterwards specialists train at service schools.

Each service has an academy for training its regular officers. The army trains short-service officers at the Third Military Academy. There is strong US influence in ROK organization, command structure, and uniforms. Weapons and equipment are still mainly of US origin or design, but ROK indigenous capabilities are constantly on the increase.

ROK paramilitary forces are numerous, well-trained and can serve as an additional reserve for the armed forces during wartime or perform rear-area security duties against the threat from North Korea's numerous special operations forces. They consist of 3.5 million citizens in the Civilian Defence Corps, 600,000 in the student Homeland Defence Corps, and 3,500 in the Coast Guard, which is equipped with 46 patrol craft, numerous boats, and nine Hughes 500D helicopters.

EQUIPMENT

Armour:
Type 88 & M60A1 MBTs
M47 & M48 medium tanks
KIFV & LVTP-7 IFVs
Fiat 6614, KM-901, & M113 APCs

Anti-Armour:
94mm LAW
90mm M67 & 106mm M40A2 RCLs
TOW ATGWs

Artillery:
105mm KH-178, 155mm KH-179,
 & 203mm M115 Hs
155mm M109 & 203mm M110 SPHs
130mm Kooryong MRLs

Air-Defence:
20mm Vulcan M167 & 35mm Oerlikon
 GDF-003 SPAAGs
Hawk, Nike-Hercules, Javelin, Stinger &
 Redeye SAMs

Aircraft:
Bell UH-1B & -1H Iroquois
Bell AH-1S HueyCobra
Cessna 0-1A Bird Dog
Hughes 500 MDH

LAOS

LAOS WAS proclaimed a People's Democratic Republic by the Pathet Lao movement after King Savang Vatthana abdicated following the Communist victories in both Vietnam and Cambodia in April 1975.

Laos is the only south-east Asian Communist state to have diplomatic relations with the United States. Its leaders have abandoned economic doctrine, but they have rejected democratic political reforms. There has been continuing ethnic unrest and insurgency, and during 1984-88 there were numerous incidents of cross-border fighting with Thailand. During one ten-week period in late 1987, fighting over a disputed border area resulted in over 200 Laotian and 50 Thai deaths. The largest group of insurgents, the United Lao National Front, has an armed strength of about 2,000.

Today's Lao People's Army (LPA, formerly the People's Liberation Army until renamed in 1982), is the successor to the Pathet Lao insurgents that fought the French and defeated the Royal Lao Army in 1975. It is organized and equipped along Vietnamese lines, and the Vietnamese have brought a strong influence to bear on the shape of Laotian counter-insurgency operations. Until recently there were three Vietnamese infantry divisions stationed there, and several thousand construction troops remain.

The LPA has 52,000 soldiers divided among four military regions and consists of five infantry divisions, seven independent infantry regiments, one armoured battalion, five artillery and nine anti-aircraft artillery battalions, two construction and one engineer regiments, 65 independent infantry companies, and one light aircraft liaison flight. Paramilitary forces consist of the 13,000 strong Police Field Force, and the 200,000 strong People's Volunteer Corps.

EQUIPMENT

Armour:
T-34 & T-54/55 MBTs
PT-76 light tanks
BTR-40, -60, & -152 APCs
Anti-Armour:
57mm M18, 75mm M20 & 107mm B-11 RCLs
Artillery:
105mm M101, 122mm D-30 & M-1938 Hs
Air-Defence:
57mm S-60 AAG
23mm ZSU-23-4 SPAAG
SA-3 & -7 SAMs

MALAYSIA

THE FEDERATION of Malaysia became an independent member of the British Commonwealth in 1957 and, with help from Britain, it defeated a Communist insurgency in a campaign often hailed as a model example of its kind. Today, Malaysia is a member of ASEAN and the Five-Power Defence Alliance (FPDA) that includes the UK, Australia, New Zealand, and Singapore. It participates in FPDA exercises and conducts bilateral patrol exercises with Indonesia and air exercises with Thailand. The first joint military exercise with Singapore was held in 1989.

The Royal Malaysian Army is organized into one corps of four divisions, which control nine infantry brigades. There is one parachute battalion and 36 infantry battalions, including one mechanized battalion equipped with British AT-105, German Condor, and US V-100/150 wheeled APCs. Regiments include five armoured recce, one special forces, five field artillery, two air-defence artillery, and five of engineers. Army reserves, 45,000 strong, form a divisional headquarters, a brigade headquarters, 12 infantry regiments (being

Below: Soldiers train in COIN at Sungai Udang Special Warfare Training Centre which is rated one of the best in the world. Recruits emerge with jungle craft skills, some based on lessons from the 1950s' "Emergency".

reorganized into three brigades), and four highway system battalions.

In 1984, the Malaysian armed forces instituted a major conventional warfare training programme. The army was trimmed to just less than 100,000 personnel, an armoured corps was developed and there are plans to field nine parachute infantry battalions. New small arms will include 65,000 Steyr AUG rifles assembled in Malaysia. A $17 billion arms acquisition programme with the UK includes Rapier and Javelin SAMs,

two Marconi-Martello 3-D radars, Royal Ordnance 105mm Light Guns, VSEL FH-70 155mm towed howitzers, and modernization kits for the army's Ferret scout cars. As in Thailand, 35mm AA guns linked with Contraves Skyguard fire-control systems have been ordered for airfield defence.

EQUIPMENT

Armour:
Scorpion light tank

SIBMAS, AML 245 H60/90, & Ferret armoured cars
Condor, V-150 Commando, Stormer & Saxon APCs
Anti-Armour:
84mm Carl Gustav & 106mm M40A1 RCLs
SS-11 ATGW
Artillery:
105mm M56 & M102 Hs
Air-Defence:
40mm Bofors L40 AAG

MONGOLIA

THE MONGOLIAN People's Republic lies in north-central Asia, sandwiched between China to the south and the Soviet Union to the north. The world's second oldest Communist state, after Russia, Mongolia recently hosted six Soviet combat divisions; a figure now reduced to one motorized rifle division.

The Mongolian armed forces consist of an army and a small air force. They exist mainly as a symbol of national sovereignty, being too small to defend the vast expanse of their country.

The army numbers 21,000, including 17,000 conscripts, and 40,000 reservists. The structure is being reduced from four motorized rifle (actually mechanized infantry) divisions, organized and equipped on the Soviet model, to probably two understrength divisions. There also are a construction brigade and an SA-2 SAM battalion, but these are controlled by the air force.

Paramilitary forces consist of 15,000 frontier guards, internal security troops, and militia who have some BTR-60/152 APCs and are under the Ministry of Public Security.

EQUIPMENT

Armour:
T-54/55 & T-62 MBTs
BRDM-2 armoured cars
BMP-1 IFV
BTR-40, -60, & -152 APCs
Artillery:
100mm T-12 ATG
122mm D-30 & 152mm ML-20 Hs
122mm BM-21, 132mm BM-13-16, & 140mm BM-14-16/17 MRLs

Air-Defence:
14.5mm ZPU-4, 37mm M-1939 & 57mm S-60 AAGs
SA-7 SAM

Below: An official parade and smart well-drilled troops cannot hide the fact that the descendants of Genghis Khan suffer from their position between the two great Communist powers of China and the USSR. The borders are disputed and armed clashes have occurred in the recent past.

MYANMAR

IN 1948, the Union of Burma — recently renamed Myanmar — was established as an independent republic. Since then it has been under military rule and plagued by a host of insurgencies involving 15,000 Communists, Kachin, Shan, Mon, and Arakanese ethnic minorities, urban students, and Chinese Kuomintang remnants. A particularly severe problem is that of the 10,000 strong Karen Liberation Army fighting for its own state along the border with Thailand. There are also heavily armed communities involved in drug trafficking,

notably that of Khun Sa, a self-styled opium warlord. It is believed that the army is fighting 19 separate rebellions, including six large insurgent armies among them.

From the foregoing, it is obvious that the primary mission of Myanmar's Army is internal security. It has experienced uneven success in its counter-insurgency operations and suffered a great many casualties.

A one-party state, the army leadership and that of the ruling Burma Socialist Programme Party are one and the same. The 210,000-man volunteer army is an infantry force influenced by the British. It has 10 regional and one garrison commands, each comprised of three to four brigade-size Tactical Operations Commands (TOC). Three TOCs form a division and each TOC has three to four infantry battalions. Three divisions are directly controlled by the Defence Ministry as a reserve force. There are nine light-infantry division HQ, each of which

controls three TOCs comprised of 10 infantry battalions, and 31 TOCs that control a total of 85 infantry battalions, two armoured battalions, four artillery battalions, and one anti-aircraft battery. Their arms and equipment are largely obsolescent.

EQUIPMENT

Armour:
Type 69 MBT
Ferret & Humber armoured cars
Anti-Armour:
84mm Carl Gustav & 106mm M40A1 RCLs
Artillery:
6-pdr(57mm), 17-pdr (76mm), 25-pdr (88mm) & 5.5in (140mm) guns
76mm M-1948 & 105mm M101 Hs
122mm MRLs
Air-Defence:
40mm Bofors L/60 AAG

NEPAL

THE KINGDOM of Nepal is situated in the Himalayan mountain range between Chinese-controlled Tibet to the north and India to the east, south, and west. It follows a policy of non-alignment and has balanced relations with China and India, who both provide aid. India provides training assistance to Nepal's armed forces.

The Nepal Army consists of 25,000 volunteer regular soldiers and 25-30,000 reservists. It is organized into two understrength divisions composed of six infantry brigades; the Palace Guard, with a cavalry squadron and garrison battalion; a parachute battalion, an armoured recce squadron, an artillery regiment and an engineer battalion.

One infantry battalion, 850 soldiers, is assigned to UNIFIL in Lebanon and the Nepalese continue to allow the British to recruit troops for their Gurkha units. There is also a paramilitary police force of 28,000.

EQUIPMENT

Armour:
AMX-13 light tank
Ferret armoured car
Artillery:
3.7in (94mm) gun
Air-Defence:
40mm Bofors L/60 AAG

PAKISTAN

THE ISLAMIC Republic of Pakistan (Urdu for "Land of the Pure" and an acronym for Punjab, Sind, Kashmir, and Baluchistan) is strategically located at the meeting point of South Asia and the Middle East and shares borders with India, China, Afghanistan, and Iran.

Tensions with India remain high, largely due to the dispute over the province of Kashmir which India controls. Clashes along the border are not infrequent, especially on the Siachen glacier, despite attempts by both governments to resolve the damaging conflict.

The Soviet invasion of Afghanistan has also had large repercussions in Pakistan. Soviet and Afghan forces both violated borders and the US and China poured in equipment, both to support Afghan resistance groups and Pakistan's military government. Pakistan has been regarded by the US as a strategic ally in the region, compensating for the fall of the Shah of Iran.

As well as generous outside support, there is considerable indigenous capability. In 1989, Pakistan successfully test-fired two SSMs it had developed, the Hatf I and Hatf II (with 80km and 300km capabilities respectively). It is also widely rumoured that Pakistan is nuclear-capable.

In mid-1990, Pakistan and Iran, with the potential long-term inclusion of Afghanistan, were planning to establish an "Islamic Defence Line" and to arrive at a common strategic consensus. Iranian officers are to attend Pakistan's Defence College.

The Pakistani Army is all-volunteer and organized along British lines. Corps are commanded by a lieutenant general and control two or more divisions. Divisions are triangular, having three brigades of three battalions each, plus artillery, engineer, signals, and supply elements.

Army recruits are trained by their units, with basic training lasting up to six months depending on the service arm. The Pakistan Military Academy trains officers via a two-and-a-half year course of academic and military subjects. An alternative is the Army Education Corps, in which university graduate officer candidates attend a short military instruction course before they receive commissions. Pakistan also has a Command and Staff College and the National Defence College at Rawalpindi for higher military education.

The army has 480,000 regulars and 500,000 reservists and is organized under nine corps headquarters. Major units include two armoured divisions, eight independent armoured brigades, 19 infantry divisions, four independent infantry brigades, three armoured recce regiments, nine artillery brigades, four air-defence artillery brigades, one special services group with three battalions, seven SAM batteries, five army aviation squadrons and some independent flights. Equipment is largely of Chinese and US origin.

Pakistan's numerous paramilitary forces consist of the 150,000 strong National Guard, which has a variety of units; the 65,000 strong Frontier Corps with its own APCs; and several other formations, including the Pakistan Rangers (15,000) and the Northern Light Infantry (9,500).

Most recently, the Pakistan government deployed an infantry brigade to the Gulf where it joined the forces assembled to liberate Kuwait.

EQUIPMENT

Armour:
T-54/55 & Type 59 MBTs
PT-76 & Type 63 light tanks
M47 & M48 medium tanks
Type 531 & M113 APCs
Anti-Armour:
75mm Type 52 & 106mm M40A1 RCLs
Cobra, TOW, & Red Arrow ATGWs
Artillery:
25-pdr (88mm), 100mm Type 59 & 130mm Type 59-1 guns
105mm M7, 155mm M109, & 203mm M110 SPHs
105mm M101, 122mm Type 54-1, & 155mm M-59 Hs
122mm BM-21 MRL
Air-Defence:
57mm S-60 AAG
35mm Oerlikon GDF-002 SPAAG
Crotale, RBS-70, & Stinger SAMs
Aircraft:
Aerospatiale SA.330 Puma
Aerospatiale SA.316 Alouette III
Bell AH-1S HueyCobra

Above: Special Services Group Commandos are the elite of the Pakistan Army. They can wage conventional warfare, as they did in the last war with India, as well as special counter-terrorist operations and hostage rescue, storming planes etc.

THE PHILIPPINES

T ODAY recovering from the political corruption of the Marcos years, the Philippines remains a country where widespread poverty and dissatisfaction at its government's ineptitude have bred unrest, insurgencies, and dissension even within the Armed Forces of the Philippines (AFP).

The AFP played a crucial role in deposing Marcos after 20 years in power but elements remain discontented and, for a variety of very different reaons, they have staged seven attempted coups against the elected government of Corazon Aquino. The most serious one, in December 1989, involved elements of the air force and élite ground forces in bloody fighting in Manila.

A significant development in recent years is the growth of the Communist insurgency by the New People's Army (NPA) which has been active since the late-1960s. It is now more than 20,000 strong, engaged in a concerted campaign, and increasingly targeting US personnel who are thought to be involved in the counter-insurgency effort. It is believed the NPA has a developed political infrastructure in place with popular support in about one-seventh of the country. In recent years, however, the AFP has embarked on a more aggressive campaign, seeking out and eliminating NPA hideouts. A more sinister development has been the emergence of so-called "death squads"

targeting left-wing activists in Manila. This, combined with internal NPA problems, appears to have halted the momentum of the insurgents, for the time being at least.

The Philippines Army has 68,000 active soldiers, all volunteers, and 100,000 reservists. In addition to a Presidential Security Group of six battalions, the six area unified commands control a total of eight infantry divisions, a light armoured regiment, eight artillery battalions, a military police brigade, a special services brigade and

Above: The army's war against the NPA is at its most intense in the jungle and tall grass of the island of Mindanao where a Muslim insurgency raged for some years.

three engineer brigades. The army's elite counter-insurgency force is the 1st Scout Ranger Regiment, recently converted into the National Manoeuvre Force.

Officers train at the Philippines Military Academy at Baguio in northern Luzon; enlisted personnel of all services are trained by the AFP Training Command. The armed forces are patterned on US lines, wear US-style uniforms and rank insignia, and use largely US equipment.

Paramilitary forces, a vital element in counter-insurgency operations and internal security, consist of the Citizens Armed Forces Geographical Units (CAFGU), with 45,000 personnel in 56 battalions; and the regular Philippine Constabulary, 43,500 strong, who will merge with the Integrated National Police to form the Philippine National Police responsible for internal security under the Department of Interior.

EQUIPMENT

Armour:
Scorpion light tank
FMC IFV
M113, V-150 Commando, & Chaimite
  APCs
Anti-Armour:
75mm M20, 90mm M67, & 106mm M40A1
  RCLs
Artillery:
105mm M101 & 155mm M114 Hs
Air-Defence:
20mm M163 Vulcan SPAAG
Aircraft:
Bell UH-1H Iroquois
Hughes 369D
MBB Bo-105

Above: This soldier in a balaclava may be a member of 1st Scout Rangers which has 2,500 men and forms the National Maneouvre Force (NMF) which can deploy to any active sectors to form a strike force or act as a reserve for local commanders.

SINGAPORE

THE REPUBLIC of Singapore has a small land size and population, yet it spends 5.5 per cent of its GDP on defence. It has a dynamic and modern industrialized economy, with Singapore's government-owned defence and related industries having been reorganized as Singapore Technology (ST) to increase exports of military equipment. For example, ST's Ultimax 5.56mm light machine gun is now used by ten nations' worldwide.

The army is 45,000 strong, 35,000 of them conscripts. There are 170,000 reservists comprising 34 reserve battalions. Since 1968, the Singapore Armed Forces (SAF) have been a unified service with Territorial, Maritime, and Air-Defence Commands. Territorial Command monitors the regular forces, the reserves, and People's Defence Force. Regular Army forces comprise the Singapore Armoured Corps, Singapore Artillery, Singapore Engineers, Singapore Signals, and the Singapore Infantry Regiment, which has nine battalions. The operational forces consist of one infantry division HQ and support units, one armoured and three infantry brigades (one of them airmobile) four artillery, two engineer, and one commando battalions.

National service began in 1967 in the hope of creating an attitude of ''nationhood'' among the Chinese, Malay, Indian, and other racial groups. All males aged 18 must serve from 24 to 30 months. The army organization is based on that of the Israel Defence Forces, and the Singapore Army has been trained by Israeli advisors.

The reserves consist of two divisions with one armoured and six infantry brigade headquarters; and 18 infantry, one commando, 10 artillery, two air-defence artillery, and three engineer battalions. The People's Defence Force consists of 30,000 part-time volunteers organized into seven brigade groups and 21 battalions. Other paramilitary forces consist of 11,600 police, Marine and Gurkha guard battalions.

EQUIPMENT

Armour:
Centurion MBT
SM-1 (Upgraded AMX-13) light tank
AMX-13VTT, M113, V-150 &
  -200 Commando APCs
Anti-Armour:
84mm Carl Gustav & 106mm M40A1 RCLs
MILAN ATGW
Artillery:
155mm FH 88 & Soltam M71 Hs
25-pdr (88mm) gun
Air-Defence:
40mm Bofors L/70 AAG
35mm Oerlikon GDF-002 SPAAG
RBS-70 SAM

Left, above: Water-borne Commando troops armed with SAR-80 assault rifles prepare to attack. This is the best unit in the SAF but it still has not been tested in combat.

Left, below: The AMX-13 SM1 is a locally upgraded version of the French light tank. It is re-engined and has an automatic loading system for its 75mm main armament.

Above: The indigenous FH88 155mm howitzer is eight times faster to use than the old M71 import. It is also ergonomically designed for the average Asian build.

SRI LANKA

FORMERLY known as Ceylon, Sri Lanka is an Indian Ocean state near the south-eastern tip of India. Since 1983, Sri Lanka has experienced ethnic violence between the mostly Hindu Tamils, who desire a separate ethnically-based state, and the mainly Buddhist Sinhalese majority; and, since 1985, between the Tamils and the Muslim community.

An India-Sri Lanka peace accord aimed at ending the civil war was signed in July 1987. In exchange for greater administrative and political power, the Liberation Tigers of Tamil Eelam (LTTE) agreed to a ceasefire and surrender of their arms. An Indian Peace-Keeping Force (IPKF) of 30,000 troops was landed to implement it but matters were only exacerbated; fighting soon broke out between Indians and Tamils, and then a Sinhalese insurgency began in the south of the island.

By mid-1990, in response to the two insurgencies, the Sri Lanka Army had expanded to 50,000, of whom 32,000 were regulars. This was four times its 1983 strength. The army has three infantry divisions, each with two three-battalion brigades, plus 10 battalions in reserve. There are also two armoured recce regiments, four artillery regiments (one light, with 120mm mortars), and one each of anti-aircraft artillery, engineers, and signals. In 1985, the 1st Special Forces Regiment was organized to provide highly-trained infantry to operate in small units during counter-guerrilla operations; these are frequent and bloody affairs. There is also a separate regiment of commandos which is based at Ganamulla, near Colombo.

The almost entirely Sinhalese Sri Lanka Army has announced its intention to recruit five infantry battalions in the predominantly Tamil north to fill the vacuum left by the IPKF withdrawal, but response was initially poor. Army officers are trained in the UK, US, and India as well as at the Sri Lanka Military Academy. Paramilitary forces consist of the 26,000 strong Police Force; a National Auxiliary Volunteer Force with 5-10,000; a Home Guard with 18,000; and 6,000 volunteers in the two-battalion National Service Regiment, five infantry battalions, two National Guard battalions, and four to five reserve battalions.

EQUIPMENT

Armour:
Saladin & Ferret armoured cars
Buffel, Saracen & BTR-152 APCs
Anti-Armour:
83mm M60 & 106mm M40A1 RCLs
Artillery:
85mm Type 56 & 25-pdr (88mm) guns
Air-Defence:
40mm Bofors L/60 AAG

TAIWAN

TAIWAN, or the Republic of China (ROC) as it prefers to be called, is one of the most significant economies in Asia. It remains isolated politically because the People's Republic of China (PRC) is recognized by most countries as the legitimate government of Taiwan.

Relations between the two Chinas are improving, albeit slowly, but because of the PRC's territorial claims Taiwan continues to devote considerable resources to its defence. It has qualitative weapons superiority (with US military technology) and its defensive strategy emphasizes: air-defence, sea control, and anti-landing operations based on its being an isolated island nation.

Taiwan's anti-landing tactical doctrine stresses continuous development of ground and air fire-support assets, mobility, prepositioned tank emplacements, deployment of SAMs and SSMs on off-shore islands, new detection/surveillance devices, patrolling against infiltration and weapons smuggling, and counter-sabotage and counter-subversion operations.

The Chungshan Institute of Science and Technology (CIST) has developed a number of sophisticated weapons, including the Kung Feng VIA MRL, as well as SAMs, an anti-ship missile, and the Ching-Kuo fighter aircraft. The Army's Fighting Vehicle Development Centre has produced the upgraded M48H MBT.

The ROC or Taiwan Army is organized along US lines. The active force numbers 270,000, and the reserves, 1.3 to 1.5 million. Major headquarters include: three armies, six corps and special forces. These control two mechanized infantry divisions, 12 heavy and six light-infantry divisions, four tank groups, one airborne brigade, four special forces groups, up to eight defence battalions, one SSM and 22 field artillery battalions, three Hawk and two Nike Hercules SAM battalions, and six aviation squadrons. Special forces include long range amphibious recce commando units, which were active on the mainland for many years. About one-third of the army garrisons the small islands of Quemoy and Matsu, off the coast of the PRC. Paramilitary forces include 25,000 militia.

Above: An M48 tank with a 90mm gun and blast deflector. The commander's cupola has a .50in Browning machine-gun. An Armoured Infantry Fighting Vehicle brings up the rear; it is a local version which mixes the M113 and the US AIFV built by FMC.

EQUIPMENT

Armour:
M60A1 MBT
M48 medium tank
M113, M2, & V-150 Commando APCs
Anti-Armour:
106mm M40A1 RCL
Dragon ATGW
Artillery:
75mm M116, 105mm M101, 155mm M114, & 203mm M115 Hs
105mm M108, 155mm Type 69, & 203mm M110 SPHs
127mm Kung Feng MRL
Air-Defence:
40mm M42 SPAAG
Improved Hawk, Nike-Hercules, Chaparral, Tien Kung-1 & -2 SAMs
Aircraft:
Bell UH-1H Iroquois
Hughes OH-6A Cayuse

THAILAND

THAILAND IS a member of ASEAN and has found itself strained because of its position bordering Laos, Kampuchea/Cambodia, and Vietnam where there has been so much warfare over recent decades. Regional instability and mistrust has led to clashes with Vietnamese troops and with Laotian forces, which inflicted heavy losses on poorly coordinated Thai air and ground forces.

The military budget has long consumed a large proportion — about 20 per cent — of the Thai national budget, reflecting the major role that the army has played in Thai politics with over a dozen coups in the past half-century. Senior generals still dominate the political process, but as a whole, the

army, which is composed entirely of native-born Buddhist Thais, is becoming smaller, more professional, and less political.

The Thai Army of 190,000 includes 80,000 conscripts. It has four regional army and two corps headquarters and is reorganizing for conventional warfare. The new "core force" will have two armoured divisions (upgraded from light-cavalry), one mechanized infantry division, seven infantry divisions (including the Royal Guard with six battalions), two special forces divisions, single air-defence and artillery divisions, three new "development" divisions, and four reserve divisions. Development divisions are a new concept that uses the army to further economic development in provinces that experience insurgencies, of which there are several now posing a significant threat to the government.

The smaller Thai units include 19 engineer and eight infantry battalions, a cavalry regiment with three air-mobile companies, and four recce companies.

Thailand has a large mix of Chinese and US equipment as well as some of European origin. The 1st Cavalry Division is being equipped with US Cadillac Gage Stingray 105mm gun light tanks, while the 2nd Cavalry Division uses a mix of Chinese Type 69 and US M45A5 MBTs.

Indigenously, the Thais produce the German HK-33 assault rifle under licence, as well as the RPS-001, a Thai design that incorporates M16 rifle features and is used by Thai special forces. The Army Weapons Production Centre has also assembled M101 howitzers, and ICI Nobel produces a variety of small arms and ammunition, thus increasing self-sufficiency.

Thailand's armed forces are backed by large paramilitary forces: Thahan Phran Rangers ("Hunter Soldiers") are 18,500 volunteer irregulars organized into 27 regiments; additionally there are 43,000 National Security Volunteer Corps, 28,000 Border Patrol Police which have heliborne units, and 50,000 Provincial Police with a 500-man Special Action Force.

EQUIPMENT

Armour:
Type-69-2 & 60 MBTs
Scorpion & Stingray light tanks
EE-9 Cascavel armoured car
M113, M3, Type 63-2, 85/YW-531H, & V-150 Commando APCs

Anti-Armour:
75mm M20, 106mm M40A1, & 94mm LAW RCLs
Dragon & TOW ATGWs

Artillery:
155mm M114 & M198 Hs
155mm M109A5 SPH
105mm Kittikachorn & 130mm Type 82 MRLs

Air-Defence:
12.7mm M55 AAG
40mm M1 AAG
20mm M163 & M167 Vulcan SPAAGs
Redeye & Aspide SAMs

Aircraft:
Bell UH-1H & AH-1S HueyCobra

Left: An instructor teaches troops on a survival training course how to trap and cook small animals using only items in the jungle — life-saving skills.

Above: A Thai special forces soldier with tiger-stripe fatigues. The special forces maintain close links with many similar units around the world, notably the Australians and South Koreans with whom they have developed exchange programmes. They also train Thai Rangers and infantrymen.

Right: A guard from the Military Security Force attending the annual joint US/Thai parachute display. He is armed with an HK33 produced locally.

VIETNAM

THE PEOPLE'S Army of Vietnam (PAVN) traces its beginnings to a mountain cave near the Chinese border in 1930 when Vo Nguyen Giap and 33 others founded a semi-guerrilla group.

By the late-1980s, it had reached a peak strength estimated at over one million, with another three million in paramilitary forces, making it the world's third largest armed force behind the Chinese People's Liberation Army and the armed forces of the Soviet Union.

The PAVN has a remarkable record: it has been to war against three of the most powerful nations on earth and defeated two of them in succession: France and the United States; most recently, it has fought China while simultaneously engaged on the Cambodian front for a decade.

Its actual combat record in each of these wars is, however, far from perfect. Frequently, it suffered tactical setbacks against technologically superior French, US, and South Vietnamese forces and inferior Cambodian guerrillas. And in terms of lives its strategic victories were costly.

Below: Asian troops come no tougher than the Vietnamese, as the French, Chinese and Americans can testify. This is an anniversary victory parade in 1985 to celebrate Saigon's liberation in ten years earlier in a war that took nearly 30 years to win.

In recent years it has become increasingly dependent upon the USSR for its military supplies, having obtained many of them previously from China. With the Sino-Soviet rapprochement it seems unlikely such largesse will be maintained. In addition, a further military challenge has to be faced — that of internal resistance. This centres principally around Montagnard and ex-ARVN (South Vietnamese Army) forces based in the south, but there are groups emerging in the north. It is thought that there may be several thousand armed insurgents within Vietnam. At present they are the responsibility of the internal security apparatus but regular PAVN and paramilitary groups have been involved in fighting.

The PAVN Commander-in-Chief is also the Chairman of Vietnam's State Council. PAVN has five general directorates, including: General Staff, Political Indoctrination, Rear Services, Economic, and Technical. PAVN have been organized primarily along traditional lines as a three-level force: Main Force or regular elements; Regional or Local Force, consisting of infantry companies with limited mobility who form a standing reserve; Militia/People's Self-Defence Force which are organized on the social structure (village, urban precinct) or economic enterprise (factory, etc.).

PAVN Main Forces are controlled by 14 corps headquarters and consist of up to 65 infantry divisions (including two training and 28 cadre divisions) whose strength varies from 5,000 to 12,000, three mechanized infantry divisions, 15 independent

Above: This picture was taken in 1986 and shows a Vietnamese infantryman before an ancient temple in Cambodia. Note his canvas and rubber combat shoes suited to jungle combat.

Above: An officer of the Viet Cong in 1972. The place is Loc Ninh, a town taken during the spring offensive as the Communists advanced on Saigon but then faltered and lost their momentum.

infantry regiments, 10 armoured brigades, 10 field artillery regiments, eight engineer divisions, about 15 economic construction divisions, two transport divisions, and 20 independent engineer brigades. There is also a Special Operations Force, including an airborne brigade and a regiment of five battalions of demolition engineers (sappers). PAVN has also raised ten brigades of Marines that saw action in the coastal provinces of Cambodia and exercised in amphibious operations with the crack Soviet Marines in 1984.

Economic construction divisions are composed of about 3,000 older soldiers, often veterans of the war in the south, who are armed and trained as soldiers but who perform economic tasks, such as building airfields, bridges, and roads, and raising rice and livestock. Many are stationed in northern Vietnam. Engineer and transport divisions are about 4,000 strong. Total Main Force strength in 1989 was about 1.15 million; the end of PAVN participation in conflicts in Cambodia and Laos, border tensions with China, and economic factors, will probably result in significant force reductions.

Paramilitary forces consist of a 60,000 strong Border Defence Force, a 500,000 strong People's Regional Force with a regimental HQ at each provincial capital, and 1 million or more in the mainly urban-based People's Self-Defence Force.

As stated, armaments are Soviet or Chinese, but there is also a considerable quantity of US materiel which was captured in 1975 and included over 1,000 tanks and APCs and several thousand artillery pieces, most still working.

EQUIPMENT

Armour:
T-34, T-54/55, T-62 & Type 59 MBTs
M48 medium tanks
PT-76 & Type 60/63 light tanks
SU-76 & SU-100 assault guns
BMP-1 IFV
BRDM-1/-2, armoured car
BTR-40, -50, -60, -152, Type 63 & 531, M113 APCs

Anti-Armour:
82mm B-10, 88mm Type 51, 90mm M67, & 107mm B-11 RCLs
AT-3 Sagger ATGW

Artillery:
105mm M101/102, 122mm D-30, 155mm M114 Hs
107mm Type 63, 122mm BM-21 & 140mm BM-14-16 MRLs

Air-Defence:
23mm ZSU-23-4 & 57mm ZSU-57-2 SPAAGs
SA-7 & -9 SAMs

OCEANIA

Edwin W. Besch

4 🪖 3,500 🛡️ none
🚚 total? 🔫 total?

2 🪖 4,700 🛡️ none
🚚 total? 🔫 4

1 🪖 30,000 🛡️ 100
🚚 700 🔫 340

5 🪖 260 🛡️ none
🚚 total? 🔫 total?

3 🪖 5,200 🛡️ 25
🚚 80 🔫 70

🪖 **Men**   🛡️ **Tanks**

🚚 **AFVs**   🔫 **Artillery**

AUSTRALIA

WITH a history of gallant service overseas Australia is a respected nation, in the military sense. A former British colony, in recent years she has adopted a more independent foreign policy. Recent army deployments were to Fiji and Vanuatu during crises in 1987-88, and in 1990 she sent naval units to the Persian Gulf to help enforce UN economic sanctions against Iraq.

A middle-ranking power in the Asia-Pacific region, its current armed forces posture reflects its new foreign policy aims, having been directed to fight as a cohesive unit, alone if necessary, rather than as separate service units attached to US or British forces. This strategic re-orientation has resulted in the establishment of a Northern Command (Norcom), to counter the only perceived land threat, and impressive defence modernization programmes. Low-intensity conflicts elsewhere in the region are considered the most likely spheres of future Australian military operations.

The missions of the army, Australia's largest service, today include: national territorial defence; regional projection of strategic forces to achieve foreign policy objectives in the south-west Pacific and south-east Asia, particularly in support of friendly nations requesting assistance; a capability to conduct combined operations with allies in a larger conflict; the ability to conduct UN peace-keeping operations; and support to the civil authorities during national disasters.

The army has 30,300 regulars and 25,000 reservists. It consists of the following major units: 10 brigade HQs (seven of them reserve), 21 infantry battalions (15 reserve), one armoured regiment, two medium artillery (155mm) regiments (one reserve), six field artillery (105mm) regiments (four reserve), one air-defence regiment (Rapier SAM), three field engineer and three construction regiments (two of each in reserve), one transport regiment, three recce regiments (two reserve), one reserve commando regiment, two aviation regiments, and many smaller independent units.

The 14,200 strong 1st Division, an infantry unit, forms the core of the Operational Deployment Force. The 1st Division has two infantry brigades (two battalions each), a mechanized brigade (one armoured, one mechanized infantry, and one parachute infantry battalion), a recce regiment, three artillery regiments, and engineer and aviation

Top: The Australian infantryman's new automatic rifle is the 5.56mm Steyr AUG A1, made under licence as the F88. It has a range of different barrels.

Right: Two infantrymen advance under cover provided by a Leopard 1 of 1st Armoured Regiment. There are over 100 Leopards in Australian service.

Above: A Wheeled Light Armoured Fighting Vehicle, LAV-25, being put through its paces.

The 2nd Cavalry Regiment currently has 15, but has eventual plans for 100 with which to conduct operations in support of the recently created Northern Command based at Darwin in Arnhem Land.

Below: Armed with lightweight F88s infantry undergo training for urban combat, known as either Fighting in Built up Areas (FIBUA) or Military Operations on Urbanized Terrain (MOUT). In a real war situation this is a form of fighting which usually results in very high loss of life on both sides.

regiments. The Special Air Service Regiment (SAS) and the Pilbara Regional Force Reconnaissance Unit in the north are also important. The 2nd and 3rd Reserve Divisions and the Training and Logistical Commands round out the ground force.

EQUIPMENT

Armour:
Leopard MBTs
LAV-25 armoured car
M113 APC

Anti-Armour:
84mm Carl Gustav & 106mm M40A1 RCLs
MILAN ATGW

Artillery:
105mm M2A2/L5 & Hamel, & 155mm M198 Hs

Air-Defence:
Rapier & RBS-70 SAMs

Aircraft:
Sikorsky S-70A-9 Black Hawk
Bell OH-58 Kiowa
Bell 206B

FIJI

FIJI CONSISTS of 320 islands in the Koro Sea, about 1,000 miles north of New Zealand. Granted independence by Britain in 1970 it is politically unstable due to ethnic tension between native Melanesians and immigrant Indians who constitute half the population. It led to a coup in 1987 led by Col. Sitiveni Rabuka of the Fijian Army who declared the islands a republic.

The all-volunteer Fijian Army is overwhelmingly indigenous in ethnic origin. Officers were trained at Sandhurst or the Australian Military College, and enlisted personnel in New Zealand; arrangements were suspended after the coup.

The army has 4,700 personnel, organized into four infantry battalions, one engineer squadron, and an artillery troop. Paramilitary forces consist of 1,500 police. In 1975, the 300-man Fiji Naval Division, which has three minesweepers, two patrol vessels, and a research vessel, was created under the army.

In the late-1980s there were 1,177 personnel deployed with UN forces: one infantry battalion of 726 soldiers was assigned to the UNIFIL, where they suffered casualties; one infantry battalion of 400 was posted in Sinai; and 51 police were in Namibia.

EQUIPMENT

Artillery:
25-pdr (88mm) gun

Above: Sinai, 1982, and Fijian members of the UN observers force stand at attention to receive their medals prior to leaving.

NEW ZEALAND

NEW ZEALAND has in the past contributed forces to fight alongside those of Britain and Australia in numerous wars, and more recently with the Americans in Vietnam. A 500-man force of the 1st Battalion, Royal New Zealand Infantry Regiment and a helicopter flight were stationed in Singapore until 1989.

A member of ANZUS, recent political difficulties with its other members — principally the US — over nuclear weapons have forced NZ to develop greater self-reliance and seek even closer cooperation with Australia. Its army is modest in size, with only 5,200 active personnel, and it consists of two infantry battalions, a light armoured squadron equipped with British Scorpion 76mm gun light tanks, a 105mm field artillery battery, a Special Air Service squadron, and a Ranger company. The reserve or territorial force is 6,300 strong and consists of six infantry battalions, four field and one medium artillery batteries, and three light armoured squadrons (one recce, one APC, one anti-tank).

New Zealand retains defence responsibilities for a number of Pacific Islands, including Niue, Tokelau, and the Cook Islands.

EQUIPMENT

Armour:
Scorpion light tank
Ferret armoured car
M113 APC
Anti-Armour:
84mm Carl Gustav & 106mm M40A1 RCLs
Artillery:
105mm Light gun
105mm M101A1 & L10A1 Hs

Left: An M113 APC against a perfect New Zealand background, a snow-capped mountain peak. There are a number of types in service, including Australian rebuilds with a T50 light recce turret.

Above: The 7.62mm FN MAG (L7 series) has been New Zealand's standard General Purpose Machine Gun for nearly 30 years. The belt holds 50 rounds and the rate of fire is 1,000/min.

PAPUA NEW GUINEA

PAPUA New Guinea (PNG) occupies half of the island of New Guinea. Its native inhabitants comprise more than 1,000 tribes speaking 700 different languages. It became independent from its status as an Australian protectorate in 1975, but it remains part of the British Commonwealth.

The PNG Defence Forces are primarily concerned with external threats to its borders, but they assist the civil authorities during national emergencies. Australia assists it and the US has provided some arms and equipment. It has some 3,500 personnel organized into two infantry battalions, engineer and signals battalions, and logistics units with light weaponry.

The border problem involves incursions by guerrillas of the Free Papua Movement (FPM) in Irian Jaya, the Indonesian half of New Guinea, who have been fighting for secession since the 1960s. Although the PNG government does not support the rebels, some of its own nationals do and it has strained relations with Indonesia. It has led to a large portion of the PNGDF's infantry being deployed along the border and on occassion they have attacked FPM camps inside PNG.

More recently a secession struggle has erupted within PNG with the Bougainville Revolutionary army demanding independence and attacking mineral sites, thus attracting involvement from Australia. Partly as a result, a new defence policy called for increased air and naval capabilities, and reorganization of the army to provide highly-mobile units trained in guerrilla and counter-guerrilla tactics.

TONGA

THE KINGDOM of Tonga is a group of islands in the South Pacific, 1,750 miles north-east of New Zealand, which are governed by a constitutional monarch.

The Tonga Defence Force (TDS) consists of Land and Maritime Forces, who have the missions of maintaining public order, patrolling coastal waters and fishing zones, and engaging in civic action and national development projects. The small army consists of 260 personnel in a headquarters platoon and a light-infantry company. Australia and New Zealand support the TDS; the US provides training.

EUROPE

David Miller and Bryan Perrett

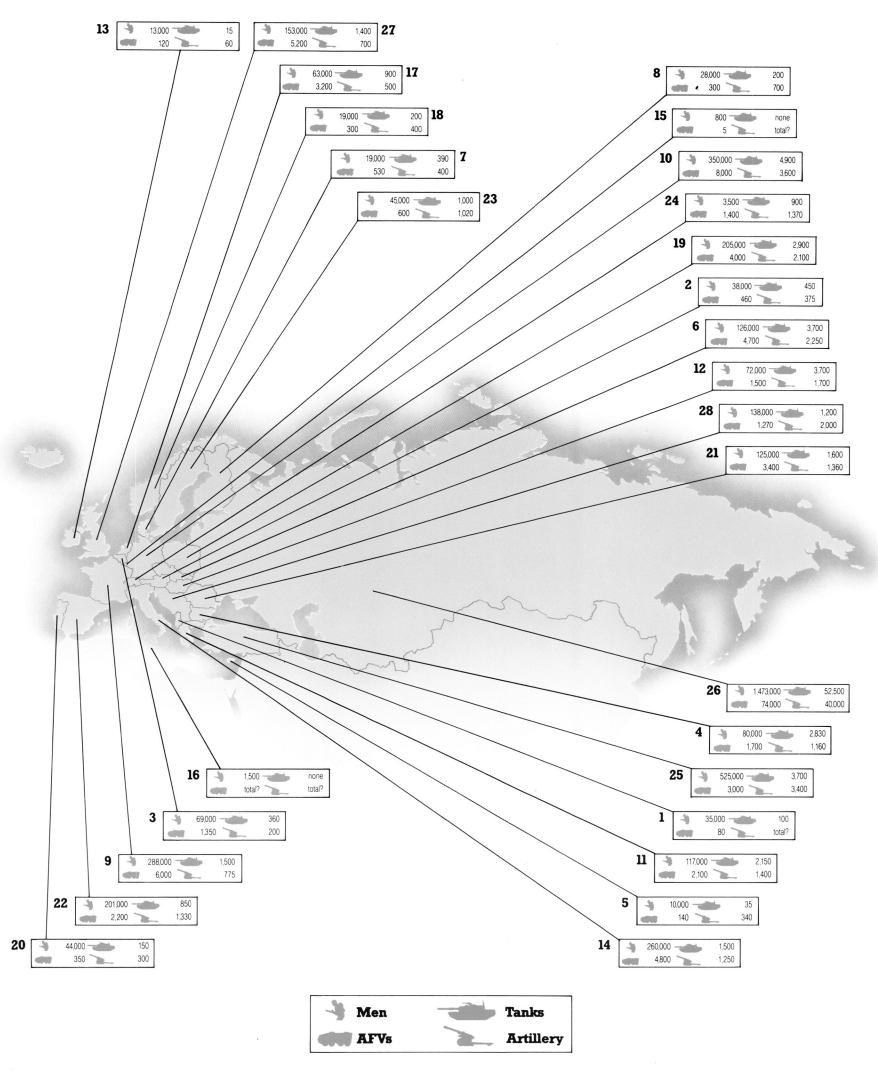

13
13,000   15
120   60

27
153,000   1,400
5,200   700

17
63,000   900
3,200   500

18
19,000   200
300   400

7
19,000   390
530   400

23
45,000   1,000
600   1,020

8
28,000   200
300   700

15
800   none
5   total?

10
350,000   4,900
8,000   3,600

24
3,500   900
1,400   1,370

19
205,000   2,900
4,000   2,100

2
38,000   450
460   375

6
126,000   3,700
4,700   2,250

12
72,000   3,700
1,500   1,700

28
138,000   1,200
1,270   2,000

21
125,000   1,600
3,400   1,360

26
1,473,000   52,500
74,000   40,000

4
80,000   2,830
1,700   1,160

25
525,000   3,700
3,000   3,400

1
35,000   100
80   total?

11
117,000   2,150
2,100   1,400

5
10,000   35
140   340

14
260,000   1,500
4,800   1,250

16
1,500   none
total?   total?

3
69,000   360
1,350   200

9
288,000   1,500
6,000   775

22
201,000   850
2,200   1,330

20
44,000   150
350   300

Men   **Tanks**
AFVs   **Artillery**

ALBANIA

THE SMALL country of Albania emerged from a long period of subjection to the Ottoman Empire in 1913, but this was followed by over a decade of near-anarchy which only ended in 1925 when one of the major chieftains, Ahmed Bey Zogu, became president. He was subsequently proclaimed King Zog I in 1928. The Italians annexed Albania in 1939 in order to use it as the springboard for the disastrous invasion of Greece in 1940.

A popular Communist resistance during the war years led to the establishment of a post-war Communist state, which for some years was part of the Soviet sphere of influence. However, the Albanian leader, Enver Hoxha, followed a particularly strict 'Stalinist' line and when the USSR deviated from that he broke with them in 1961 and in 1968 Albania withdrew from the Warsaw Pact in protest at the invasion of Czechoslovakia. For a time there were close relations with Communist China, but even that ended, this time because of Albanian support for Vietnam over its border clashes with China in 1978, and thereafter the Albanians followed a policy of strict, hard-line Communism which turned their country into one of the most isolated and backward in the whole of Europe. After Hoxha's death his successors endeavoured to continue the same policies but have been forced into a gradual easing through the relaxation of tension in the rest of Europe, even to the extent of taking observer status at the CSFE Conference on Human Rights in 1991. Most recently there have been free elections.

The Albanian Army, which has secured continued party rule, is some 35,000 strong, of which about 57-60 per cent are conscripts serving for a period of two years. It is possible that reserves total over 100,000 and these can be supplemented by 5,000 Interior Troops and 7,000 Frontier Troops. Albania has two military regions, north and south, and the field army is organized into one tank brigade and four infantry brigades, supported by three artillery regiments and an engineer regiment. There are also six lightly-armed coastal-defence artillery battalions.

These units are equipped with very elderly weapons, which were originally obtained from the USSR or the PRC. It can be assumed that all the equipment is in relatively poor condition and that spares and ammunition are in very short supply. The Albanian Army would be of limited value in anything other than guerrilla defensive operations, or in maintaining order in support of the existing political structure.

EQUIPMENT

Armour:
T-34, T-55, Types 59 & 63 MBTs
BRDM-1 & BA-64 armoured cars
BTR-40, -50, -152, & Type 531 APCs
Anti-Armour:
45mm M1942 & 57mm M1943 ATGs
82mm T-21 RCL
Artillery:
85mm D-44 & Type 56, & 122mm
  M1931/37 guns
122mm M1938 & Type 60, & 152mm
  M1937 & D-1 Hs
107mm Type 63 MRLs
Air-Defence:
23mm ZU-23-2, 37mm M1939, 57mm S-60,
  & 85mm KS-12 AAGs
SA-2 SAM

AUSTRIA

AFTER THE disastrous experience of WWI the Republic of Austria was created in November 1918 from the remnants of the once-proud and extensive Austro-Hungarian Empire. After some years of independent existence it was forcibly annexed into Hitler's Germany in March 1938. Austria was thus involved with Germany throughout WWII and in 1945, having suffering its second massive defeat in 28 years, it was occupied by the Allies for a decade. It then regained its independence in 1955, but this time with its neutral status and territorial integrity guaranteed by the former Allied powers.

Austria maintained its neutrality throughout the Cold War, poised uneasily between the major blocs, sharing borders with two Warsaw Pact countries (Czechoslovakia and Hungary) and two NATO countries (the Federal Republic of Germany in the north and Italy in the south). Also to the south was the non-aligned Communist state of Yugoslavia. To counter these threats the Austrians have developed a similar defence concept to that of their other neighbour — Switzerland — with a small regular army, a somewhat larger conscript element and a large number of reserves (242,000) capable of very rapid mobilization.

There is effectively only one armed service, since the air element is part of the army and operates not only the small fighter component but also provides all helicopters

and the bulk of the air-defence artillery and radar systems. The tiny Danube waterborne service is operated by army engineers. However, the land element of the force is some 38,000 strong, of which about 20,000 are conscripts.

Above: A well-camouflaged NCO prepares to break out of cover as the smoke clears during an exercise. The officer carries a Type HG78 grenade and the Steyr AUG rifle which has a plastic see-through magazine to enable ammunition checks.

Below: As befits a nation of skiers the Austrians have some tough Alpine forces. The elite are the graduates of the Ranger School at Hainburg, fully trained in mountainous combat and survival arts.

Above: Young conscripts working their way through an obstacle course. A good quality, quickly mobilized force is vital for a country dependent on reserves for the bulk of its combat strength.

operational role, becoming, in effect, divisional HQs with an infantry brigade together with a number of the Cadre Force territorial defence regiments and battalions, guard units, artillery units and anti-tank companies — the actual mix depending upon the area and the operational tasks.

The army obtains its equipment from a variety of sources. Tanks and SP artillery come from the USA, while some light weapons are obtained from Sweden. However, there is also a small but efficient domestic industry, which produces the successful 105mm Kürassier self-propelled tank destroyer as well as Steyr-Daimler-Puch APCs, light guns and the very successful Steyr AUG 5.56mm rifle. Part of the Austrian defence plan is to ambush advancing tanks by fire from static strongpoints for which complete turrets from obsolete M48 and Centurion tanks have been set in concrete emplacements.

The leading element of the Austrian Army is the 15,000-man Standing Alert Force, consisting of a mechanized division and two additional independent battalions, one airmobile and the other a mountain unit. The mechanized division is a strong and highly-mobile force, composed of three brigades (each with one tank battalion), one mechanized infantry battalion and an artillery battalion. Two of the three brigades also have an anti-tank battalion, equipped with Kurassier tank destroyers.

The two remaining elements are the Standing Field Units (SFU), which act as a regional defence force, and the Cadre Force which contains the territorial reserve forces. The SFU consists of a field army HQ, together with two subordinate corps HQs, which are only fully manned and implemented in wartime. The country is divided into nine provincial commands whose principal responsibility in peacetime is to train conscripts and maintain equipment. In the event of war these HQs would have an

EQUIPMENT

Armour:
M60A3 & Centurion Mk5 MBTs
Steyr SK-105 tank destroyer
Saurer 4K4E/F APC
Anti-Armour:
84mm Carl Gustav & 106mm M40A1 RCL
90mm M-47 & 105mm Centurion L7A2 :
both static turrets
Artillery:
85mm M52 & 105mm M59 guns
105mm IFH (M2A1) & 155mm SFK M2 Hs
155mm M109A2 SPH
128mm Steyr 680 M51 MRL
Air-Defence:
20mm GAl-B0l & 35mm Oerlikon
   GDF-002 SPAAGs
40mm Bofors L/70 AAG
40mm M42 SPAAG

BELGIUM

HAVING suffered invasion and been overrun twice this century, Belgium has more reason than most small nations to value the concept of collective security and shortly after WWII she signed the Benelux mutual assistance treaty with the Netherlands and Luxembourg. As the concept evolved the Benelux countries became founder members of NATO and since then the Belgian armed forces have been committed to the defence of western Europe within that organization's overall framework.

There have, nevertheless, been occasions when the Belgian Army has provided troops for out-of-area operations. A volunteer battalion distinguished itself fighting with the United Nations' forces during the Korean War, but it was in the Belgian Congo, now Zaire, that the army's major post-WWII operations took place. The most spectacular of these was the rescue of some 2,000 hostages by two battalions of paracommandos dropped into Stanleyville (Kisangani).

Above: The maroon berets and Battalion Belge badges signify the 1st and 3rd Battalions of the para-commando regiment.

Below: A Scorpion or Scimitar awash with mud as it fords a stream at high speed on maneouvres. Nearly 300 are in service.

Above: Infantrymen aim a 5.56mm FNC and 7.62mm MAG, excellent weapons that maintain Belgium's reputation for quality firearms.

Below: In the field an officer receives or gives instructions on the battlefield radio set, a vital element in modern warfare.

This action has come to be regarded as a role-model for subsequent hostage-rescue operations and the Belgians have repeated it on several occasions. In May 1978 paracommandos participated in a joint operation with French troops to rescue hostages held in Shaba and in October 1990 paracommandos and French paratroopers were flown into Rwanda to protect foreign nationals during an invasion by dissident exiles based in Uganda.

The present strength of the army is 68,700 men, of whom 29,100 are conscripts who serve one year in Belgium or ten months if posted to Germany. There are also an estimated 160,000 reserves who receive annual refresher training for five years after leaving the colours.

The active element of the army consists of one armoured brigade, three mechanized infantry brigades, a paracommando regiment of three battalions and supporting sub-units, a recce group, one independent tank battalion, three self-propelled artillery battalions, a missile battalion, four air-defence battalions, four engineer battalions and three light aviation squadrons.

Reserve forces subject to immediate mobilization and maintained at cadre strength include two mechanized infantry brigades, two infantry and one self-propelled artillery battalions, plus 11 motorized infantry regiments and four infantry battalions for territorial defence. The NATO commitment is designated I Belgian Corps and consists of two divisions. The paracommando regiment is retained under army command, one battalion being assigned permanently to the rapid-reaction role should it be required.

The recent easing of tension in Europe has led to the General Staff carrying out a wide-ranging review of the army's future role and deployment. The results depend upon a number of factors, but if the process of disengagement continues it is possible that reduction in size and equipment holdings could follow, coupled with the withdrawal of Belgian troops from Germany. Due to the problems of accomodation inherent in any such relocation it is unlikely in the short term that there will be anything more than a partial withdrawal.

EQUIPMENT

Armour:
Leopard 1 MBT
M41, Scorpion & Scimitar light tanks
90mm Jagdpanzer tank destroyer
AMX-VCI & BDX(S) IFVs
M113A2 & Spartan APCs
Anti-Armour:
MILAN & Swingfire ATGWs
Artillery:
155mm M59 gun
105mm M101 H
105mm M108, 155mm M109 & 203mm M110 SPHs
Air-Defence:
20mm M167 Vulcan, HS-804 & 35mm Gepard SPAAGs
Hawk SAM
Aircraft:
Aerospatiale SA.313/318 Alouette II

BULGARIA

BULGARIA obtained its independence from Turkey in 1878 and then became a central element in the Balkan Wars. It sided with Germany in WWI and also gave Germany limited support in WWII, albeit without participating in the military efforts on the Eastern Front. It was invaded by the USSR in September 1944, which led to the establishment of a Communist-dominated government in 1946 and to membership of the Warsaw Pact.

Bulgaria has a lengthy coastline on the Black Sea and lies between Romania to the north, and Greece and Turkey to the south, with its western border being with Yugoslavia. With a population of nine million, it was the smallest member of the now defunct Warsaw Pact, and had a European war ever broken out it would have provided the base from which Soviet forces would have attempted to capture the Dardanelles.

The Bulgarian Army is 80,000 strong, all bar 10,000 conscripts serving two years, and can call upon 200,000 reserves plus 15,000 Frontier Troops and 150,000 volunteer Territorial People's Militia. Organizational patterns have until now followed the Soviet model closely. The Ministry of Defence exercises direct command over three territorially divided military districts, an

airborne regiment (which is manned by air force personnel), and four missile brigades (four with Scud or SS-23 Spider, one with SAMs). The three military districts would become fronts in wartime: one commands three motorized rifle divisions and two tank brigades, while the other two each command two motorized rifle divisions and one tank brigade.

As with the Soviet Union, the air force is under the operational command of the army and provides all air support, including battlefield helicopters. It also provides an air-defence division, equipped with SA-2, SA-3, SA-5, and SA-10 SAMs, which gives air-defence cover over the entire country with the missiles being located at some thirty dispersed sites. This air-defence division is under the direct command of the Ministry of Defence, as is the airborne regiment. This leaves the Army responsible for its own mobile air-defence.

Bulgaria has been one of the most loyal members of the Warsaw Pact since its inception, and its armed forces are organized on Soviet lines and equipped with exclusively Soviet equipment. This might well continue after the formal dissolution of the Warsaw Pact.

Below: The ZPU-2 is now a rather elderly anti-aircraft gun and is more likely to be found serving with second-line units in defence of targets rather than front-line units which will have more modern guns. It is used all over the Third World.

EQUIPMENT

Armour:
T-34, T-54, T-62 & T-72 MBTs
BRDM-1, & -2 armoured cars
BMP-1 IFV
BTR-60, MT-LB & OT-62 APCs
Anti-Armour:
73mm SPG-9 RCL
100mm T-12 ATG
AT-3 Sagger & AT-1 Snapper ATGWs
Artillery:
76mm M1942, 85mm D-44 & SD-44 guns
122mm D-30 & M 1938 Hs
152mm 2S3 SPH
122mm BM-21 & 130mm RM-130 MRLs
Air-Defence:
14.5mm ZPU-2, 23mm ZU-23, 57mm S-60, & 85mm KS-12 AAGs
23mm ZSU-23-4, & 57mm ZSU-57-2 SPAAGs
SA-4, -6, -9, & -13 SAMs

CYPRUS

PREDOMINANTLY Greek in character, Cyprus has a substantial minority of Turks. The island gained its independence from Britain in 1960, but in July 1974 Turkey invaded and in 1983 it unilaterally established the Turkish Republic of Northern Cyprus. The remaining two-thirds of the island is the state of the Republic of Cyprus, the only internationally recognized government there. The two ethnic communities have not yet managed to re-establish a single state.

Formed in the late 1960s the Greek Cypriot National Guard has a strength of 10,000 with a first-line reserve of 65,000. It is predominantly a conscript force and consists of one under-strength armoured brigade, 13 small infantry battalions, four of which are reserve units, one special forces battalion and seven artillery battalions. In recent years the quality of the force, and that of its equipment, has improved beyond recognition. The Greek Army seconds two infantry battalions plus some 1,300 instructors to the National Guard.

The Turkish-Cypriot Security Force is a conscript force believed to be 4,000 strong with 11,000 first-line reservists. It is armed and equipped by the Turkish Army and wears the same uniform. Organized into infantry battalions, it lacks heavy weapons and performs the role of a paramilitary Gendarmerie.

EQUIPMENT

Armour:
T-34/85 & AMX-30 MBTs
EE-9 Cascavel & EE-3 Jaracara armoured cars
VAB-VCI IFV
BTR-50P, VAB-VTT & Steyr 4K 7FA APCs
Anti-Armour:
57mm M18 & 106mm M40 RCLs
MILAN & HOT ATGWs
Artillery:
25pdr (88mm) gun
75mm M116, 105mm M101 & M56 Hs
128mm M-63 MRLs
Air-Defence:
40mm Bofors L/60 AAG
20mm M55 & Oerlikon GDF-002 SPAAGs
SA-7 & Mistral SAMs
Aircraft:
Aerospatiale SA.342 Gazelle

CZECHOSLOVAKIA

CZECHOSLAVAKIA was created in 1918 from the western Slavonic provinces of the former Austro-Hungarian Empire. The new state was made up of a multiplicity of races, including approximately seven million Czechs, two million Slovaks, 750,000 Germans, 700,000 Hungarians and 450,000 Ruthenians, together with some smaller groups, including Russians and Gypsies. It quickly became relatively prosperous, but was hampered by racial tensions and the external threat from Germany. The latter led to annexation of the Sudetenland in 1938, and of the remainder of the country in 1939. At the end of the war the country was overrun by the USSR and her pre-1938 frontiers were restored, except for Ruthenia which was annexed by the Russians.

The democratic government was overthrown in a Communist coup in 1948, following which Czechoslovakia became a Soviet satellite and a founder-member of the Warsaw Pact. There was, however, an undercurrent of resistance, which eventually led to the 1968 "Prague Spring" under Dubcek which was brutally suppressed by invading forces from the USSR, Bulgaria, Poland and Hungary. In the late 1980s, as the Soviet grip loosened, the Czechoslovak Communist Party was eased out of power, with President Havel taking over in 1989. Today, the country's armed forces have already adopted a more all-round defensive posture, in contrast to the previous concentration on the western border.

Czechoslavakia is divided into two military districts on the Soviet pattern, one in the west and the second in the east. Wartime combat strength would be seven motorized rifle and six tank divisions, of which four are now maintained at full strength in peacetime. Centrally controlled formations include a Scud brigade, two air-defence (SAM) brigades and an airborne brigade. The latter in particular have a high reputation for being tough, competent and well-trained.

Like many other European armies, the Czechoslovakian Army is in the throes of a post-Cold War rundown. Four tank regiments have been disbanded and some 850 MBTs are due to be destroyed, although the process is proving to be slower and more difficult than predicted. Current strength of the army is some 125,700, of which some 80 per cent are conscripts on an 18-month engagement, with reserves of 250,000. The People's Militia, a 120,000 strong part-time force, has been disbanded, but the Border Troops (some 13,000 men) remain.

Czechoslovakia has long had a successful and efficient arms industry and although much Soviet equipment is still used, the OT series of APCs and Dana SP wheeled howitzers have all been exported in some numbers. (However, the notorious explosive Semtex has given the industry a bad name and it has been announced that the export of all arms will cease.) During the Gulf War the Czech Army deployed a chemical warfare company to the war zone.

Above: A troop assault with BVP-1s. Both marks of this infantry vehicle are manufactured in the Czech state arsenal, a large arms enterprise.

Below: T-72 MBTs by streetlight. The Czechs possess about 100 but tank numbers are now being reduced in post Cold-War Europe.

EQUIPMENT

Armour:
T-54, T-55, & T-72 MBTs
PT-76 light tank
BRDM-1 & OT-65 armoured cars
BVP-1 (BMP-1) & BMP-2 IFVs
OT-62, OT-64, & OT-810 APCs

Anti-Armour:
82mm RCL
AT-3 Sagger, AT-4 Spigot, & AT-5
  Spandrel ATGWs

Artillery:
76mm M1942, 85mm M52, &
  100mm M53 guns
122mm D-30 & M1938 Hs
122mm 2S1 & 152mm DANA SPHs
152mm D-20 & M1937 Hs
122mm RM-70 & 130mm RM-130 MRLs

Air-Defence:
14.5mm ZPU-4, 23mm ZU-23, 30mm M53,
  & 57mm S-60 AAGs
23mm ZSU-23-4 & 30mm M53/59 SPAAGs
SA-4, -6, -8, -9, & -13 SAMs

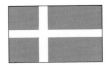

DENMARK

THE Danish Army has an active strength of 19,400 of whom some 9,900 are conscripts serving a nine or twelve month tour of duty followed by five years on the reserve. Total reserves available amount to 72,400 men, of whom 24,000 belong to the Local Defence Forces. There is also a 55,300 strong all-volunteer Home Guard with an establishment of over 500 companies.

The regular element consists of five mechanized infantry brigades, each with one tank battalion, two mechanized infantry battalions (one reserve), an artillery battalion and supporting units; one independent infantry brigade; two recce battalions; and light aviation and helicopter squadrons. In addition to these there are troops designated "Regional Defence" who are maintained on a cadre basis until mobilization. These include two infantry brigades and seven regimental combat teams each consisting of two or three infantry battalions, an artillery battalion and a tank company.

The army is organized administratively into Eastern and Western Commands, with the island of Bornholm a separate region garrisoned by an independent infantry battalion. An infantry battalion is also permanently available for UN peace-keeping forces, but apart from this, and units taking part in NATO exercises in northern Germany, the Danish Army remains within its own territory. It is a small but efficient and highly trained force which, in the event of hostilities, would commit to NATO its five small armoured infantry brigades, plus a tank battalion, an armoured infantry battalion and an artillery battalion, all being augmented from the reserves on mobilization.

EQUIPMENT

Armour:
Centurion Mk5 & Leopard 1 MBTs
M41 light tank
M113 APCs
Anti-Armour:
84mm Carl Gustav &
   106mm M40A1 RCLs
TOW ATGW
Artillery:
105mm M101, 155mm M59 & 203mm M115
Hs
Air-Defence:
40mm Bofors L/60 AAG
Redeye SAM
Aircraft:
Hughes OH-6A Cayuse

Left: These Jaegers have to pass a very demanding process of selection before they are accepted.

Below: The Danes equip their army well. These men have G3A5 rifles, an MG42 and a Carl Gustav RCL.

FINLAND

THE qualities and determination of the Finnish soldier were demonstrated during the Winter War of 1939-40 when, for a while, the mighty Soviet Red Army was fought to a standstill. Finland then joined in the German attack on the Soviet Union, but sued for peace when it became clear that Germany was close to defeat. As a result of the subsequent Treaty of Paris, her status of permanent neutrality was established and her standing armed forces were restricted to a maximum of 42,000 men; at the present time they number approximately 25 per cent below this figure. Finland's topography favours defensive operations and, with her aircraft numbers strictly limited and only a minor part of the land suitable for tanks, appropriate plans have been developed to make best use of it. Artillery is much favoured, together with obstruction and ambush tactics.

The strength of the army is about 27,800 men, including 22,300 conscripts serving an eight-month tour of duty (eleven months in the case of officers and NCOs). Total reserves amount to 700,000 men, of whom the great majority belong to the army, and of these some 50,000 report for re-training courses each year. The country is divided into seven military areas, which are in turn sub-divided into 23 military districts. Currently, this is being reorganized and it is thought that three large areas with 12 new districts will be the outcome.

The active element consists of one armoured brigade, eight infantry brigades, four independent infantry battalions, one artillery regiment, two coastal artillery regiments and three independent coastal artillery battalions, four air-defence regiments and two engineer battalions. Finnish contingents from this active force are also supplied regularly to UN peace-keeping forces. Reserve formations which would become active on mobilization include two armoured brigades, 11 Jäger and 14 infantry brigades, 50 independent infantry battalions and 200 local defence units. The Jägers possess the most modern infantry equipment and the armoured force is having its T-55s upgraded.

As might be expected, most of the army's heavy weapons are imported from the Soviet Union, with whom Finland has a reciprocal security arrangement, but small arms are manufactured locally and the highly-regarded Tampella organization not only produces its own mortars but also adapts imported artillery weapons to the army's requirements.

EQUIPMENT

Armour:
T-55M & T-72MI MBTs
PT-76 light tank
BMP-1 & -2 IFVs
MT-LB, BTR-50 & -60, & XA-180 Sisu APCs
Anti-Armour:
95mm SM58-61 RCL
AT-4 Spigot & -5 Spandrel, TOW & SS-11 ATGWs
Artillery:
105mm M-61/37 & M-37/10 Hs
122mm D-30 & 155mm K-83 Tampella Hs
122mm BM-21 MRL
Air-Defence:
40mm Bofors L/60 AAG
35mm Oerlikon GDF-002 SPAAG
23mm ZSU-23-4 & 57mm -57-2 SPAAGS
SA-3 & -7 SAMs

Above: The Finns too have Jaegers, but these men may well be members of the Sissi. This means "partisan" and harks back to the very effective light infantry ski units which fought so well against the Red Army.

Below: An exercise involving a massed armoured assault. Not a typical Finnish preference because of unfavourable country, but they do still have a lot of armour such as these T-72 MBTs and BMP-1 IFVs

FRANCE

THE French Army's experiences in the two decades following WWII were not happy ones. A protracted war in Indo-China was followed by a savage counter-insurgency campaign in Algeria. In both these conflicts the army could claim numerous tactical successes but political expediency proved to be the critical factor which resulted in a French withdrawal from both countries. Elsewhere, because of its involvement in Indo-China, the army could commit no more than one volunteer battalion to the UN forces in Korea. In 1956, however, it made a substantial contribution to the successful Anglo-French landings during the Suez Canal crisis. Again, however, there was no satisfactory outcome to this involvement.

Once these troubled years had ended the army quickly recovered its morale and customary élan, enabling it to concentrate on fulfilling its principal task as one of the major forces available to NATO. It provides garrisons for overseas French territories in the West Indies, the Pacific and the South Indian Ocean, and has also maintained French influence in former colonial territories in Africa. Since 1962, the latter role has involved active service in Djibouti on the Gulf of Aden, intervention three times in Chad, the rescue of hostages from Kolwezi, Zaire, in 1978 and, in October 1990, the despatch of troops to Rwanda to protect French nationals during an invasion by exiled dissidents. In addition, a large contingent was supplied for peace-keeping duties with the Multi-National Force in Beirut (1982-84) where many French soldiers were killed and injured.

The present strength of the army is 288,500. This includes 6,000 women and 180,500 conscripts, the latter serving one year with the option of voluntarily extending their service to 16 months or two years. From the total of 915,000 reservists available, some 325,000 are due for immediate recall on mobilization. The army is well-trained and is equipped by a highly-developed defence industry which not only supplies all but a tiny proportion of its requirements but also conducts a flourishing export trade. Much emphasis is placed on the store of accumulated tradition as a means of generating esprit de corps, and in this connection it is interesting to note that, as in the British service, regiments are normally of battalion size. Save in the direst emergency, the army is unlikely to be called to the assistance of the Civil Power in internal security matters, as this function is executed by the paramilitary Gendarmerie, which has an active strength of 91,800 (plus reserves) and is equipped with its own

Above: War in the desert armed with MILAN and the 5.56mm FAMAS bullpup rifle.

Below: A VAB wheeled APC plus some of the AMX family: AMX-30, AMX-10, and Roland.

Right: Gazelles armed with HOT missiles show their low-level attack potential.

Above: A Mistral SAM is prepared while to the rear a 155mm TR-F-l gun is fired.

Above: A Super Puma unloads its troops. The Mark II can carry 29 infantrymen.

AFVs, heavy weapons, aircraft and helicopters.

The present structure of the army contains four major elements: a Pre-Strategic Nuclear Force; a Manoeuvre Force intended for use in Europe; a Rapid Reaction Force (Force d'Action Rapide or FAR) capable of speedy deployment overseas; and a Territorial Defence Force which, as its name suggests, is primarily but not exclusively concerned with the mobilization of reserve formations, the provision of reinforcements and defence of France itself. The composition of these four elements might vary in a war situation, but in peacetime there is comparatively little movement of formations between them.

The smallest of these four is the Pre-Strategic Nuclear Force, which has a strength of 6,100 men and 40 Pluton SSM launchers. The Manoeuvre Force consists of the First Army which has three corps, one with two armoured divisions and two with one motorized infantry and two armoured divisions each. Altogether, these eight divisions can deploy 16 armoured regiments, two armoured reconnaissance regiments, 12 mechanized infantry regiments, nine motorized infantry regiments, ten artillery regiments and six helicopter anti-tank squadrons. Army and corps troops include three armoured recce regiments, one special operations regiment, one parachute regiment, one infantry regiment, five artillery regiments, five SSM regiments, eight air-defence regiments, seven engineer regiments, one electronic warfare regiment and three combat helicopter regiments.

The Rapid Reaction Force has a strength of 47,000 and contains a parachute division with six parachute regiments, one armoured cavalry regiment and one artillery regiment; an air-portable Marine division with three infantry regiments, two light armoured regiments, one artillery regiment and two engineer companies; a light armoured division with two armoured cavalry regiments, two mechanized infantry regiments, one artillery regiment and one engineer regiment; a mountain division with six Alpine infantry regiments, one light armoured regiment, one artillery regiment

and one engineer battalion; and an airmobile division consisting of three infantry regiments and one command, one support and three combat helicopter regiments. This means the FAR possesses a flexibility which will enable it to deal with almost any situation which it is likely to encounter, and it can be supplemented by troops already serving overseas or outside France.

These additional forces include the all-regular 8,500 strong Foreign Legion, consisting of one armoured, one parachute, four infantry and two engineer regiments; the French elements of a Franco/German brigade, which are a light armoured regiment, a mechanized infantry regiment and a recce squadron; and 12 Marine infantry regiments. (An unusual feature of the French order of battle is that, despite their title and uniform, Marine units and formations are army rather than naval troops. Although the navy also possesses a 2,600 strong force of Fusiliers-Marins, the bulk of this is employed in naval base protection, but it also includes one commando battalion trained for helicopter assault and underwater attack.)

The active strength of the Territorial Defence Force (FDT) includes one infantry division assigned to the defence of the country's Strategic Nuclear Forces, plus six regiments of frontier guards. On mobilization its immediate task is to provide 101,000 individual reinforcements from the reserve for the First Army and FAR. Simultaneously, two light armoured divisions, each with two armoured regiments, two infantry regiments and one artillery regiment, will be mobilized from the personnel of instructional schools. A territorial engineer division, with infantry and air-defence elements, is already maintained at cadre strength on the Rhine. The bulk of the (FDT) consists of 22 divisions recruited geographically throughout the country, each based on a combined-arms regimental combat team. These, in turn, are supported by seven defence zone brigades, each containing two infantry regiments and one armoured regiment plus recce, anti-tank and heavy mortar units. Two such brigades are based in one of the FDT's six military regions, and one each in the remainder. Plans are being discussed which would harmonize these six regions into

three major geographical zones: North-North East, Mediterranean, and Atlantic (including Paris). The regional headquarters would be at Metz, Lyon and Bordeaux respectively. Under this scheme, named Armed Forces 2000, the 22 divisions of the Territorial Defence Force would be reduced to 10 Circonscriptions de Défense. The improved command structure would almost certainly increase efficiency.

France had a large contingent of troops which served with great distinction in the Gulf War, performing a deep-thrusting armoured offensive with considerable skill which contributed much to the victory. She also has a number of garrisons around the world to which the army deploys: Central African Republic (1,200), Chad (1,100), Djibouti (3,650), Gabon (550), Cote d'Ivoire (500), Mayotte and La Reunion in the Indian Ocean (3,300), New Caledonia (3,800), Polynesia (5,400), Senegal (1,250) and the West Indies and Guiane (8,800). There is also a force of 500 men serving in southern Lebanon with UNIFIL.

EQUIPMENT

Armour:
AMX-30 & LeClerc MBTs
AMX-13 light tank
AMX-10RC, Panhard AML-90
 armoured cars
AMX-10P & VAB-VTT APCs

Anti-Armour:
89mm ACL-STRIM &
 112mm Apilas RLs
MILAN & HOT ATGWs

Artillery:
105mm Light & 155mm TR-F-l guns
155mm M50 H
105mm AU-50, 155mm AU-F-l & -3 SPHs
227mm MLRS

Air-Defence:
20mm Terasque 53T2 & 30mm
 HSS-831A AAGs
Hawk, Roland I/II, & Mistral SAMs

Aircraft:
Cessna 0-1 Bird Dog
Aerospatiale AS.332M Super Puma
Aerospatiale SA.316/319 Alouette III
Aerospatiale SA.341/342 Gazelle

GERMANY

AT THE END of WWII Germany was partitioned into four zones, each controlled by one of the Allies; a division that became institutionalized with the onset of the Cold War. The three western zones were given increasing authority and in 1949 two new states come into being, the Federal Republic of Germany (FRG) and, in a Soviet response, the German Democratic Republic (GDR). The apparent threat from the Soviet Union (USSR) led to the belief among the western powers that the FRG should re-arm in order to bear its share of the defence burden, especially in manpower terms. This eventually took place in 1956 with the formation of the Bundeswehr (Federal Armed Forces), which were composed of the Bundesheer (Federal Army), Luftwaffe (Air Force) and Bundesmarine (Federal Navy). The USSR strongly protested and then retaliated by forming the Warsaw Pact.

The Bundesheer gradually gathered strength, despite considerable domestic protests in the early days. It was organized partly on US lines, but also included elements of traditional German military practice. There was, however, a very strong emphasis on what was known as "Innere Führung", a form of inner-discipline and leadership which was intended to ensure that the new democratic German armed forces did not become blind political tools like their predecessors in 1914-18 and 1939-45. The GDR's Nationalen Volksarmee (NVA), however, showed fewer inhibitions about the past. It organized on Soviet Communist lines, but with a much stronger element of traditional Prussian militarism (for example, the retention of the "goose-step").

During the Cold War the two adversarial powers came to regard the German armies (the Bundesheer and the NVA) as the linchpins of the ground forces of their respective alliances, at least on the central front. They were well-disciplined, well-organized, equipped with the latest weaponry, and both tended to follow the precepts of their respective mentors more closely than the other members of the alliances.

The GDR actually became a byword for blind devotion due to the way in which it followed the instructions of its Soviet masters. It came, therefore, as a very considerable shock that the Soviets offered it no support whatsoever when the régime in the GDR began to falter in 1988/89. The

reunification process which followed, however, was no coming together of two equal partners; the FRG was clearly much the stronger of the two economically and it just swallowed the other up. This was particularly visible in the area of the army, where the Bundesheer simply took over the NVA. All NVA senior officers were pensioned off (there were no known exceptions), and officers and senior NCOs from the Bundeswehr were sent into the territory of the former GDR to reorganize its army and to retrain it.

The situation is currently somewhat complicated. The area of what was the GDR is now known as the "Fünf Neue Länder" (the five new states or FNL). It has been agreed in the Reunification Treaty that the forces of the USSR will take some four years to vacate the FNL and that during that time the territory will not come within NATO's purview. As a result, the German government has established OberKommando Ost (Headquarters East), whose forces are under German-national and not NATO command, at least until the final departure of the Soviet forces. The garrisons of the Western Allies in Berlin have been reduced, but some elements will remain until the last Soviet troops leave the FNL.

A major outcome of the situation in which

Below: Now no longer needed, two soldiers of the National Volks Armee patrolling the border area prior to German unification.

Below: A Bundeswehr soldier with an MG3 machine gun. It has a high fire rate, with up to 1,300/min, and a quick-change barrel.

Above: The pride of the Bundeswehr is the Leopard 2. Some 2,000 are in service.

Below: The Gepard SPAAG has two 35mm cannon and a radar on a Leopard 1 chassis.

Faced with the prospect (at least during the Cold War) of a very large-scale Soviet armoured attack the Bundesheer, remembering the experiences of WWII, has always paid considerable attention to anti-tank defences. One of the principal missions of the tank force is to destroy enemy armour but there are also many dedicated anti-tank weapons, among them the Jagdpanzer Kanone and Jagdpanzer Rakete which are self-propelled anti-tank guns and missile launchers, respectively. MILAN and HOT missiles are also in service in considerable numbers.

The Bundesheer operates its own helicopter force, which consists of 750 machines. There are over 200 MBB Bo-105P attack helicopters among them (also known as the PAH-1), which have a crew of two and are armed with six Euromissile HOT launchers.

In the process of integration with the NVA the Bundesheer has become the involuntary possessor of a considerable amount of Soviet equipment. Some very sensitive electronic equipment is believed to have been removed, but other than that not only did the Soviets let the FRG take the equipment over but they have insisted that existing GDR orders should stand, even for aircraft such as the MiG-29! Most of this equipment has proved to be of little value and in a few years time almost none of the Soviet equipment will remain to show that part of the German Army was once the Soviet Union's closest ally in the Warsaw Pact.

EQUIPMENT

Armour:
Leopard 2, Leopard 1A1, M48 & T-72M* MBTs
90mm Jagdpanzer
Marder A1/A2, & BMP-1/-2* IFVs
SPz-2 Fuchs armoured car
TPz-1 Fuchs (NBC), M113, M577 & BTR-60/-70* APCs

Anti-Armour:
Milan, TOW, HOT, AT-4 Spigot* & AT-5 Spandrel* ATGWs

Artillery
105mm M-56 & M-101, 122mm D-30* & M-1938 HS
130mm M-46*, 152mm D-20* & 155mm FH-70 Hs
122mm 2S1 Gvodzika* & 152mm 2S3 Acatsia* SPHs
155mm M-109A3G & 203mm M-110A2 SPHs
110mm LARS MRL

Air-Defence:
40mm Bofors L/70 & 57mm S-60 AAGs
23mm ZSU-3.4 & 35mm Gepard SPAAGs
Patriot, Roland, SA-4, -6, -8, & -9* SAMs

Aircraft:
Aerospatiale SA.313/318 Alouette II
Bell UH-1D Iroquois
MBB Bo-105 (PAH-1)
Mil Mi-8 Hip*
Mil Mi-24 Hind*
Sikorsky CH-53G

Note: * indicates equipment formerly operated by the East German NVA at the time of German reunification.

the German Army finds itself is that it must conduct a number of separate but concurrent activities. Of these, by far the most important in the short term is that it is contracting as a result of the lessening of tension in Europe — and the resultant post-CFE environment — while also re-training and absorbing the NVA and expanding its activities into the FNL. The pre-unification strengths of the Bundesheer and NVA were 308,000 and 96,300 respectively, and these must not only be combined but also run-down to the 1994 target of 255,000.

While there are still some uncertainties about the Bundeswehr's future some elements are now becoming clear. It has been announced that from 1994 the grand total of the Bundeswehr will be 370,000, of which the army's share will be about 255,000 men, with 82,000 in the Luftwaffe and 32,000 in the navy. In the army the regular and territorial elements will be treated as one

force and there will be three major commands: two corps headquarters and one territorial command. The army will be designed to field up to 28 brigades and it is intended that in the regular army the proportion of regular soldiers to conscripts will be raised. Almost alone among the major armies, however, the Bundesheer will continue to refuse to permit women to serve, except in a very few medical posts; this is strongly supported throughout German society and enshrined in the Basic Law (Constitution).

After the post-CFE reductions the Bundesheer will be the second largest army in Europe after that of the USSR. It is Germany's firm intention that she will remain tied into NATO and closely allied with the USA, but by the very facts of its size and geographical location the Bundesheer must inevitably become the most influential army in Europe.

GREECE

IN the immediate aftermath of WWII the re-constituted Greek Army was plunged into a bitter and protracted civil war which ended with the defeat of its Communist opponents in 1949. Given the circumstances of its re-birth, it is not surprising that the army was heavily politicized and in 1967 this resulted in a military coup following which the country was ruled by a corrupt and inefficient junta until 1974. The junta fell from power when, having created the

Below: Greek para-commandos in a

PLB 370 boat for light Aegean island raiding.

situation which provoked the Turkish invasion of Cyprus, Greece was humiliated by her inability to respond. As both Greece and Turkey were members of NATO, the incident gave rise to serious tensions within the alliance.

Since then, the army has been expanded and equipped with expensive modern weapons. It regards its major roles as being not only to guard against invasion from eastern Europe, but also to defend the country against aggression by its traditional enemy, Turkey. For these reasons, the bulk of its strength is deployed in the north and north-east of the country. Two infantry battalions and 1,300 advisers are seconded to the Greek Cypriot National Guard.

The army's present strength amounts to some 117,000 men, of whom 101,000 are conscripts serving a 20-month tour of duty. There are approximately 230,000 reservists, who are in turn backed by a Territorial Army of 30,000 and a 120,000 strong National Guard. Included in the army's order of battle are: 10 infantry divisions; one paracommando division; five independent armoured brigades; two independent mechanized brigades; four armoured battalions; 18 artillery battalions; 10 air-defence artillery battalions; two surface-to-surface missile (SSM) battalions; three army aviation battalions; and one independent aviation company. Units are maintained at three levels of operational readiness: Category A — immediate; Category B — 60 per cent within 24-hours of mobilization; Category C — 20 per cent within 48-hours of mobilization.

In view of the continuing state of mutual suspicion which exists between Greece and Turkey, it seems unlikely that any cuts will be made in the army's strength.

EQUIPMENT

Armour:
AMX-30 & Leopard 1 MBTs
M47 & M48 medium tanks
Steyr SK-105 tank destroyer
AMX-10P, MOWAG Roland, M113, M2, M3, & Steyr 4K 7FA APCs
Anti-Armour:
90mm EM-67 & 106mm M40A1 RCLs
MILAN ATGW
Artillery:
105mm M56 & M101 Hs
155mm M114 & 203mm M115 Hs
105mmM52 SPH
155mm M109 & 175mm M107 SPHs
Air-Defence:
20mm Rheinmetal Rh-202 & 30mm Artemis AAGs
Hawk & Redeye SAMs
Aircraft:
Bell AH-1 HueyCobra & UH-1 Iroquois
Agusta A.109
Hughes NH-300
Boeing-Vertol CH-47C Chinook

HUNGARY

HUNGARY was an equal partner with Austria in the Hapsburg Austro-Hungarian Empire from 1867 onwards, but, in the post-WWI era, Hungary became an independent republic, although it lost some land it claimed as its own in the process. These territories were recovered in 1939-40 when the Germans gave it control of southern Slovakia, Ruthenia and part of Transylvania. Hungary joined the Axis powers in the war, but then tried to negotiate a separate armistice with the Allies, as a result of which it was invaded by Germany before being overrun by the Soviet Army.

The Soviets returned Hungary to its pre-1938 borders and, after a brief period of democratic rule, encouraged the Communists to take power in 1948. An anti-Communist uprising in 1956 was brutally

suppressed by Soviet troops. From that time onward Hungary was a loyal member of the Warsaw Pact, although frequently exhibiting a more adventurous spirit than most of the other satellites.

The 72,000 strong (42,500 conscripts) Hungarian Army can call upon 120,000 reserves and is currently organized on Soviet lines, with an army HQ and three corps, each possessing one tank brigade, three motorized rifle brigades, an artillery brigade and an SA-6 regiment. There are also army-level supporting formations of an artillery brigade, an SSM brigade (armed with Scud missiles), a heavy air-defence brigade armed with SA-4 Ganef SAMs, and an airborne battalion.

During the post-CFE activities the Hungarian Army has been reducing, with an initial target of cuts of some 35 per cent in overall manpower. Four brigades have already gone and the length of service for conscripts has been reduced from 18 to 12 months. 600 MBTs are due to go, which will presumably include a few T-34s still held in store, as well as the T-54s and T-55s. The last Soviet soldier was scheduled to leave Hungary in mid-1991.

The Hungarian Army has a small number of officers with the United Nations observer group on the Iran/Iraq border.

EQUIPMENT

Armour:
T-54/55, & T-72 MBTs
PT-76 light tank
BRDM-2, PSzH-IV, & FUG armoured cars
BMP-1 IFV
BTR-50, -60, -80, MT-LB, & OT-64 APCs
Anti-Armour:
73mm SPG-9 & 107mm RCLs
57mm M1943 & 100mm T-12 ATGs
AT-3 Sagger, AT-4 Spigot, & AT-5 Spandrel ATGWs
Artillery:
76mm M1942 & 85mm D-44 guns
122mm 2S1 & 152mm 2S3 SPHs
122mm D-30 & 152mm D-20 Hs
122mm BM-21 & 240mm BM-24 MRLs
Air-Defence:
14.5mm ZPU-2, 57mm S-60, & 100mm KS-19 AAGs
23mm ZSU-23-4 & 57mm ZSU-57-2 SPAAGs
SA-4, -6, -7, -8, -9, -13, & -14 SAMs

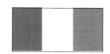

IRELAND

ALTHOUGH the Irish Army defines its primary function as being to defend the country against external aggression, it lacks the strength to impose more than a temporary check on an invader. The army's major peacetime role is to serve as the ultimate guarantor of the Civil Power, providing assistance, when requested, for the Garda Siochana (Civil Police) who have responsibility for maintaining or restoring law and order as well as for internal security. In these circumstances the most probable threat is presented by the illegal Irish Republican Army (IRA) which is active in the northern border areas of the country. With the terrorists receiving increasingly sophisticated weapons the army has responded by purchasing modern equipment suitable for the counter-insurgency role. In conjunction with the Garda and the British security forces, it is regularly engaged in joint security operations along the border with Ulster and has numerous successes to its credit.

Contingents are also sent to UN peacekeeping forces, earning an excellent reputation for their ability to handle difficult situations. notably in the Congo and Cyprus, in both of which casualties were incurred. They continue to serve the UN today, notably in Lebanon where the Irish have been at the forefront of the UNIFIL presence.

The army is composed of some 13,000 regular volunteers who serve a minimum term of three years, and can also call on 16,000 reservists. It is organized into Eastern Command (HQ Dublin), Curragh Command (HQ Curragh), Southern Command (HQ Cork), and Western Command (HQ Athlone), and consists of 11 infantry battalions, one Ranger company, one tank squadron, one recce squadron, three artillery regiments, one independent artillery battery, one air-defence regiment and three engineer companies. The largest formation is the infantry brigade, of which four exist, but as some units within these have reserve status they are maintained below full operational strength. The army's second-line reserve is provided by An Forsa Cosanta Aitiuil (FCA), a volunteer force whose structure parallels that of the regular army and has a strength of 22,000 of whom some 15,000 are engaged in active training. Altogether, the FCA can produce 18 infantry battalions, six artillery regiments, three armoured cavalry squadrons, three engineer squadrons and three air-defence batteries.

EQUIPMENT

Armour:
Scorpion light tank
Panhard AML-60/90 armoured cars
Panhard VTT, M3 & Timoney APC
Anti-Armour:
84mm Carl Gustav RCL
MILAN ATGW
Artillery:
25-pdr (88mm) & 105mm Light guns
Air-Defence:
40mm Bofors L/60 AAG
RBS-70 SAM

Above: The need for the Browning .50in HMG was learned on UN peace-keeping duty.

Below: Ireland's Army Ranger Wing is their well-trained flexible deployment force.

ITALY

ALTHOUGH the Italian Army's performance during WWII tended to attract critical comment, this was partly due to the fact that it was under-equipped for the type of conflict in which it was engaged, partly from political intervention in its affairs, and partly from poor motivation arising from the troops' lack of conviction in their cause. The army's subsequent task, therefore, was to correct these faults and it has succeeded in becoming an efficient, highly-trained and well-equipped force supported by an extensive armaments industry which is capable of producing its own weapon systems or manufacturing many imported designs under licence.

Rather than continuing to rely on the latter, however, Italy has decided to commence construction of her own family of AFVs, including the C1 Ariete MBT armed with a 120mm smoothbore gun, the B1 Centauro tank destroyer armed with a 105mm rifled gun, the VCC-80 APC/IFV armed with a 25mm cannon, the Puma wheeled recce vehicle with ATGW and SAM derivatives, and the SIDAM 25 self-propelled air-defence system consisting of quadruple 25mm cannon on an M113 APC chassis. All of these have either reached the prototype or user-trials stage and will begin entering general service shortly, providing Italy with a formidable array of modern armour.

The Italian Army is committed to NATO and its primary task is the defence of the country's north-eastern frontier, although the volatile situation in the Middle East and proximity of a potentially hostile Libya also affect its internal deployment. As is the case with many other European armies, its secondary role is aid to the Civil Power should this be required, although the main responsibility for this has been assumed by the para military Carabinieri, Public Security Guard and Finance Guards.

With the exception of medical support units despatched to the UN army during the Korean War, no Italian troops served outside the country until 1982, but from June of that year until February 1984 a 2,000-man Italian contingent formed part of the Multi-National Force in Beirut. Italy has also contributed troops to the UN forces in Sinai, southern Lebanon, the Iran/Iraq and the Indo/Pakistan ceasefire lines.

The army's active strength amounts to 260,000 men, of whom 207,000 are conscripts who serve one year. Reserves number approximately 520,000 including 240,000 subject to immediate recall on mobilization. Operationally, the army is divided into the Field Army and the Territorial Army. The former consists of three corps, one with three armoured and four mechanized brigades, an SSM and a heavy artillery battalion; the second with one

Above: Members of the "Lagunari", an army amphibious infantry unit based at Venice where they were formed 100 years ago.

Below: Leopard MBT built under licence by OTO Melara. Italy has nearly 1,000 and upgrades have kept them battleworthy.

armoured, four mechanized and one motorized brigade; and the third with five Alpini mountain brigades and an armoured cavalry battalion. It also has an air-defence group containing six air-defence artillery and four SAM battalions. The aviation element of the Field Army consists of four wings, plus 15 multi-role and four medevac helicopter squadrons.

The Territorial Army's duties include training, mobilization and internal security, but the Rapid Intervention Force (RIF) also comes within its area of responsibility when uncommitted. The RIF consists of an airborne brigade which includes a special forces battalion, a motorized brigade, a Marine battalion (navy), a helicopter squadron and an air transport unit (air force). Other formations serving with the Territorial Army include two independent

mechanized brigades, three independent motorized brigades, an amphibious regiment, an armoured battalion, an armoured recce battalion, four artillery and three engineer battalions.

Following the easing of European tension, senior Italian officers are pondering the full implications of the cuts in force levels proposed during the Conventional Forces in Europe (CFE) discussions. For the Armed Forces Staff, attempting to plan for the next century, the equation is complicated by a drastic cut in the defence budget, coupled with demographic factors which are reducing the size of the conscript intake. The latter have already led to units being disbanded and, when economic considerations are also taken into account, the cumulative result of further unit disbandments could result in the loss to the army of an entire corps. All in all, the Armed Forces Staff believe that this would place it below its minimum defensive requirements. One solution being considered is to increase the size of the regular element by offering better incentives to volunteers. Another is to abolish conscription in favour of a smaller, all-regular professional army, but preliminary costings indicate that this would be many times more expensive than the present conscript-based force.

EQUIPMENT

Armour:
Leopard 1, C-1 Ariete, & M60A1 MBTs
Fiat 6616 armoured car
M106, M113, & VCC-1/2 APCs
Anti-Armour:
112mm Apilas RL
MILAN & TOW ATGWs
Artillery:
105mm M56 H
155mm M114 & 203mm M115 Hs
155mm M109, FH-70, & 203mm M110 SPHs
227mm MLRS
Air-Defence:
25mm Sidam & 40mm Bofors L/60 AAGs
Hawk & Stinger SAMs
Aircraft:
Cessna O-1E Bird Dog
Agusta A.129 Mangusta
Agusta-Bell AB.206 JetRanger
Boeing-Vertol CH-47C Chinook

Above: Alpini troops with supply column pack mules; modern technology has only a limited effect in this combat terrain. Still recruited from the mountainous north, their corps' combat record is one of distinction. The five brigades are "Cadore", "Taurinese", "Orobica", "Tridentia" and "Julia". Some of the corps are airborne qualified.

LUXEMBOURG

THE Grand Duchy maintains a small, 800 strong, all-volunteer force of one infantry battalion which is committed to NATO. It possesses few heavy weapons and imports infantry small arms from its NATO allies. In immediate reserve is a 500 strong Gendarmerie. During the Korean War one infantry company served with the UN forces.

EQUIPMENT

Armour:
V-150 Commando APC
Anti-Armour:
94mm LAW 80
TOW ATGW

Below: Troops armed with FN weapons, a FA1 and MAG, man a commanding position overlooking a typical village in the Duchy.

MALTA

SINCE achieving her independence Malta has pursued a policy of strict neutrality. A 1,500 strong all-volunteer defence force is maintained, consisting of two nominal regiments. One of these contains an infantry company, an inshore patrol squadron, an airport security company and a helicopter flight; the second contains an air-defence battery, a general duties company, a supply company and an engineer company.

Obviously a force of this size and composition is clearly incapable of offering anything more than token resistance and its roles are therefore limited to internal security or aid to the Civil Power, should the need for either arise. The force is equipped with small arms but has few heavy weapons.

EQUIPMENT

Anti-Armour:
RPG-7 RL
Air-Defence:
14.5mm ZPU-4 & 40mm Bofors L/60 AAGs
Aircraft:
Agusta-Bell AB.206 JetRanger

NETHERLANDS

BETWEEN 1945 and 1949 the Royal Netherlands Army fought a protracted guerrilla campaign against nationalist elements in the Dutch East Indies, and subsequently a volunteer infantry battalion served with the UN army during the Korean War. Since then, however, the army has not been engaged in active operations and has concentrated on fulfilling its commitment to NATO, which consists of a corps of two divisions.

The army has a strength of 63,000 men, of whom 39,600 are conscripts serving a 14- or 16-month tour of duty, and there is a 135,000 strong reserve. Unfortunately, the fact that with the exception of one armoured brigade based in Germany the army spends its time in home garrisons has resulted in boredom

Below: For decades the Dutch armoured commitment to NATO has been crucial.

With Germany united the role of countries like the Netherlands awaits redefinition.

that can affect the morale of individual units. On the other hand, the army has a long tradition of stubborn fighting in defence of its homeland, and in the event of it being involved in hostilities it is probable that the recovered sense of purpose would resolve many of its problems. In this context, too, it should be noted that the army has high standards of technical training and that its equipment is excellent.

The structure of the army consists of one corps and three mechanized divisional headquarters; three armoured brigades (one at cadre strength); six mechanized infantry brigades (two at cadre strength); and one independent infantry brigade (at cadre strength). Including corps and divisional troops, these consist of 17 mechanized infantry battalions; two infantry battalions; 12 tank battalions; four recce battalions; 19 artillery battalions; one surface-to-surface missile battalion; three air-defence battalions; and three helicopter squadrons (Air Force). The Netherlands also has a 2,800 strong Marine corps which maintains the highest operational standards (and which is the oldest in the world) and the 4,700 strong Royal Military Constabulary.

In common with other NATO allies which have troops based in Germany, the army is studying the implications of the reduced tension in central Europe. Unlike its Bene-

lux partner, Belgium, or the United Kingdom, both of which maintain large forces in Germany, the withdrawal of the Dutch element is unlikely to pose major accomodation problems since it numbers only 8,000 men. It also seems probable that the government is contemplating a reduction in the army's strength, which in turn would mean re-structuring to provide a more flexible response to potential threats, but the details involved in such a move have yet to be finalized.

EQUIPMENT

Armour:
Leopard 1 & 2 MBTs
M113, YP-408 & YPR-765 APCs
Anti-Armour:
106mm M40A1 RCL
Dragon & TOW ATGWs
Artillery:
105mm M101 & 155mm M114 Hs
155mm M109 & 203mm M110 SPHs
227mm MLRS
Air-Defence:
40mm Bofors L/60 AAG
35mm Gepard SPAAG
Stinger SAM
Aircraft:
Aerospatiale SA.316/319 Aloutte III
MBB Bo-105

NORWAY

DESPITE her neutral status, Norway was invaded and occupied by Nazi Germany during WWII and this experience has left a deep scar on the national consciousness. The questions of NATO membership and defence are taken very seriously and in the event of war every able-bodied man is expected to turn out, either with the army or with his local Home Guard unit. This motivation, coupled with harsh terrain and an inhospitable climate for much of the year, ensures that any potential aggressor would have an extremely difficult task on his hands.

Norway is, in fact, one of only two NATO members to share a common frontier with the Soviet Union, and much of her military effort is directed to the north of the country where exercises are carried out regularly with other NATO forces, notably the British Royal Marine Commandos. During the Korean War a medical unit served with the United Nations army and subsequently Norway has contributed regularly to UN peace-keeping forces, usually in battalion strength.

The 19,000 strong Norwegian Army possesses a small cadre of regular officers and NCOs, but the bulk of its strength consists of some 13,000 conscripts who serve one year with the colours. Reserves number approximately 146,000 and the Home Guard has a strength of about 75,000. The country is divided into Northern and Southern Military Commands with most of the training establishments, depots and mobilization centres being located in the latter where the majority of the population live. Permanently based in the north is a mechanized

Above: The Leopard 1 has to function in the cold Norwegian north as efficiently as it does on the plains of northern Germany.

Below: Modern mortars are becoming more sophisticated with computerized fire-control systems such as that in use here.

brigade group consisting of two infantry battalions, one tank battalion, one self-propelled artillery battalion, an engineer battalion and an air-defence battery; a reinforced infantry battalion task force with armoured, artillery and air-defence sub-units; and a battalion of border guards. Independent infantry battalions, armoured squadrons and artillery units are stationed elsewhere throughout the country, reserve units being maintained at cadre strength.

EQUIPMENT

Armour:
Leopard 1 MBT
M48 medium tank
NM-135 & M113 APCs
Anti-Armour:
84mm Carl Gustav & 106mm M40 RCLs
TOW ATGW
Artillery:
105mm M101 & 155mm M114 Hs
155mm M109 SPH
Air-Defence:
20mm Rheinmetall Rh-202 & 40mm
 Bofors L/60 AAGs
RBS-70 SAM
Aircraft:
Cessna O-1A Bird Dog

POLAND

POLAND IS an ancient country, whose existence always seems to be somewhat precarious, lodged as she is between Russia and Germany. She was partitioned in 1772, 1793, 1795 and 1815, the latter resulting in her disappearance for just over one hundred years. Reconstituted in 1918 she had to fend off Soviet attacks in 1920, but was attacked by Germany in 1939 and partitioned for a fifth time between Hitler's Germany and Stalin's USSR. Having suffered greatly throughout the war Poland was then occupied by the Soviet Army, losing some of her eastern territory to Russia but gaining considerable ground from defeated Germany.

During the Cold War Poland remained an uneasy ally of the USSR, with periodic riots and the gradual but inexorable rise of Solidarity. Today, Poland is independent, but she is unavoidably still stuck between the USSR and Germany, and while this may

Below: Elite Polish paratroops assemble on a mountainside after a drop onto the top. They are trained to use the long ropes for abseiling down sheer rockfaces. The red beret is the universal paratroopers' symbol.

not seem too grave a problem at the moment she could find herself in problems again in the future.

The Polish territory is split into three military districts, each of which becomes an Army HQ on mobilization. The standard division, recently introduced, consists of two tank and two motorized rifle regiments. Two of the military districts command four such divisions, the third just one. There are a number of formations controlled at a high level, of which the most important is a strong and efficient airborne brigade composed of four parachute infantry battalions and one artillery battalion. For many years the Polish sea-landing brigade, organized on the same lines as the Soviet naval infantry, was a major element in the Warsaw Pact threat in the Baltic area, but this has now been re-designated a coastal defence brigade and has had its battalion of amphibious tanks removed.

The army's normal strength is some 205,000, of which 168,000 are conscripts whose term of service has recently been reduced from 24 to 18 months. However, it is quite probable that these strengths will reduce further, possibly to 175,000, if tensions in Europe continue to ease. The Polish Army has long contributed small numbers of officers to United Nations peace-keeping and currently has some 50 with the observer group in Syria. The USSR has a major HQ and a number of troops in Poland and it seems highly likely that these will be withdrawn in the near future.

There is an increased emphasis on all-round defence needs, thus forces have been redeployed from west to east to counter potential threats from that direction.

Most of the equipment currently in use by the Polish Army is of Soviet origin. However, Poland has cooperated with Czechoslovakia in the development of a tracked APC and an 8-wheeled APC; Polish designations for these are TOPAS (OT-62) and SKOT (OT-64) respectively. Poland is also seeking to acquire armoured vehicles from Austria, as well as anti-tank and anti-artillery items.

EQUIPMENT

Armour:
T-54/55 & T-72 MBTs
PT-76 light tanks
FUG & BRDM-2 armoured cars
BMP-1 IFV
TOPAS (OT-62), & SKOT (OT-64) APCs

Anti-Armour:
85mm SD-44 & 100mm T-12 ATGs
AT-1 Snapper, AT-2 Sagger, AT-4 Spigot, AT-5 Spandrel, & AT-7 Saxhorn ATGWs

Artillery:
122mm D-30, 152mm D-1 & M1937 Hs
122mm 2S1 & 203mm 2S7 SPHs
122mm BM-21 & RM-70 MRs
140mm BM-14-16 & -17, WP-8, & 240mm BM-24 MRs

Air-Defence:
14.5mm ZPU-2 & -4, 23mm ZU-23, 57mm S-60, & 85mm KS-12 AAGs
23mm ZSU-23-4 & 57mm ZSU-57-2 SPAAGs
SA-6, -7, -8, -9, & -13 SAMs

PORTUGAL

PORTUGAL was not directly involved in WWII but her armed services gained considerable experience in counter-insurgency operations during the period of de-colonization after it. At first the army was forced to fight on the defensive but, having studied American methods in Vietnam and reinforced the troops in the field to the point at which by the end of the 1960's no less than 150,000 men were serving in Africa, the situation was brought under control if not entirely resolved. Portugal, however, is a small and less than wealthy nation, and by the beginning of the 1970s the public was of the opinion that the African colonies were simply not worth the treasure expended and lives lost. This view was reflected by senior army officers, a group of whom formed the Armed Forces Movement which, in 1974, removed the dictatorship which ruled the country and granted independence to Guinea-Bissau the same year and to Angola and Mozambique in 1975. During the period of internal unrest which followed, the army, and in some areas the Roman Catholic Church, provided a stabilizing influence. With the return of calm, the army, its strength reduced, retired to barracks and concentrated on its NATO role.

At the present time the army numbers 44,000 men, of whom 35,000 are conscripts serving a 12- or 15-month tour of duty with the colours. Substantial reserves exist, but it is unclear what role these are intended to perform. The task of aid to the Civil Power, should it be needed, is already carried out by the paramilitary National Republican Guard (19,000 men equipped with APCs and helicopters), the Public Security Force (17,000) and the Border Security Guard (8,500). Administratively, the country is divided into six military commands.

At present, the army is undergoing a major reorganization and modernization programme which will increase its air-portable and mechanized potential, but at the time of writing it consists of one composite brigade containing one mechanized and two motorized infantry battalions, a tank battalion and an artillery battalion; one airborne light-infantry brigade containing one special forces battalion and three airborne battalions; one airborne brigade (Air Force); two infantry brigades; three cavalry regiments; 12 infantry regiments each with one armoured and three infantry battalions; one field artillery, one air-defence and one coastal artillery regiment; and two engineer regiments. Three infantry regiments, two coastal artillery battalions and two air-defence batteries are based in Madeira and the Azores.

Above: A sergeant in a Portuguese armoured unit, probably aboard an M113 APC, prepares to load a belt of ammunition into his heavy calibre .50in Browning machine gun.

EQUIPMENT

Armour:
M48 medium tank
Saladin & Panhard AML60/-90 armoured cars
Chaimite & M113 APCs
Anti-Armour:
106mm M40A1 RCL
TOW, SS-11 & MILAN ATGWs
Artillery:
105mm LFH-18 & M101 Hs
155mm M114 H
155mm M109 SPH
Air-Defence:
20mm Rheinmetall Rh-202 & 40mm Bofors L/60 AAGs
20mm M163 Vulcan SPAAG
Blowpipe SAM

ROMANIA

ROMANIA was led during the 1930s by a strong fascist party which led her into an alliance with Italy and Germany and in 1941 the attack on the USSR. When Soviet troops reached Romanian borders in 1944 the country changed sides and declared war on Germany. In November 1945 the USSR imposed a Communist government and since then the country has been ruled by the Communists, although the Romanian régime, particularly under Ceaucescu, took a line which was increasingly independent from Moscow. The Ceaucescu régime was toppled in December 1989, although the country remains under Communist control.

The Romanian Army is 125,000 strong, three-quarters of them conscripts serving 16 months. It can call upon 180,000 reserves upon mobilization, and can be supplemented by a paramilitary Border Guard of 14,000. It remains, however, in a confused state following the revolution. The country is divided into four military areas, which command the ten divisions (two tank, eight motorized rifle), of which only two (one tank, one motorized-rifle) are fully manned in peacetime. There are also three mountain brigades, four airborne regiments, two artillery brigades, an anti-tank brigade, four air-defence and two Scud brigades.

The Romanian Army uses a greater mixture of equipment than any of the other Eastern bloc forces and seems to have kept obsolete equipment in service even longer than usual in those armies. A large quantity of pre-war artillery pieces are still in use, as are a few JSU-152 heavy assault guns of WWII vintage. The Romanians have their own armaments industry which produces tanks and artillery.

EQUIPMENT

Armour:
T-34, T-55, T-72, TR-80, & TR-580 MBTs
SU-100 assault gun
BRDM-2 & TAB-C armoured cars
MLI-84 IFV
BTR-40, -60, TAB & MLVM (MT-LB) APCs
Anti-Armour:
76mm & 82mm RCLs
57mm M1943, 85mm SD-44 & 100mm T-12 ATGs
AT-1 Snapper & AT-3 Sagger ATGWs
Artillery:
100mm Skoda, 105mm Schneider, & 122mm M1938 Hs
152mm D-20 & M1938 Hs
122mm APR-21 & -40, 130mm R-2, & ZIL-157 MRLs
Air-Defence:
14.5mm ZPU-2, 30mm M53, 37mm M1939, 57mm S-60, 85mm KS-12, & 100mm KS-19 AAGs
57mm ZSU-57-2 SPAAG
SA-6 & -7 SAMs

SPAIN

APART FROM the all-volunteer 250th or Blue Division which fought for Hitler on the Eastern Front, the Spanish Army has seen virtually no active service for the past 50 years. Spain, it is true, has been troubled by Basque extremists for over a decade but the responsibility for dealing with these has rested with the 63,000 strong Guardia Civil, which has its own APCs, helicopters and heavy weapons. Indeed, because of conscription, the army is regarded as a stabilizing influence which has served to re-emphasize the national identity after the traumatic differences of the past. Following the introduction of a constitutional monarchy, Spain was admitted to NATO in 1982 and this has tended to reinforce the army's sense of purpose.

The army has a strength of 201,400 men, including the all-regular Spanish Foreign Legion which is 7,000 strong. There are 158,500 conscripts who normally serve a one-year tour of duty but, if they enjoy the life, they are permitted to extend their service for various periods up to a total of three years. Administratively, the army is divided into eight regional operational commands, but for operational purposes it is split into the Field Army or Intervention Force and the General or Territorial Reserve Force.

The Field Army is capable of being deployed where required and consists of one armoured division, one mechanized division, one motorized division, two mountain divisions, two armoured cavalry brigades, one air-portable brigade, one independent infantry battalion, six special operations battalions, and five engineer battalions. The General or Territorial Reserve Force's primary function is to defend the national boundaries; its title is somewhat misleading, for while some of its formations do indeed require the mobilization of reservists to bring them up to strength, others are

at immediate readiness and are assigned to the Army element of Spain's Rapid Action Force (Fuerza de Accion Rapida) should this be activated.

Included in the General Reserve Force is the Royal Guard Regiment which contains elements of all three services; the Foreign Legion, with a strength of three regiments; an airborne brigade of three battalions and supporting units assigned to the Rapid Action Force; an air-defence command with six regiments; a field artillery command; a coastal artillery command; and an engineer command of two regiments. Army aviation units consist of an attack battalion, a transport battalion, three general purpose units, support and training squadrons. Spain also possesses a 7,500 strong Marine Corps which, as well as its infantry element, contains its own organic armoured, artillery and anti-tank sub-units.

A prime defensive consideration for Spain is the potential threat posed by northern African states — something they have persuaded NATO to recognize as very real with Islamic fundamentalism and poverty growing in the Maghreb. Spain guards the

back door to Europe and has oriented her defence needs to that end, as witnessed by the Joint Strategic Plan of 1984 which has been accepted by NATO partners who agree on Spain's value as a rear-area logistic base sheltered behind the Pyrenees in the event of war in central Europe.

Overseas garrisons are maintained by the Army on the Balearic Islands (5,600), the Canary Islands (10,000) and in the North African territories of Ceuta and Melilla (15,800). Observers are also attached to UN teams in Angola and Central America.

EQUIPMENT

Armour:
AMX-30 MBT
M47 & M48 medium tanks
Scorpion light tank
Panhard AML-60 & -90, BMR-VEC
    armoured cars
BMR-600, M113, BLR, LVTP7, M3 &
    UR-416 APCs
Anti-Armour:
106mm M40A1 RCL
MILAN & HOT ATGWs
Artillery:
105mm M26 M56, M108
    155mmM114,& 203mm M115 HS
155mm M109 & 203mm M110 SPHs
140mm Teruel MRL
Air-Defence:
20mm & 35mm Oerlikon GDF-002 &
    40mm Bofors AAGs
Nike Hercules, Improved HAWK, Roland and Skyguard/Aspide SAMs
Aircraft:
Aerospatiale AS.332B Super Puma
Bell OH-58 Kiowa
Bell UH-1B & 1H Iroquois
Bell 206 JetRanger
MBB Bo-105
Boeing CH-47 Chinook.

Left and below: With their battle-cry of "Long Live Death" the Spanish Foreign Legion take their training seriously. Despite the name, the Tercio de Extranjeros consists almost entirely of native Spaniards. It is imbued with tradition and takes a tough and die-hard approach to soldiering. A two-man team fire an MG3 over the heads of colleagues.

Top: The CETME L assault rifle is light because of its modern composite materials.

Above: A Jeep armed with a 106mm recoilless rifle built by VIASA. It is an effective weapon.

SWEDEN

THE LAST battle in which elements of the Swedish Army were involved was at Leipzig in 1814. Since then, Sweden has pursued a policy of strict neutrality and to maintain this she has adopted the philosophy of the nation-in-arms, armed to the teeth by a highly-developed defence industry which produces the majority of the armed services' requirements as well as conducting a profitable export trade.

Given this tradition and the fact that the role of the army is an entirely defensive one in concept, its structure differs in some

Below: Swedish armour and infantry staging a combined assault. The Stridsvagn 103 MBT (foreground) is unusual because of its main gun in the glacis. The Pbv-302 APCs are amphibious and can carry 10 men.

important respects from that of other armies. At the present time it has an active peacetime strength of 44,500, of whom approximately 37,700 are conscripts serving between eight and 15 months depending upon their rank and the technical nature of their branch of service. On discharge, conscripts remain on the reserve until they are 47, undergoing regular mobilization exercises and refresher training to maintain their skills. In this way it is anticipated that if the country was to be attacked, no less than 700,000 trained soldiers could be mobilized within 72-hours. These, in turn, would be supported by the 120,000-man Home Guard, a strong Civil Defence Corps in which all between 16 and 25 are liable to serve, and volunteer auxiliary organizations including a Motor Cycle Corps, Radio Organization, Women's Motor Transport Corps, and the Women's Auxiliary Defence Services.

The army's regular officers and NCOs receive their training in central academies and schools, following which they form the permanent staff of the 44 armoured, recce, artillery, air-defence, engineer, signal and supply regiments which constitute its

peacetime strength. The responsibility of these regiments include local defence, training conscript intakes, providing refresher courses for reservists, and forming mobilization cadres. Administratively, the country is divided into six military commands which are further sub-divided into 26 defence districts. A 2,650 strong Coast Defence Force, including artillery and infantry elements, also exists but this is the responsibility of the navy.

On mobilization to war establishment the army is divided into the Field Army and Local Defence Units. The Field Army consists of four armoured brigades, one mechanized brigade, 10 infantry brigades plus one on the island of Gotland, five Norrland (Arctic) brigades, 100 independent armoured, infantry, artillery and airdefence battalions, one aviation battalion and nine artillery aviation platoons. The Local Defence Units include 60 independent battalions (between 400 and 500 independent companies) supplemented by the Home Guard, which normally occupies static positions.

Despite its lack of operational experience, the Swedish Army has been

Above: The Ikv 91 tank destroyer has a laser rangefinder and computerized fire- control system for its 90mm gun. it may be uprated with a low recoil 105mm gun

Below: A MAG machine gun team belonging to an independent jaeger battalion trained to serve in the harsh arctic climate in the north of Sweden.

involved with UN peace-keeping missions since 1947 and its contingents have served in many areas around the world, earning a fine reputation for discipline, efficiency, courage and resolution in difficult and dangerous situations. At the present time Swedish troops or military observer teams are acting on behalf of the UN in Central America, Afghanistan, Cyprus, India/Pakistan and Korea, with the largest contingent being based with UNIFIL in southern Lebanon.

EQUIPMENT

Armour:
Strv-101 & -103 MBTs
Ikv-91 tank destroyer
Pbv-302 APC

Anti-Armour:
74mm Miniman, 84mm Carl Gustav, & 90mm Pv-1110 RCLs
RB-53 Bantam & TOW ATGWs

Artillery:
105mm 4140, 150mm M-39, & 155mm FH77A/B Hs
155mm BK-1A gun

Air-Defence:
40mm Bofors L/60 AAG
Redeye, RBS-70, & RB-77 Improved Hawk SAMs

Aircraft:
MBB Bo 105
Agusta-Bell 206 JetRanger

SWITZERLAND

DESPITE THE fact that during two world wars Switzerland provided a useful channel of communication between belligerents, an intelligence clearing centre of use to both sides, financial facilities and a base for humanitarian agencies, the Swiss are under no illusion that their neutrality has been preserved by any other means than remaining a fully-equipped nation-in-arms. The role of the army, therefore, is to protect Swiss neutrality by deterring any potential aggressor with the knowledge that he would be forced to commit immense resources to a hard fight in impossible terrain and receive little or no reward at the end of it. Thus, the structure and composition of the army, like that of Sweden, is entirely defensive and based on every able-bodied man turning out in time of national emergency. It is augmented by a formidable system of fortifications and bunkers situated throughout the country, plus explosives already laid at strategic locations to hamper any invader.

The purely regular element of the army is very small and consists of senior and staff officers, and about 3,500 regimental officers and NCOs. These are responsible for training conscript intakes and providing refresher courses for reservists. Every year two intakes, each containing some 18,000 conscripts, receive 17 weeks basic training. Following this, they are liable to undergo a decreasing period of annual reserve training until they are aged 50 when they are transferred to the 438,500 strong Home Guard, which also trains annually.

Each reservist is allocated to a local unit to which he reports on call-out, and as he keeps his personal arms at home the whole process of mobilization is extremely efficient. Furthermore, because shooting is a national sport (almost every village possesses a shooting club and rifle range) a high standard of marksmanship is almost ensured. It is calculated that when fully mobilized the army would have 625,000 men under arms, backed by an armaments industry which can supply the majority of its requirements. There is also a 480,000 strong Civil Defence organization, some 300,000 members of which are fully trained.

The major part of the army would consist of four corps, three of which contain one mechanized and two infantry divisions plus corps troops and supporting arms, while the fourth contains three mountain divisions and corps troops. In addition to army troops, at the disposal of senior commanders, there are also 11 border brigades and a number of independent infantry battalions whose function is to fight a delaying action from the frontier back to the mountain redoubt which would become the core of the national defence. Finally, the ground troops of the air corps (Switzerland does not possess an independent air force) include three air defence regiments each of four battalions, stationed at air bases, and an air defence brigade consisting of one two-battalion SAM regiment and seven air-defence artillery regiments each of three battalions.

Left: Her soldiers were once feared throughout Europe and today they remain a formidable force. These mechanized infantry are armed with new-issue SG550 Sturmgewehr 90 assault rifles. The M113 Armoured Personnel Carrier seen here is armed with a 20mm gun, and there are over 1,000 similar vehicles in service today.

Above: These infantry belong to one of the three specialist divisions which contain men living in the Alpine regions. The army's combat strategy seeks to make best use of such ideal ''active defence'' terrain, for maintaining sovereignty over a part of Swiss territory throughout any conflict is vital. The Alpine Massif has only several possible invasion routes and on these the Swiss have built large fortresses which house artillery. They help to make the mountainous areas of Switzerland nigh impregnable.

Below: The Swiss infantry are equipped with robust, high-performance modern weaponry. Each battalion has ATGWs such as the Dragon seen here.

EQUIPMENT

Armour:
Pz-55/57 (Centurion), Pz-61,Pz-68, & Pz-87
  (Leopard 2) MBTs
MOWAG Piranha tank destroyer
MOWAG Spy armoured car
MOWAG Improved Tornado IFV
MOWAG Roland & Grenadier, M63/73
  (M113 with 20mm gun),& M113 APCs

Anti-Armour
83mm M80, 90mm PAK 50, & 106mm
  PAK-58 (M40A1) RCLs
TOW-2, B/B-65 Bantam & B/B-77
  Dragon ATGWs

Artillery:
155mm M50 H
155mm Pz Hb-66/74 (M109) SPH
81mm RWK-014 MLR

Air-Defence Weapons:
35mm Oerlikon GDF-002 AAG
Rapier & Stinger SAMs

Aircraft:
Aerospatiale SA.315 Alouette II
  & SA.316/319 Alouette III
Aerospatiale AS.332 Super Puma

TURKEY

TURKEY remained neutral during WWII but subsequently joined NATO and is, in fact, one of only two of the alliance's members to share a common frontier with the Soviet Union. Because of a historical tradition of enmity with her Russian and Greek neighbours, particularly the latter, she maintains a large peacetime standing army. There is also a tradition of military involvement in national politics, and as recently as 1960 and 1980 the army was responsible for internal coups.

In other respects, the army has seen comparatively little active service during the post-WWII era. One infantry brigade served with the UN army in Korea, displaying the traditional Turkish military virtues of toughness and aggression to earn itself a formidable reputation.

In July 1974, however, following a pro-Greek coup in Nicosia, a 40,000-man task force was despatched to Cyprus, ostensibly to protect the lives and property of the Turkish-Cypriot community but also to prevent the island becoming a Greek military base. Despite the weakness of the opposing Greek-Cypriot forces, the performance of the Turks, especially at the higher levels, was not impressive and they only overran one-third of the island before a ceasefire was imposed. The incident created serious tensions within NATO, of which Greece is also a member, and relations with the United States, which supplies much of Turkey's military hardware, were badly damaged. Since then Turkey has felt compelled to maintain a garrison in the occupied portion of Cyprus, currently estimated to consist of about 30,000 men plus supporting armour and artillery. This means an unwelcome diversion of troops and a continuously heavy burden on the national exchequer, but to Turkish minds, constantly suspicious of Greek intentions in Cyprus and the Aegean, it is not regarded as being a sterile exercise.

The army has a strength of 525,000 men, of whom 475,000 are conscripts serving an 18-month tour of duty with the colours. There are 950,000 men on the reserve who remain eligible for call-out until aged 46, but little provision seems to be made for refresher training and in an increasingly technical age this can only be regarded as a serious weakness. Four army Commands exist, one of which has permanent responsibility for the Soviet frontier, and these contain three or four corps of the ten available. The exception is the smaller Fourth Army at Izmir which has only two infantry divisions and an infantry brigade under its command. Altogether, the Army consists of one mechanized division, 13 infantry divisions, seven armoured brigades, six mechanized brigades, 10 infantry brigades, one airborne brigade, two commando brigades, five coastal defence battalions, 10 independent tank battalions, and 50 independent artillery battalions — of which 20 are air-defence units. It is believed that a number of these formations are maintained some way below their war establishment. Other troops available include a Marine regiment (navy) with three infantry battalions, an artillery battalion and support units. Turkey also possesses a paramilitary Gendarmerie/National Guard with an active strength of 70,000 and a further 50,000 on the reserve. This contains infantry and commando formations and is equipped with its own heavy weapons, APCs and helicopters.

Below: A soldier pauses on patrol in a Kurdish village. A guerrilla campaign has been active in areas like Anatolia since 1984 and firefights are not infrequent.

EQUIPMENT

Armour:
Leopard 1 MBT
M47 & M48 medium tanks
M2/3 & M113 APCs
Anti-Armour:
57mm M18 & 106mm M40A1 RCLs
Cobra, SS-11, TOW & MILAN ATGWs
Artillery:
105mm M101, 155mm M114 &
   203mm M115 Hs
105mm M52 & M108, 155mm M44, &
203mm M110 SPHs
70mm RA-7040 & 227mm MLRS
Air-Defence:
40mm Bofors L/60 AAG
20mm GA1-DO1 & 35mm Oerlikon
   GDF-003 SPAAGs
   Rapier & Redeye SAMs
Aircraft:
Cessna O-1E Bird Dog
Agusta-Bell AB.205
Bell UH-1H Iroquois

Above: Turkey has a large number of tanks and armoured vehicles which form part of the CFE talks; but, due to her geography, she will be able to redeploy any excess to other areas outside the treaty's control, such as the Iraq border, rather than destroy them.

Below: Preparing to resist an assault just as their forefathers did at Gallipoli, these modern Turks are equipped with a German Heckler & Koch G3 rifle and a missile-less MILAN anti-armour guided weapon system. The red bands are for exercise purposes.

USSR

DESPITE the development of "glasnost" and "perestroika" there should be no doubt that the Communist Party of the Soviet Union (CPSU) remains in charge of the USSR and that the Red Army constitutes the Party's main instrument for controlling Soviet society as a whole. The Red Army is also, as has been demonstrated several times in practice in recent years, the ultimate guarantor of the cohesion of the Union. Within the Soviet organizational hierarchy the Red Army is a separate arm of service, second only in importance to the Strategic Rocket Forces, although senior even to them in influence; the Minister of Defence, for example, is always an army man.

The Red Army was a crucial element in revolutionary Russia, its actual date of birth being 28 January 1918, with compulsory military service becoming an essential part of its ethos from 22 April of that year. Since that time the Red Army has taken part in numerous wars and campaigns, although it has always had just one essential mission — to protect the soil of the USSR from invasion by a foreign power.

Following WWII, or The Great Patriotic War as it is known in Russia, the Red Army's first task was to occupy that territory of the defeated Germany which had been allocated to the USSR. Next, they supervised a return to normality in the other European countries allocated to the Soviet sphere-of-influence, which led to the establishment of Communist governments in all of these states — a process which the Red Army did much to assist.

The Red Army put down numerous insurrections during the Cold War period, the most important of which were those in East Berlin in 1953, in Hungary in 1956 and in Czechoslovakia in 1968. It deployed large numbers of troops in Afghanistan for the ten-year war from 1979-89, an ill-advised and ill-fated intervention that has proved instructive for the military leadership as well as the rank and file. Today, however, the Red Army is in the throes of a number of major developments. Firstly, it is withdrawing to Soviet territory as part of the CFE Treaty — a process not eased by the obvious delight of the local people at seeing the Soviet soldiers depart. Secondly, and as a consequence of the first, the Red Army is having to reorganize in order to accommodate the reductions in men and equipment agreed in the various recent treaties. Thirdly, it finds itself being deployed to deal with unrest within its own territory, a duty which all armies, and especially conscript ones, find very distasteful. Fourthly, the Warsaw Pact has terminated its existence and thus the Soviet Union no longer finds itself the principal partner in a military coalition.

The latest pressure, however, arises from the recent campaign in Kuwait and Iraq, where the Iraqi Army, which was equipped with Soviet weaponry and trained according to Soviet doctrines, was totally smashed in just 100 hours. While it was the Iraqis who took the major strategic decisions, the generals are thought to feel serious disquiet both because their weaponry showed up so badly and also because the US Army's "AirLand Battle 2000" doctrine worked so extremely effectively. The Soviet General Staff and its especially effective Military History Bureau will analyze the war in minute detail with a view to developing a Soviet counterstrategy.

The principles of Soviet military doctrine, which dictate the shape and form of the ground forces, are heavily influenced by the geography and economics of the country. The USSR is so vast and the population density so low, even in European Russia, that the cost of fixed fortifications along its

Left: Volgagrad War Memorial, a tribute to the dead of 1941-45.

Below: T-72s in exact formation during the annual May Day parade.

borders could not be borne, even assuming that such defences could be made effective. Almost all of European USSR is a vast plain, bounded by the Baltic Sea to the north and the Black Sea to the south; eastward only the rolling range of the Urals lie between Moscow and the Tien Shan mountains on the border with China.

The greatest obstacles to any military operations within the USSR are the massive size of the country, the large rivers which dissect it, and the weather, particularly the winter. Soviet military planners must reckon with these factors, which affect attacker and defender alike, and plan the development of the Red Army accordingly. Throughout the period of the Cold War these geographical circumstances, allied to Russia's historic experience of being the victim of attack, led the Soviet planners to stress the absolute primacy of the offensive as the means of waging war. Today, however, even that is being reassessed and a less aggressive operational doctrine is to be adopted.

The Soviet Army is comprised of four elements. First, are the combat arms: the motorized-rifle troops, tank troops and airborne troops. These are supported by the artillery, which has long been a large, efficient and very influential element of the Red Army. Next come the specialists: engineers, communications and chemical troops. Finally, but by no means the least important, come the rear services: transport, medical, police, supply troops, etc. All these are controlled and coordinated by the all-powerful General Staff, an élite body of carefully selected and well-trained officers.

In wartime the Soviet forces would be commanded at the highest level by the Supreme High Command, located in or near Moscow. From there the operations of the land/air forces would be organized into "Teatr Voennykh Deistvii" (TVD, which is normally translated as a "strategic direction"), a unique type of headquarters which is responsible for planning, coordination of intelligence and strategic direction, but is not actually a command HQ as such. It is believed that four such land/air TVDs might be planned for general war: Western, South-Western, Southern and Far East, with a central reserve in the Moscow/Urals area and a Northern Front which covers the Scandinavian area.

At the next level the Soviet forces would be organized into fronts, each of which would normally comprise four or five armies and a tactical air force ("frontal aviation"). The commander of the front would thus be able to deploy his airpower in coordination with his ground forces, allotting it to whichever section of the battlefield he considered to be the most important. He also controls medium-range surface-to-surface nuclear-armed missiles and any paratroops who are allocated to him.

The USSR is divided in peacetime into 14 military districts which provide an administrative framework for raising, training and commanding military units, and for the organization and supply of military formations in their designated geographical areas. The military district is also respon-

Above: Airborne blue beret elite troops. The weapon nearest is an AKR sub-machine gun.

Right: A textbook air and land assault with mobile air-defence protection.

sible for mobilizing units and formations when war threatens, and some may also have a field command function in war.

The Red Army is huge; it consists of some 1,473,000 men and women, of whom just over one million are conscripts. Its combat strength lies in its divisions, of which there are four principal types: tank, motorized-rifle, airborne and artillery. These are at four stages of readiness for war: Category A divisions are at the highest state of readiness, with over 75 per cent of their manpower strength in place, equipped with the latest weapons and systems, complete to scale, and ready for war within one or two days at the most. Category B divisions have between 50 and 75 per cent of their manpower, are also fully equipped and could

be ready for war within three days. Category C, however, are somewhat less capable, being between one-quarter and one-half manned, having older equipment and requiring an estimated seven days to reach full manning, following which they would need some 60 days of training. Lowest of all are Category D divisions which have only some 5-10 per cent of their manpower in peacetime (ie, a small cadre) and would take some months to be fully manned, properly equipped and trained for war.

The cutting-edge of the Red Army are its 46 tank divisions; of these 17 are Category A, 19 Category B and the remainder Category C or D. Each tank division consists of two tank and two motorized-rifle regiments, supported by two artillery regiments (one field artillery, one air-defence), together with an armoured recce battalion. The more important of the tank divisions are equipped with the T-80, T-72 and T-64 MBTs, these are highly mobile vehicles armed with a 125mm gun. Divisions in the less crucial areas are still equipped with T-62 and even T-54/-55 MBTs.

There are some 142 motorized-rifle divisions which have recently been reorganized so they contain four motorized-rifle regiments, losing their tank regiments to form extra tank divisions and leaving only an independent tank battalion. This is a somewhat surprising decision as it appears to have robbed the motorized-rifle divisions of their main "punch". Combat-support is much the same as for the tank division with a field artillery regiment, a SAM regiment and an armoured recce battalion, but with an anti-tank battalion added in an effort to overcome the loss of the MBTs. Of these 142 divisions, 23 are in Category A, 27 in Category B, 82 in Category C and the remainder in Category D.

Of great importance to the Soviet state authorities are the seven airborne divisions, six of which are Category A, (the other being a training formation). These are the Red Army's élite force, specially trained and maintained at a particularly high state of readiness to deal not only with international crises, but also with domestic problems. In view of these roles, the airborne divisions come directly under the command of the Ministry of Defence. They have a large amount of specially designed equipment, such as the excellent BMD tracked infantry combat vehicle, which can be dropped by parachute, and there is a huge force of fixed-wing and helicopter transports to move them around.

Of additional importance are the Soviet special forces, known even in the West by their Russian name of "Spetsnaz". Now believed to number some 30,000, these carefully selected and exceptionally well-trained men (and some women) are intended to operate in many clandestine roles in war. They are known to specialize in foreign languages and would also be used for deep-penetration missions, raiding an

Left: Troops using an implausible assault technique to take a mountain position.

Top: Large, mediocre tank forces have been developed rather than small, skilled ones.

The Soviets have designed some highly-capable attack helicopters, of which the most successful to date has been the Mil Mi-24 Hind. This helicopter was widely used in Afghanistan where the Mujahideen treated them with considerable respect. The Mil Mi-28 Havoc attack helicopter is now in production as the first rotary-winged aircraft designed from the outset for air-to-air combat.

The question is often asked: Just how good is the Red Army? The US Army has fought three major campaigns since 1945, the first in Korea, the second in Vietnam and the third, albeit a very brief one, in the Gulf. It was successful in the first, unsuccessful in the second and spectacularly successful in the third. In contrast the Soviet Army has only had one major external campaign — in Afghanistan — and that proved to be only just short of a disaster. Much is made of the ethnic variety in the Soviet Army and of the effect this might have in war. The fact is, however, that the Soviet Army of 1941-45 fought exceptionally well against the best combat force in the world at that time and triumphed. Thus, if there was to be another such threat to the USSR, one that the junior officers and soldiers could believe in, then the Soviet Army would almost certainly fight as well as it has done in the past.

Above: T-54/55s remain the most numerous type of tank in service and would provide the backbone for armoured assault waves.

opponent's rear-area logistical bases, setting ambushes etc. They have historical roots in the guerrilla units which fought Napoleon and later proved so effective against the Germans.

The USSR is a country which can neither feed nor clothe its people adequately, nor can it organize an effective domestic transportation and distribution system. Despite this it has produced some of the finest military equipment in the world, and the fact that Soviet weaponry is sometimes not used to great effect by Third World countries may tend to disguise its inherent quality. For example, the ZSU-23-4 self-propelled anti-aircraft gun system was a relatively cheap and simple combination of three existing pieces of equipment: the ZU-23 quad 23mm cannon, the Gainful tracked chassis, and a valve-technology radar. Despite these origins the "Shilka" system proved devastating in use and earned the respect (if not fear) of every pilot who has ever flown near one; indeed, for many years it was the yardstick by which other such systems was judged.

The Iraqi Army was equipped with large numbers of Soviet air-defence systems which failed to deter or destroy the Allied air effort. This should not be taken to mean, however, that the Soviet weapons would not be effective in a European environment. Over Iraq the Allied air forces had total air supremacy from early in the combat and were able to deploy a mass of very sophisticated electronic counter-measures

in a "Suppression of Enemy Air Defences" (SEAD) role. There can be no question of the Soviet air force permitting such circumstances to arise.

Soviet small arms are characterized by their simplicity, ease of manufacture and effectiveness. The AK-47, for example, has become a guerrilla symbol throughout the world and must be the most widely used weapon in history. It has been replaced in Soviet service by the 5.45mm AKS-74 assault rifle, which promises to repeat its success. Other infantry weapons are equally simple and robust, such as the 30mm AGS-17 automatic grenade launcher and the PK/RPK series of light machine-guns.

Red Army planners realized early that the proper execution of combined-arms operations at the high tempo they envisaged would require a very efficient performance from combat engineers. As a consequence, there are a large number of them and their primary functions are to help in maintaining a speedy advance by clearing and maintaining routes, crossing obstacles and eliminating mines. In defence they would assist in preparing the position, lay minefields and create obstacles to the enemy's advance. To achieve all this they are equipped with a considerable amount of hardware, most of it excellent quality.

Air support for Red Army operations is provided by frontal aviation which is manned by air force officers and men, and includes helicopters. Thus, there is no separate army aviation corps as there is, for example, in the United States, British and French armies; although the helicopter regiments may be placed under the operational command of local commanders.

EQUIPMENT

Armour:
T-54, T-55, T-62, T-64, T-72 & T-80 MBTs
PT-76 light tank
BRDM-2 armoured car
BMP-1, BMP-2, BMP-3 & BMD IFVs
BTR-50P, BTR-60P, BTR-70, BTR-80, BTR-152 & MT-LB APCs

Anti-Armour:
57mm ASU-57 & 85mm ASU-85 SPATGs
85mm D-44S & D-44 guns
100mm T-12 ATG
AT-2 Swatter, AT-3 Sagger, AT-4 Spigot, AT-5 Spandrel, AT-6 Spiral, & AT-7 Saxhorn ATGWs

Artillery:
120mm S-120 & 122mm 2S1 SPHs
152mm Dana, 2S3 & 2S5 SPGs
100mm M-1944 (BS-3) & 130mm M-46 FGs
152mm M-1976, 180mm S-23 & 203mm M-1975 (SO-203) guns
122mm D-30, 152mm M-1937, M-1938, D-1, D-20 & 203mm B-4M Hs
122mm BM-21, M-1975,M-1976, 140mm BM-14, BM-16, 220mm BM-27, 240mm BM-24 & 300mm Smerch MRLs

Air-Defence:
23mm: ZU-23, 57mm S-60, 85mm M-1939, 100mm KS-19 & 130mm KS-30 AAGs
23mm ZSU-23-4, 30mm ZSU-30-2 & 57mm ZSU-57-2 SPAAGs
SA-4 Ganef, SA-6 Gainful, SA-7 Grail, SA-8 Gecko, SA-9 Gaskin, SA-11 Gadfly, SA-12A Gladiator, SA-13 Gopher, SA-14 Gremlin, SA-15, SA-16, SA-17, SA-18 & SA-19 SAMs

Aircraft:
Mil Mi-6 Hook
Mil Mi-8/Mi-17 Hip
Mil Mi-10 Harke
Mil Mi-24/Mi-25 Hind
Mil Mi-26 Halo

UNITED KINGDOM

DESPITE the fact that since the end of WWII the primary task of the British Army has been the defence of western Europe within the overall framework of NATO, the periods when it has not been involved in active operations somewhere in the world can be measured in days rather than weeks. These have involved full-scale conventional warfare in Korea, the Suez Canal crisis of 1956, the recovery of the Falkland Islands in 1982 and, in 1990, the deployment of an armoured division and other troops to Saudi Arabia for the liberation of Kuwait. There have been numerous counter-insurgency campaigns, with the 20-year old campaign in Northern Ireland an ongoing example. Britain has also despatched contingents to UN peace-keeping forces, most recently in Lebanon and Namibia. To each of these diverse and often unexpected challenges the army has responded with flexibility, demonstrating its versatile nature by adapting its tactics and techniques to each situation as its arose. No army in the world possesses so great a store of successful counter-insurgency experience.

One intangible feature unique to the British Army, although it also exists to a lesser extent in the older Commonwealth armies, is the regimental system, which is admired and sometimes copied with varying degrees of success by others throughout the world. Regiments, normally of battalion size, are recruited within specific geographical areas and their members remain with them for the greater part of their service. The regiment thus becomes a closely-knit community which takes immense pride in its achievements, traditions and customs, each regiment being convinced that it is better at its job than others in the same arm of service. The great strength of the system is that in terms of morale it extends beyond simple esprit de corps, recognizing as it does the fact that a soldier fights best among his neighbours and kin. At the regimental level, therefore, the British Army has an edge which is seldom apparent elsewhere and this has been demonstrated numerous times, generally in desperate circumstances.

The regular army is a professional, all-volunteer force with a strength of 153,000. Of these, 8,900 are recruited abroad, including 7,400 Gurkhas, and 6,700 are women. There are 181,600 ex-regular reservists available. The army's present order of battle includes one corps headquarters with corps troops consisting of an artillery brigade (one SSM, three heavy artillery and two air-defence regiments); two armoured recce and four engineer regiments; three armoured divisions (two with three armoured brigades, one with one mechanized and two armoured brigades; all with

Above: Soldiers from the 1st Battalion of the Staffordshire Regiment practise trench assaults in a live fire exercise in the desert before the Gulf land war begins.

Below: Air-mobile abilities have grown in recent years. The army now has over 100 Lynx helicopters alone, each one capable of carrying 10 fully armed men into battle zone.

three artillery, one engineer and one aviation regiments, plus an air-defence battery); an infantry division with one air-mobile brigade, two infantry brigades and an artillery regiment; one mechanized brigade; one airborne brigade; 11 infantry brigade headquarters; and three engineer brigade headquarters. It is equipped with the latest in military technology from a highly-developed defence industry.

The combat element of these formations consists of 13 armoured regiments; five armoured recce regiments; 16 mechanized infantry battalions; four armoured infantry battalions; 32 infantry battalions, of which five are Gurkha; three airborne battalions; one special forces (SAS) regiment; 18 artillery regiments (composed of one surface-to-surface missile, three heavy, eight self-propelled and six field); three air-defence regiments; 13 engineer regiments,

including one amphibious, one armoured and one Gurkha; and four aviation regiments.

On mobilization regular formations would receive substantial reinforcements from the 73,000 strong all-volunteer Territorial Army, the combat units of which include two armoured recce regiments; three light recce regiments; 41 infantry battalions; two special forces (SAS) regiments; two field artillery regiments; one artillery recce regiment; four air-defence regiments; eight engineer regiments; and an aviation squadron. Those elements not allocated to the British Army of the Rhine (BAOR) are constituted into United Kingdom Land Forces (UKLF) and United Kingdom Mobile Forces (UKMF).

On a somewhat different footing are nine battalions of the Ulster Defence Regiment (UDR). With a strength of 6,200, of whom 3,300 are part-time volunteers, the UDR is

Above: As part of European defences British troops train to fight with other armies. This Fusilier has been airlifted to the wintry north of Norway in a German UH-1D.

Below: The 5.56mm L85A1 is now the standard infantry rifle issued to the British Army. The Bullpup design entered service in 1985 with a first order of 170,000.

Above: The Vickers Challenger MBT with its 120mm L11A5 gun has shown in the Gulf that it can perform as ably as the Abrams, which is still the choice of many experts.

the largest regiment in the army and was raised to perform the internal security role in Northern Ireland, to which it is restricted. (The remainder of the army generally has six battalions on regular tours of the troubled province, with other units undertaking short tours at any given time.) There is also a 3,000 strong, volunteer Home Service Force organized in 47 companies for local defence duties. Other ground troops available to the United Kingdom include the Royal Marines' Commando Brigade and specialist units.

At the present time the army's major overseas commitment is the provision of I British Corps for NATO defence in Europe. Based in Germany, the normal peacetime strength of BAOR is some 53,000. In the event of hostilities in Europe, I Corps would be heavily reinforced with regular and territorial troops from the United Kingdom, the elements involved being an infantry division, a mechanized brigade, SAS, infantry and air-defence units. Some 2,300 men have also been allocated to the Allied Command Europe (ACE) Mobile Force for defence of the flanks and a number form the UK/Netherlands Amphibious Force which will deploy on NATO's northern flank.

The army's other overseas commitments include Belize (1,500), Brunei (900), Cyprus (3,000 including one battalion group serving with UNFICYP), the Falkland Islands (700-1,000), Gibraltar (800, soon to be reduced by the withdrawal of an infantry battalion), Hong Kong (5,900) and Nepal (1,200 at Gurkha training depot). There are also several hundred military instructors and advisers attached to the armies of 33 countries around the world, and a detachment serving with the peace-keeping Multi-National Force and Observers (MFO) in Sinai.

Since WWII the army has been progressively reduced in strength to a point which some feel is already dangerously low. Nevertheless, following the sudden

Above: Troops deploy from the latest IFV in British service, the Warrior. It has a 30mm cannon and carries seven soldiers.

Below: Scottish soldiers of the Royal Highland Fusiliers in Belize to deter the Guatemalans. A Mayan temple can be seen in the distance.

collapse of the Warsaw Pact as an offensive alliance, politicians and media persons were quick to clamour for a "peace dividend" which could be achieved by force reductions and the withdrawal of troops from Germany. Unfortunately, another unique feature of the British Army is that the bulk of it has always served overseas, and quite simply the United Kingdom no longer possesses the barracks or training areas in which troops can be housed in such numbers. Nor could such barracks, together with their infrastructure of married quarters and schools, be provided save at enormous expense. Thus, when the 1990 Defence Review was produced, it proposed cuts far greater than could be justified by the lessening of tension in Europe, cuts which on average would mean a reduction of one-third in the strength of the army's principal fighting arms. However, no sooner had the review been published than Iraq invaded and occupied Kuwait and it became necessary to despatch troops to join the international force assembling in Saudi Arabia. In the resultant war, Britain's 25,000 troops and the untested Challenger MBTs, as well as other armoured support, performed excellently and with a high degree of professionalism. Losses were minimal and heavy punishment was inflicted on the Iraqis, leading to their early surrender. In difficult desert conditions it was a remarkable victory.

This proved to be a sobering reminder of the speed with which conflicts can arise, a reminder which should not have been necessary, given the recent memory of the Falklands War in 1982. In the circumstances, it is difficult to see how the proposals contained in the review can possibly be implemented in the short term, although it seems inevitable that in due course some reductions will be made.

EQUIPMENT

Armour:
Challenger & Chieftain MBTs
Scorpion & Scimitar light tanks
Warrior & FV 432 IFVs
Saxon APC
Anti-Armour:
94mm LAW 80
MILAN & Swingfire ATGWs
Artillery:
105mm Light gun
155mm FH-70, 105mm Abbot & 175mm
  M107 SPHs
155mm M109 & 203mm M110 SPHs
227mm MLRS
Air-Defence:
35mm Oerlikon GDF-002 SPAAG
Blowpipe, Javelin, & Rapier SAMs
Aircraft:
Westland Lynx
Westland Gazelle
Westland Scout

YUGOSLAVIA

AN INCREASING desire for a union of the southern Slavs was finally realised in 1918 when the Kingdom of the Serbs, Croats and Slovenes was established, the title being changed to Yugoslavia in 1929. The pre-WWII government was increasingly pro-German and when a military coup was successful in March 1941 the Germans invaded and quickly overran the country. Strong resistance, however, came from the Communist guerrillas under Tito and after the war he established a Communist government. It was not long, however, before Tito split with Stalin and the country followed an independent course.

Tito's death in 1980 did not provoke the East-West clash that had been forecast in some quarters. However, increasing internal stresses among constituent national republics have meant that the Yugoslav People's Army (YPA) has again become very involved in domestic matters. It is predominantly Serbian and it regards itself as the guarantor of national unity under the leadership of Serbia.

The army is some 138,000 strong, of which two-thirds are conscripts on a one-year

Below: An assault crossing on the Danube, one of the great European rivers.

engagement. There are approximately 440,000 army reservists who are available on mobilization at short notice, and a further 1.5 million in the Territorial Defence Force, a militia armed with obsolescent weaponry. There are also some two million men and women in the Civil Defence Corps, although this is not under army control. Additionally, there is a paramilitary Frontier Guard of 15,000 which would fall under YPA operational control.

The country is divided into four military regions, one of which is a joint land/sea command covering the extensive Adriatic coastline which is particularly vulnerable. On mobilization the country can field 16 corps HQs with 42 combat brigades (eight tank, five mechanized, 23 infantry, four light-infantry, one mountain and one airborne). There is also a considerable artillery force of 14 field artillery brigades, six anti-tank regiments, four air-defence artillery and six SA-6 Gainful regiments.

Absorbing lessons from their WWII experience, all Yugoslav soldiers are trained to operate as partisans if required. It is the skilled climbers and skiers of the mountain brigade, however, that would most clearly replicate the roles adopted by modern Yugoslavia's founding fathers.

Much equipment is of Soviet design and some, such as the SA-6 Gainful missiles, launchers and radars, are purchased direct from the USSR. Other equipment is produced by Yugoslavia's relatively large and sophisticated defence industry. For example, the M-84 MBT design has been developed from the Soviet T-72 and is being produced in Yugoslavia both for its own

army and for export, one of the most recent deliveries being to Kuwait.

Yugoslavia looks set to maintain its independent status and to avoid joining any future European defence community. However, the internal stresses between Yugoslavia's disparate ethnic groups are such that the army's attention is more likely to be on domestic matters for the foreseeable future.

EQUIPMENT

Armour:
T-54, T-55, & M-84 MBTs
M47 & Sherman Firefly medium tanks
PT-76 light tank
SU-76 & SU-100 assault guns
M-80 IFV
BTR-40 & -50, OT-810, & M-60P APCs

Anti-Armour:
57mm & 82mm RCLs
57mm M1943, 75mm PAK-40, & 100mm
  T-12 ATGs
AT-3 Sagger, AT-4 Spigot, & AT-5
  Spandrel ATGWs

Artillery:
105mm M56, M101, & M18/40 Hs
122mm D-30 & M1938, 152mm D-20 &
  M1937 Hs
155mm M65 & M114 Hs
122mm 2S1 SPH
128mm M63 & YMRL32 MRLs

Air-Defence:
12.7mm & 20mm M55, 57mm S-60 AAGs
40mm M1 & Bofors L/70 AAGs
20mm BOV-3, 23mm ZSU-23-4, 57mm
  ZSU-57-2 SPAAGs
SA-6, -7, -8, -9, & -13 SAMs.

NORTH AFRICA AND MIDDLE EAST

John W. Turner

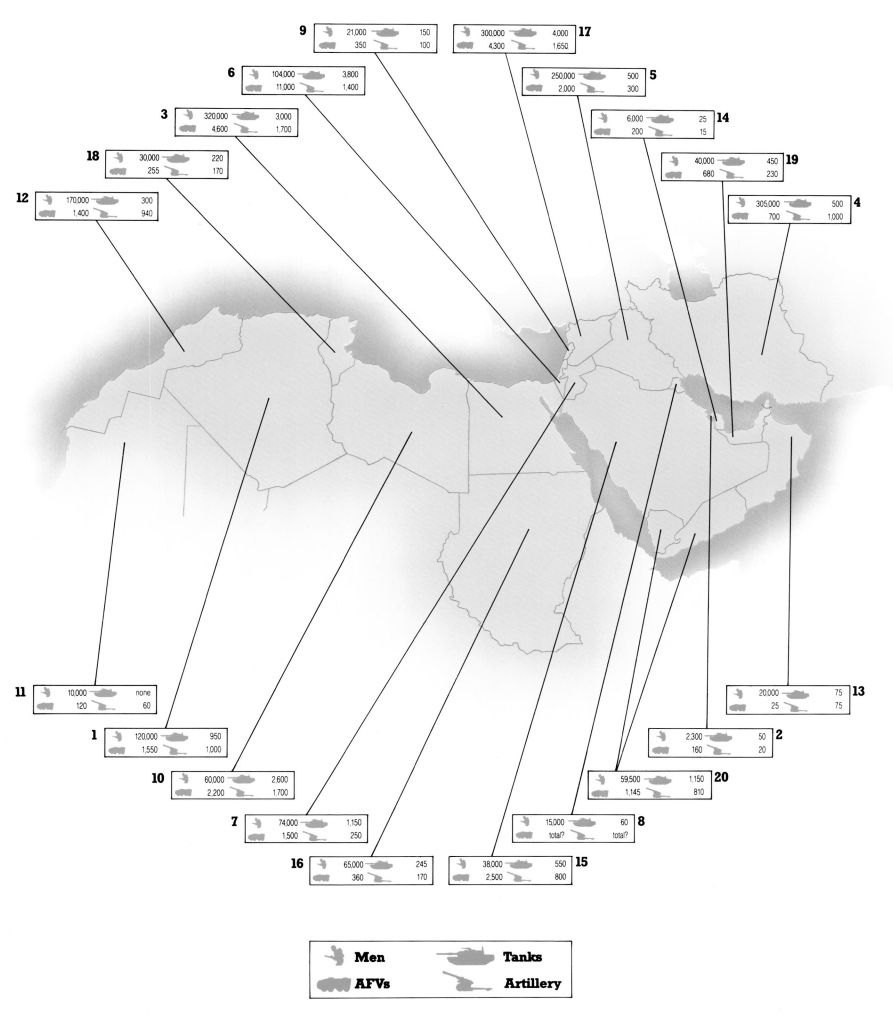

9 21,000 150
350 100

17 300,000 4,000
4,300 1,650

6 104,000 3,800
11,000 1,400

5 250,000 500
2,000 300

3 320,000 3,000
4,600 1,700

14 6,000 25
200 15

18 30,000 220
255 170

19 40,000 450
680 230

12 170,000 300
1,400 940

4 305,000 500
700 1,000

11 10,000 none
120 60

13 20,000 75
25 75

1 120,000 950
1,550 1,000

2 2,300 50
160 20

10 60,000 2,600
2,200 1,700

20 59,500 1,150
1,145 810

7 74,000 1,150
1,500 250

8 15,000 60
total? total?

16 65,000 245
360 170

15 38,000 550
2,500 800

Men	Tanks
AFVs	Artillery

111

ALGERIA

The Algerian Army or Ground Force (Force Terrestre) is, with 120,000 personnel, the largest service of the nation's armed forces which are collectively called the People's National Army (Armée Nationale Populaire or ANP). It is the third largest ground force in northern and Saharan Africa, after Egypt and Morocco. The primary mission of the army is territorial defence; its secondary mission is internal security which is the primary responsibility of the 23,000 strong Gendarmerie Nationale or GN.

The Algerian president is supreme commander of the ANP through the Minister of Defence and the ANP General Staff (EMG ANP). The latter is responsible for operations, training, administration, and logistics. Military intelligence and security is handled by a separate directorate, that of Military Security (Sécurité Militaire or SM) which is directly subordinate to the minister of defence.

Subordinate to the EMG ANP are the military regions and ground force brigades. The six military regions into which Algeria is divided have their HQs at Blida, Oran,

Bechar, Ouargla, Constantine, and Tamanrasset, respectively. Most units are stationed in First Region (Oran) or Third Region (Bechar). Army units include three armoured, five mechanized, 12 motorized infantry, and one airborne/special forces brigades, plus 49 independent battalions (31 infantry, five artillery, five air-defence, four paratroop, and four engineer) and 12 companies of desert troops, the latter

deployed in Third, Fourth, and Sixth Regions. With the exception of brigades, all army units are subordinate to the regions in which they are stationed.

Army conscripts serve 18 months, which consists of 6 months' basic training and the remainder in civic action projects. The relative benefits of military life attract sufficient voluntary personnel so that only about 10 per cent of the available military man-

Above: A ZSU-23-4 Shilka self-propelled anti-aircraft gun with four 23mm cannon. Algeria has about 200 SPAAGs in total.

Below: The French Army fought a hard war against Algeria. These paratroopers of a new generation will be just as capable.

Right: The SA-6 Gainful SAM carries three missiles in ready-to-launch position on a 360deg traversable table. It is for low/medium altitude defence and has effective minimum and maximum ranges of 3,700m and 24,000m.

Below: T-72 tanks in desert paint scheme. Algeria is thought to have 100 in service.

power pool is called to service.

Military training aims to develop a professional officer and NCO corps. The former receive candidate training at the Combined Services Military Academy (Cherchell). Subsequent training in combat-arms is at specialized schools for armour (Batna), artillery (Telergma), infantry and commando (Biskra), and desert operations (Ouragla). Support training includes schools for communications (Bougarea), engineering (Hussein Dey), and technical support, logistics, and administration (El Harrach). The main NCO academy is at Boghari.

EQUIPMENT

Armour:
T-62 & T-72 MBTs
PT-76 light tank
BRDM-2 armoured car
BMP-1 & -2 IFVs
BTR-50/-60/152 APCs
Anti-Armour:
82mm T-21 & 107mm B-11 RCLs
AT-3 Sagger & MILAN ATGWs
57mm ZIS-2 & 100mm SU-100 ATGs
Artillery:
122mm D-30 & M1931/37 Hs
152mm ISU-152 SPH
122mm BM-21 & -24 MRLs
Air-Defence:
14.5mm ZPU-2, -4, 23mm ZU-23
 & 57mm S-60 AAGs
23mm ZSU-23-4 & 57mm ZSU-57-2
SPAAGs
SA-6, -7, -8, & -9 SAMs

BAHRAIN

The small Sheikhdom of Bahrain has an army of 2,300 built around a single brigade of four battalions (two infantry, one tank, one special forces) augmented with an armoured car squadron and two batteries each of field artillery and mortars. Terms of service are voluntary.

It is also one of the six members of the Gulf Cooperation Council set up in 1981 which has led to a degree of standardization of equipment and inter-operability of units and personnel among the states involved. It contributes less than a battalion of men but is committed eventually to increasing its role.

Below, left: To assist its regular forces Bahrain also has paramilitary police.

Below, right: These troops are practising fixed-bayonet combat with their M16 rifles.

EQUIPMENT

Armour:
M-60A3 MBT
Saladin, & Ferret armoured cars
Saxon & M3 APCs
Anti-Armour:
106mm M40A1 & 102mm MOBAT RCLs
TOW ATGW
Artillery:
105mm Light Gun
155mm M198 H
Air-Defence:
RBS-70 & Stinger SAMs

EGYPT

THE Egyptian Army's primary mission is the land defence of Egypt. Its secondary mission is to promote internal security for the government and nation. However, a regional and ideological mission exists as well for a country which regards itself as leader of the Arab world.

The army's 3rd Mechanized Division, 15,000 strong, and 3rd Infantry Division were among 20,000 troops which fought to liberate Kuwait from Iraqi occupation. This is in keeping with the tertiary mission of the EAF: one of acting to defend, either individually or as a participant, the perceived interests of the greater Arab nation. Past commitment to this mission has led Egypt to deploy forces abroad, for instance in North Yemen in the mid-1960s, or offer direct or indirect military support to other Arab nations, such as to Iraq during the recent war with Iran. The main impact of this mission in the past was to involve Egypt in Arab coalitions against Israel in four wars. Since the Camp David accords and peace with Israel, it is likely that the regional aspect of the mission will outweigh the ideological (Arab nationalist) aspect.

The army consists of the Army General Headquarters (GHQ), field units, and military zones or districts. The GHQ consists of the staff, arms branches or departments, and administrative branches/departments. Each is headed by a major-general. The arms branches are infantry, armour, artillery, combat-engineer, paratroop, and commando ("Ranger"). The administrative or services branches are supply, transport, arms and ammunition (ordnance), military works and surveys (the National Service Projects Organization), signals, intelligence/recce, electronic warfare, chemical warfare, medical, provost, Data Systems Administration, the Training Authority, officers' affairs, military personnel, the Organization and Management Authority, insurance and pension, and moral affairs. Administrative services offices, also called departments or authorities, administer corps (military occupation specialties).

Major field units are organized into the GHQ reserve force and two armies (corps equivalent). The GHQ reserve force, located in the Delta region, comprises a number of mobile units, many organized under a headquarters of special forces. The two, 2nd at Ismailia and 3rd at Suez, are deployed along the Suez Canal. The remainder of Egypt's forces are deployed in six military districts in the Nile Valley, Red Sea coast, and the Western Desert.

Most of the army is organized into divisions or independent (non-divisional) brigades. Divisions are under field army HQs, and total 12 (four armoured, six mechanized, and two infantry). Each division consists of manoeuvre brigades, an artillery brigade, and battalion-size, or smaller, support units. Independent brigades total 28 (one Republican Guard armoured, one armoured, four infantry, three mechanized, two air-mobile, one paracommando, 14 artillery, and two heavy mortar). There are also seven commando groups of roughly brigade size. Most army missile assets are contained in one of the SSM regiments possessing FROG-7 or Scud-B.

The army has 320,000 active duty personnel, of whom about 180,000 are conscripts chosen via a selective service system performing three-year obligatory tours of duty. The army has reserves available of at least 500,000 personnel.

Training is administered by the Army GHQ Training Authority, and consists of basic, NCO, officer and staff, general and specialty courses at various installations. A number of army personnel are regularly trained abroad (500 in 1989), with the US, UK, France, Brazil, and Germany the the major

Above, left: Soldiers wear their favoured leopard-spot pattern fatigues as they take up prone positions on an impromptu firing range in the desert. The small arms are all of Soviet origin; most are rifles.

Above, right: Men from a paracommando unit (shown by the padded jump helmets) prepare to fire a round from an RPG-7V rocket launcher, a capable and fairly accurate weapon.

foreign powers providing such facilities. The US role in financing and training the Egyptian Army does not please Israel.

Army personnel receive specialty or advanced training at either MOD/EAF schools or army-administered schools, of which there are several dozen. The latter schools train army personnel in arms or services specialties not available at MOD/EAF schools. Specialty training is open to all qualified officer and enlisted applicants. EAF and other schools, through Egyptian military assistance programmes to other Arab and African nations, regularly train large numbers of foreign military personnel too. At least 20 nations either send military personnel to Egypt for training or host Egyptian training personnel.

At the national level the Army Staff Section for Logistics, as well as the GHQ Logistics Authority, oversees logistical support for the army. Tactical logistics are handled at division and brigade level with these echelons being supported by supply and transport battalions or companies.

Egypt's varied arms inventory, especially for ground equipment, complicates logistical support. However, national policy in the 1970s and 1980s has been the development of a domestic arms industry capable of indigenous maintenance and upgrades to existing equipment, with the ultimate aim of Egyptian production of major ground systems. Major ground force arms purchases continue, however, to be made from foreign suppliers, with the largest recent ones being 700 M60A1 MBTs from the US (March 1990), plus nearly 500 Hellfire anti-tank missiles.

Ground force doctrine draws upon a mixed heritage reflecting the army's roots in British colonial times, Soviet military assistance and the shift to more Western support. Since the mid-1970s there has emerged an increasingly Egyptian doctrine (or perhaps it can be called a re-emergence of ancient warfare beliefs in manoeuvre etc). In the 1973 Yom Kippur War the army proved itself and indicated its ability to adapt its tactics to changed situations.

The armour-heavy Egyptian units have evolved to counter what is perceived to be the regional threat: Israel. Concurrently, anti-armour tactics were also developed to counter Israeli armour and these proved quite successful during the 1973 Yom Kippur War. Despite innovation in tactics and doctrine, however, improvement is still needed in the timeliness and decisiveness of operational response to changing battlefield situations. This may well be remedied with improvements in educational levels of enlisted personnel and continuing improvements in officer training. Emphasis on combat-support and combat-service support continues to upgrade the force and its operational capabilities. The officer corps is highly professional and probably the best in the Arab world.

Egypt has a chemical warfare (CW) capability, one it shares with its neighbour to the west, Libya. As a result, the Egyptian Army has chemical defence units attached to all major formations.

The Egyptian Army is currently capable of defending the nation against attack from its neighbours, although its offensive potential may not be what it was in 1973. Of note is the increasing ability to project power (i.e., militarily intervene) in select actions throughout the region, a trend likely to continue.

Above: Used to the desert, Egypt's army is among the best in the region but had no recent experience until the Gulf War.

Below: Infantry line up at Cairo West air base. Egypt's role as a regional power, with the ability to act as one, looks set to grow.

EQUIPMENT

Armour:
T-54/55 & T-62 MBTs
M60 & M1A1 MBTs (on order)
PT-76 light tank
BRDM-2 armoured car
BMP-1 IFV
BMR-600, M113, BTR-50, OT-62, Walid, & Fahd APCs

Anti-Armour:
107mm B-11 RCL
AT-2 Swatter, & -3 Sagger, MILAN, Swingfire, & TOW ATGWs

Artillery:
122mm M1931/37 & 130mm M46 guns
122mm D-30, M1938, & 152mm M1937 Hs
155mm M109 SPH
80mm VAP-80-12, 122mm BM-21 & Saqr-18 & -30 MRLs
130mm M51/Praga V3S, 132mm BM-13-16 MRLs
140mm BM-14-16, 240mm BM-24 MRLs

Air-Defence:
14.5mm ZPU-2 & -4, 23mm ZU-23-2 & Sinai AAGs
37mm M1939 & 57mm S-60 AAGs
23mm ZSU-23-4, 35mm Oerlikon GDF-002 & 57mm ZSU-57-2 SPAAGs
SA-6, -7, Chaparral, & Crotale SAMs

IRAN

IRAN'S military, which had been carefully built up into a powerful fighting force in the 1970s under the late Shah Reza II, maintained its status immediately after the revolution in 1979. Iranian forces initially took the advantage during the eight-year Iran-Iraq War. Subsequently, they lost it and were unable to make significant gains against well-established Iraqi lines of defence. In the offensive process of trying to breach these lines, the Iranian armed forces (Army and Revolutionary Guard) incurred massive personnel and equipment losses which still cripple it as a military power. Currently, Iranian military strength is at its lowest point since WWII; however, recent contacts with the Soviet Union may lead to increased arms supplies.

The Islamic Republic of Iran Ground Force (IRIGF) has about 305,000 of the country's 605,000 military personnel. It is assisted in its ground mission of national defence by the Revolutionary Guard and paramilitary groups. Two ministries handle operational matters, the Ministry of Defence and that of Pasdaran (Revolutionary Guards). With the war against Iraq over, a system of regional commands is being set up.

At present, personnel are divided among three Army HQs. To these are assigned four mechanized and six infantry divisions, one airborne brigade, one special forces division, and 12 Improved Hawk SAM batteries. Some independent armoured and mechanized units exist as well. The army also has an aviation unit at Esfahan, equipped with combat helicopters (about 350) and some fixed-wing aircraft.

The Revolutionary Guard (RG or, in Farsi, Pasdaran Inquilab) ground forces consist of some 250,000 personnel in 11 regional commands. There are eight divisions, comprised of about 40 infantry, five armoured, and a number of other brigade-sized units under these commands. Sub-brigade level units are battalions that vary widely in their make-up. In addition to the regional commands and their units, there are a large number of independent RG units, including those for border defence, air-defence, missile, special forces, and various combat arms.

Assisting the regular Iranian ground forces are a number of paramilitary organizations. The largest of these is the Basij, or "Mobilization of the Oppressed" a volunteer force of Iranian youth loosely organized into about 500 battalions. These units, for the most part infantry, are in turn divided into three companies of four line platoons and one support platoon each. There are about three million members. The 2.5 million-man Home Guard is, like the Basij, under the control of the RG. The Gendarmerie, with 45,000 personnel, have an internal security and border guard mission,

and possess an air and a naval wing. In addition to these more organized paramilitary bodies, there are a number of "Tribal Guards" or militias of which about 40 are being formed. The Kurds in Iran are organized into the Kurdish Democratic Party (KDP) military wing, or the Pesh Merga, with about 12,000 or so personnel.

Relatively few details of training programmes are known. Military training is focused on conscripts, who have an average 50 per cent literacy rate and often do not speak Farsi. Most NCOs come from the urban middle-class and conscripts from the rural areas. Traditionally, officers came from the upper strata of Iranian society, but battlefield promotions as well as a move to augment the officer corps with personnel from the better-educated middle-class has altered its composition. Officers are trained at the National Military Academy; they were formerly trained abroad in the US and other Western countries, but since 1979 such outside training has been limited to a few countries such as China and North Korea.

Iranian military tactics are derived from a combination of Western doctrine (in which US military assistance contributed significantly from the 1950s to the 1970s) and indigenous doctrine. RG tactics in the Gulf War were marked by operations that resulted in extensive losses of men and materiel. However, they should not be thought of as representative of all ground force doctrine. It should be noted here that Iranian forces, like their Iraqi opponents, used chemical weapons and the Iranian military still possesses this capability.

A major drawback to Iranian military capabilities has been the diverse sources of equipment. This has compounded logistical difficulties. Support for high-tech weapons maintenance and training was provided by the US prior to 1979, but the end of such aid after the revolution resulted in a degradation of Iranian military capabilities. This has remained so, despite Iran's attempts to seek sufficient spare parts and supplies in the international arms market.

Partly as a result of Western embargoes, as well as a perceived desire for self-sufficiency in some areas of military production, the Islamic revolutionary govern-

Above: During the war with Iraq, religion inspired many to acts of suicidal bravery.

ment formed the Defence Industries Organization (DIO) in 1981. It is responsible to the Deputy Minister of Defence for Logistics who controls national or strategic logistics. By the mid- to late-1980s the DIO was overseeing the production of infantry weapons (rifles, machine guns, mortars) and ammunition. At the same time, efforts were made to develop a domestic maintenance capability for more sophisticated equipment held by Iran, an effort that has been partially realized.

While Iran's army, like its other military services, is experiencing a period of weakness, there is little doubt that the force can be built anew. Iran's oil assets and extensive borders requires that national defence pose a credible deterrent. The main mission of the Iranian military in the 1990s will be to rebuild this military capability, and even perhaps strive to regain its lost role as the major power in the Persian Gulf region. The outcome of the Gulf War will have assisted this process.

EQUIPMENT

Armour:
T-54/55, T-72, Type 59, Chieftain, & M60 MBTs
M47 & M48 medium tanks
Scorpion light tanks
EE-9 armoured car
BMP-1 IFV
BTR-50 & -60, & M113 APCs
Anti-Armour:
106mm M40 RCL
Dragon, ENTAC, SS-11 & -12, & TOW ATGWs
Artillery:
130mm M46 & Type 59 guns
155mm M101, M56, FH-77B, G-5 Hs
155mm M109 & 203mm M110 SPHs
107mm Type 63 & 122mm BM-21 MRLs
Air-Defence:
23mm ZU-23 & 37mm M1939 AAGs
23mm ZSU-23-4 & 57mm ZSU-57-2 SPAAGs
SA-7, RBS-70 & Improved Hawk SAMs
Aircraft:
Boeing-Vertol CH-47C Chinook

IRAQ

THE world was abruptly made aware of Iraq's military power when on 2 August 1990 they invaded and conquered Kuwait. Within hours the country had been overwhelmed and occupied by elements of Iraq's armed forces, spearheaded by élite armoured and mechanized units.

The Iraqi ground forces are characterized by their large size and by the quality and quantity of their armament. As a result of the war with Iran, Iraq had the eighth largest army in the world, and certainly the largest in the Middle East. Prior to the invasion of Kuwait, it was known to have about 955,000 personnel, with a variety of modern equipment and well-trained, making it a formidable fighting machine.

Subordinate to the state president is the Iraqi Armed Forces General Staff (GHQ), which includes the Military Control Directorate and Deputy Chiefs of Staff for Operations, Instruction and Training, and Administration. Directly subordinate to the GHQ are the Republican Guard Forces Command (RGFC), eight army corps (seven regular army corps and one special corps) and GHQ army unit assets (primarily artillery battalions), reserve army divisions, and Iraqi army aviation.

There are 49 divisions attached to the seven regular corps HQs of the army proper (42 infantry and seven armoured or

Below: T-55 tanks with 100mm guns occupying Kuwait soon after the invasion. Although T-72s were in Kuwait it seems most were kept in Iraq.

mechanized). The RGFC is comprised of six divisions (three armoured, one mechanized, one infantry, and one commando). In addition to these forces there are at least 20 special forces brigades and two SSM brigades (one FROG-7 and one Scud-B).

Army corps comprise divisions and independent brigades, including: a brigade-sized commando force; an artillery brigade with 130mm, 152mm, 155mm guns and MRLs; and a brigade-sized grouping of various types of air-defence battalions (SAM and ADA). Combat-support and combat-service support back similar structures in subordinate units. Each subordinate division has about 10,000 personnel; a corps has four divisions plus corps assets, thus comprising some 45,000 troops in all.

Prior to the occupation of Kuwait, Iraqi corps were distributed along the Iranian border from north to south in five fronts: Northern, North-central, Central (Baghdad), South-central, and Southern (Basra). The huge force which is displaced through these fronts is manned by a conscription system that requires personnel to serve for 21 to 24 months, with reserve obligations thereafter. The post-war situation is more chaotic with Iraq's command and control structure broken down and widespread insurgencies raging in the Kurdish north and Shiite south.

Training is the responsibility of the Deputy Chief of General Staff HQs for Instruction and Training. Officers are trained at the Military College in Baghdad and advanced training is available at the Al Bakr University for Higher Military Studies, also located in the capital. Army officers are also trained at the Reserve College. Details of enlisted training are not available in detail, but an analysis of operations indicates that Soviet military doctrine and tactics are followed to a considerable degree, with modifications that take into consideration local terrain and climate.

Logistics poses a potential problem for the Iraqi military machine. The diversity of sources of supply during the Iran-Iraq War has resulted in a plethora of equipment of varying types and maintenance specifications. However, to date the Iraqis appear to have been able to operate and maintain this diverse assortment of hardware, even producing their own spare parts and some ammunition. The arms embargo imposed after the occupation of Kuwait degraded Iraqi military capabilities significantly as repair parts for sophisticated electronic and other high-tech equipment could not be manufactured locally. This situation was massively exacerbated by the destruction incurred during the surprisingly brief hostilities between Iraq and the international coalition forces led by the US.

Iraq has developed an extensive indigenous arms industry, partly as a result of the Iran-Iraq War, and among Iraqi arms production projects are the assembly of the T-72 variant called the Assad Babil, or Lion of Babylon, and two gun-howitzer systems, the 210mm Majnun and the 133mm al-Fao. Domestic production of 155mm extended-range full-bore base-bleed ammunition has also been reported.

After the crushing defeat at the hands of the Allies it is hard to tell how much of Iraq's equipment was destroyed, although most estimates suggest 100,000 men were killed and tens of divisions dismantled. The ability to fight back against the uprisings has shown that many of Iraq's best troops were never in Kuwait and that the army which remains, albeit much smaller and depleted of some armour, may be an able force for defensive operations at least.

EQUIPMENT

Armour:
Types 59, 69, T-54/55, T-62, T-72, M60 & Chieftain MBTs
PT-76 light tanks
Steyr SK 105 tank destroyer
AML-60/-90, EE-3 Jaracara & EE-9 Cascavel, BRDM-2, ERC-90, & FUG-70 armoured cars
BMP-1 IFV
BTR-60 & -152, MOWAG Roland, OT-62-64, M113, M3, & EE-11 Urutu APCs

Anti-Armour:
73mm SPG-9, 82mm B-10, & 107mm RCLs
AT-3 Sagger & -4 Spigot, SS-11, MILAN & HOT ATGWs

Artillery:
105mm M56, 122mm D-30, & M1938 Hs
130mm M46 & Type 59 guns
152mm M1937 & M1943 Hs
155mm G-5, GHN-45, & M114 Hs
155mm AU-F-1 SPH
122mm BM-21, 128mm Ababil, 132mm BM-12-16, 180mm Astros SS-40 & 300mm Astros SS-60 MRLs

Air-Defence:
14.5mm ZPU-1, -2, & -4 AAGs
23mm ZU-23, 57mm S-60, & 100mm KS-19 AAGs
23mm ZSU-23-4 & 57mm ZSU-57-2 SPAAGs
SA-2, -3, -6, -7, -9, -13, -14, & Roland SAMs

ISRAEL

THE Israeli Army is the main component of the Israel Defence Force (IDF, in Hebrew the Zavah Haganah l'Yisrael, or ZAHAL), and is the most modern and capable ground force in the Middle East. The Israeli navy and air force are part of the IDF and not separate services. The IDF was officially created on 26 May 1948, but its roots go back to a number of underground Jewish groups that had become established in British-ruled Palestine from the 1920s onwards. Its mission is the defence of Israel's borders as well as the defence of the Jewish state. The army has also been used to reinforce the Israeli police during periods of civil disturbance, most recently since 1988 because of the "Intifadah" or Palestinian uprising on the occupied-West Bank and Gaza Strip. However, the main role remains one of national defence.

The IDF consists of a General Staff, Territorial Commands, Ground Forces Command, Navy and Air Force Service Commands, and the Functional Commands. The General Staff, subordinate to the Chief of the General Staff, comprises two elements. The first is the Coordinating Staff (General Staff Branch, and Intelligence, Manpower, Logistics, and Planning Branches; and the Training, Research and Development, and Operations Departments); the second is the Operational Staff, which has 16 offices that are formed around the ground force arms of service, or military specialization fields. The three Territorial Commands are the Northern, Central, and Southern. The Functional Commands are the NA'HAL Command (No'ar Halutzei Lohem, or Fighting Pioneer Youth), and the Gadna Command (Gdudei Noar, or Youth Battalions).

Ground Forces Command is in charge of army units. This control is exercised through the OC Armoured Corps, the Chief Infantry and Paratroop Officer, the OC Artillery Corps, and the OC Engineering Corps. The IDF ground force consists of an active component of two corps HQs, three armoured divisions, five mechanized brigades (one airborne-capable), three regional infantry divisions HQs (for each military command), one SSM battalion, and three artillery battalions. The reserve component consists of nine armoured divisions, an air-mobile mechanized division, 10 regional infantry, each with border sector responsibilities in the event of mobilization, and four artillery brigades.

The IDF's manpower needs are filled through a system of conscription (male and female) for Jews and Druze, while Christians, Circassians, and Muslims are permitted to volunteer for service. Officers are obligated for 48 months, male enlisted 36 months, and female enlisted 24 months. The active component, or Sherut Sadir (career soldiers and conscripts), has about 104,000 personnel of whom 88,000 are conscripts. The reserve component (Sherut Miluim) can expand the army dramatically. The force on full mobilization could number as high as 598,000.

Conscripts remain reservists through to the age of 55 for males and 39 for women. Although the training obligation for reservists is a day per month and a month per year, longer periods for some occupations are not uncommon. An extensive military training establishment as such does not exist, but many civilian colleges and vocational schools offer courses in military specialties to supplement the specialization training offered by the military. Those who finish conscript duties may opt to become career soldiers, signing renewable contracts for three, five or more years.

IDF ground force personnel, especially career soldiers and reservists, pursue military specializations in any one of the 16

Above: Golani troops armed with Galils and M16s stand beside their M113 APC during the withdrawal from Lebanon in 1982.

Below: A mechanized NA'HAL paratroop unit prepared for chemical attack during maneouvres in the hot and dusty Negev.

Above: An M60 with protective Blazer reactive armour panels attached to the glacis plate and turret. These detonate when struck by incoming shells and negate the penetrative power of an armour-piercing round.

ground forces corps or arms of service. These are: armoured, artillery, infantry and paratroop, engineer, signals, ordnance, supply and transport, general services, women's corps, medical, military police, education, the Rabbinate, the Judge Advocate's Branch, military intelligence, and the Fighting Pioneer Youth. The heads of some of these corps, such as intelligence and armour, are also at the same time in command of higher staff elements.

Although the IDF's mission is one of national defence, this does not mean a passive or static defence. On the contrary, the Arab-Israeli conflicts are marked by a history of bold pre-emptive strikes spearheaded by armoured units supported by massive air and artillery bombardments. The most recent example of this was during the 1982 invasion of southern Lebanon. The pre-emptive doctrine used by Israel is one of the major factors that has served to negate the vast superiority in personnel and equipment possessed by hostile neighbouring powers.

Israeli tactical logistics is simplified by the relatively small size of the country and its relatively well-developed transportation network. Movement of troops and supplies to the frontiers, as well as mobilization in time of war, have been greatly enhanced by these geographical factors. Israel's size is, of course, also a weak point.

Historically, the IDF has had three major sources of weapons. The high-tech source of modern weaponry has been the West, specifically the US and Europe. However, a significant amount of military equipment has been captured from Israel's Arab opponents in war. This is, for the most part, of Soviet-Warsaw Pact make. More recently, the IDF has cultivated indigenous Israeli suppliers of ground equipment in a move to promote self-sufficiency in a number of military areas, and to obtain weapons suited for the Middle Eastern battlefield. The strategy has also led to the development of a thriving domestic arms industry with a large export market. The most prominent major ground system produced indigenously for the IDF has been the Merkava tank.

Israel's military establishment is still perceived at home as a citizen force. The sense of mission, high morale, state-of-the-art equipment, and high standards of training and education enable the force to carry out effectively its mission of protecting Israel from being overwhelmed by foes many times more numerous than itself.

EQUIPMENT

Armour:
Merkava II, M60, T-54/55, T-62, & Centurion MBTs
M48 medium tank
Ramta RBY & BRDM-2 armoured cars
M2, M3, M113, Nagmashot, & BTR-50 APCs

Anti-Armour:
84mm Carl Gustav & 106mm M40A1 RCLs
Ramta, Dragon, Picket, & Mapats TOW ATGWs

Artillery:
M46 gun
105mm M101, 122mm D-30, & 155mm Soltam M71 Hs
122mm BM-21, 160mm LAR-160, 240mm BM-24, & 290mm MAR-290 MRLs

Air-Defence:
23mm ZU-23 & 40mm Bofors L/70 AAGs
20mm M163 Vulcan & 23mm ZSU-23-4 SPAAGs
Chaparral & Redeye SAMs

JORDAN

ALTHOUGH the army of the Hashemite Kingdom of Jordan, with 74,000 personnel, is of comparable size to that of its neighbours, it is about 2.5 per cent of the country's total population. Built upon the old Arab Legion (al-Jaysh al-Arabi) established during the days of British rule, the Jordanian Army of today is a well-trained and capable ground force commanded by the King of Jordan himself.

The force consists of four divisions (two armoured, two mechanized), two independent brigades, and 16 artillery battalions. Deployment in general is along the western border with Israel, the Syrian border, and around the capital, Amman. The combat units are recruited from the Bedouin of the Trans-Jordanian Desert, while the settled population of Jordan, much of its descended from West Bank Palestinians, is represented in the administrative and support elements. Despite the fact that the Kingdom of Jordan has suffered a number of military defeats at the hands of Israel, including that of the 1967 war, the Jordanian Army remains loyal to the monarchy. Service is voluntary, with no lack of volunteers. A draft is authorized if it is required, with two years' service for conscripts.

During the Iran-Iraq War of 1980-88, Jordan assisted Iraq and since the end of the war military relations between the two states have increased markedly. These close military ties may in part explain the Jordanian position taken during the Iraq-Kuwait crisis of 1990-91.

Jordan has long been an ally of the West, and much of its ground inventory is British. Most of the equipment can be assumed to be in good repair and with high rates of availability.

EQUIPMENT

Armour:
M60, Khalid (Chieftain), & Tariq (Centurion) MBTs
M47 & M48 medium tanks
Scorpion light tank
Ferret armoured car
EE-11 Urutu, M113, & Saracen APCs
Anti-Armour:
106mm M40A1 & 112mm Apilas RCLs
Artillery:
105mm M101, 155mm GHN-45 & M114, & 203mm M115 Hs
155mm M44 & M109, & 203mm M110 SPH
Air-Defence:
20mm M163 Vulcan & 23mm ZSU-23-4 SPAAG
SA-7, -8, -13, -14, & Redeye SAMs

Below: Troops aboard a transport aircraft. The unit is unknown but may well be the airborne special forces' Storm Brigade which is composed of Bedouins loyal to the king.

KUWAIT

THE Kuwaiti Army of 16,000 was destroyed during the August 1990 invasion and conquest of the country by Iraq. The force, which consisted of two armoured, one mechanized, and one artillery brigade, was unable to withstand the multi-division attack spearheaded by the Republican Guard.

Some elements of the Kuwaiti armed forces, including 4,500 army personnel were able to escape into Saudi Arabia with their equipment and join units already there as part of the GCC. Others who were not killed or taken prisoner remained in Kuwait as part of the underground resistance.

The Kuwaiti Army was rebuilt in exile from the core of 4,500 personnel who managed to flee to Saudi Arabia. Seeking volunteers from the exile community, 10,500 Kuwaitis signed up and were formed into two brigades and trained at facilities in Saudi Arabia or the United Arab Emirates. It deployed with the multi-national force in the Gulf and took part in the successful war of liberation.

The major ground force equipment is of western origin. An unspecified amount, including some Chieftain tanks, was taken to Saudi Arabia. The Kuwaiti government has begun to re-equip its forces, but little information has been released about how this is being done. However, it is known that 300 Yugoslav tanks (probably the M-84, a T-72 variant) have been ordered to re-equip the armoured units and these are being delivered at a reasonable rate.

Right: Kuwaiti troops atop one of their Mk 5/2 Chieftain tanks in the Saudi desert. It is armed with a 120mm gun and possesses a computerized fire-control system.

LEBANON

WITH the establishment of Syrian hegemony in Lebanon in late-1990, the Lebanese Army is in the process of being re-built slowly. However, rival militia forces, especially in and around Beirut, still overshadow the force in terms of capability and armament. Many units have seconded themselves to the various militias, although army personnel are still paid from state accounts.

On paper, the Lebanese Army consists of about 21,000 personnel who are divided into 10 brigades, of which six, with Ranger and special forces battalions (total of 12,000 personnel), are controlled by the Christians; three, with 8,000 personnel, are controlled by Muslims; and one, with 1,000 personnel, is controlled by the Druze. Two of the Muslim brigades are Sunni, and one is Shi'a, controlled by the Amal militia.

In late 1990, Syria had 30,000 troops in Lebanon, concentrated mainly in Beirut, Metn, the Beqa'a Valley, and at Tripoli.

Despite their presence the militias are the real local military powers in Lebanon. Militias, like the Lebanese Army brigades, are either Christian, Muslim, or Druze. All are equipped with a variety of weaponry, including tanks, APCs, and armoured cars, and an assortment of artillery.

They include the Lebanese Forces Militia which is Christian and has about 35,000 personnel, of whom 6,000 are full-time militiamen. The force is armed with 150 MBTs, mostly T-55s and M48s, M113 APCs, and a variety of artillery up to 155mm calibre. The Phalange is also Christian and has a force of 6,000, with about 800-1,000 full-time. It is armed with M113 APCs, 120mm mortars, and various infantry weapons.

The Shi'a Muslims have two principal groups. Amal has some 15,000 personnel, a third of whom are active fighters. It is armed with at least 50 MBTs, most of them T-54/-55, various APCs and armoured cars, and artillery up to 155mm calibre. Hizbollah, also with 15,000 personnel, has 3,500 full-time militia. Their equipment includes APCs, artillery, various infantry and anti-tank weapons. Shias also join the Iranian Revolutionary Guards which have based themselves is the Beqa'a Valley and number some 2,000. In Lebanon, there also remains the PLO which has 10,000 or so active fighters.

The Druze dominate the Progressive Socialist Party which has 12,000 personnel and 5,000 fighters; their equipment includes 70 older (T-34/T-54/-55) MBTs and BTR-60/-152 APCs.

Finally, there is the South Lebanese Army (SLA) supported and equipped by Israel. The force has about 1,200 full-time soldiers and a reserve of 1,500 militia in the self-styled Israeli "Security Zone" in southern Lebanon. Its equipment includes about 70 MBTs (M4, T-54/-55), M113 APCs, and an assortment of towed artillery up to 155mm calibre. It is particularly keen to halt Palestinian border raids.

EQUIPMENT

Armour:
M48 medium tank
AMX-13 light tank
Ferret & Saladin armoured cars
M113, Saracen, & VAB-VTT APCs
Anti-Armour:
85mm RPG-7 & 106mm Type 60 RCLs
ENTAC, MILAN, & TOW ATGWs
Artillery:
105mm M101, 122mm D-30 &
    155mm M114 Hs
Air-Defence:
20mm Oerlikon K63 & 23mm ZU-23 AAGs
40mm M42 SPAAG

LIBYA

THE Libyan Army currently reflects the organizational philosophy of their commander, Col Mu'ammar Ghadaffy, and other top members of the governing hierarchy. The army mission is one of national defence, especially against Egypt, as well as the maintenance of internal security. During the 1980s Libyan forces were sent into northern Chad to defend territorial claims there in the Aozou Strip.

Head of State, Ghadaffy, also heads the General Secretariat of the General People's Congress and is de facto Armed Forces Chief of Staff. Estimates of Libyan Army strength vary considerably, ranging from 55,000 to 85,000. A reserve force (the Popular Resistance Force) of 30,000 to 40,000 personnel exists, and it is believed that the 85,000 figure represents a regular base plus a reserve augment of 30,000. Despite these relatively large figures, Libya still cannot provide crews for over half of its armoured vehicles. Selective conscription exists for two or four years, but even so Libya is hard pressed to maintain an armed force that is at least 2 per cent of its small population (4.4 million).

The army consists of three divisions (one armoured, two mechanized), 38 tank battalions, 54 mechanized infantry battalions, 41 artillery battalions, a National Guard battalion, and 12 paratroop and commando battalions. Air-defence is charged to two ADA battalions and three SAM (SA-9/-13 and Crotale) brigades. Ground forces are augmented by seven Scud-B and FROG-7 brigades. The Libyan Army also has organic air assets.

Libyan ground forces are deployed in at least six military regions (Tripoli, Surt, Benghazi, Tobruk, Kufra Oasis, and Sabha Oasis). The balance of forces are deployed to guard the border with Egypt. The logistics bases in the oases support formations that operate in the southern border/Aozou Strip area. In 1990, two mechanized and two tank battalions, with support elements, were still deployed in the Aozou Strip, claimed by Chad.

The Libyan military inventory reflects the basic Eastern bloc alignment of Ghadaffy since 1971, with such weaponry dominating, and many advisers from there having trained Libyans. Approximately two-thirds of the Libyan tank inventory and half of its armoured vehicles are in storage. The force has offensive chemical capabilities, and employs protective equipment.

EQUIPMENT

Armour:
T-62 & T-72 MBTs
BRDM-2 & EE-9 Cascavel armoured
    cars
BMP-LIFV
BTR-50 & -60, OT-62 & -64, EE-11 Urutu,
    & Fiat 6614 APCs
Anti-Armour:
106mm M40A1 RCL
Vigilant, MILAN, & AT-3 Sagger ATGWs
Artillery:
105mm M101 & 122mm D-30 Hs

Above: Libyan T-72s, the pride of their armoured division. Its abilities are now known in the West after the IDF knocked some out in Lebanon and Iraq's proved no match for Allied tanks such as the M1 Abrams in Kuwait.

122mm 2S1 & 130mm 2S3, 155mm
    Palmaria & M109 SPHs
107mm Type 63, 122mm BM-21 & RM-70
    & 180mm SS-40 Astros II MRLs
Air-Defence:
40mm Bofors L/70 & 57mm S-60 AAGs
23mm ZSU-23-4 & 30mm M59 SPAAGs
Crotale, SA-6, -7, -9, -13, & -14 SAMs
Aircraft:
Aerospatiale Alouette SA.315 II
Agusta-Bell 412
Boeing-Vertol CH-47 Chinook

MAURITANIA

THE small (10,400-man) Mauritanian Army is organized and equipped primarily for an internal security mission. Assisting it are the paramilitary Gendarmerie National 2,200 strong.

The military is controlled by the president of Mauritania through the Ministry of Defence. Army units are deployed throughout seven designated regions. Principal units consist of four battalions (two infantry, one paratroop, one artillery), a recce camel corps, three armoured recce squadrons, four air-defence batteries, and an engineer company.

Although a two-year conscription system exists, the force is currently filled through volunteers, with military duty viewed as prestigious by Mauritanians. All former service members are considered reservists available if needed.

EQUIPMENT

Armour:
AML-60 & -90, EBR-75 armoured cars
M3 APC
Artillery:
105mm M101 & 122mm D-30 Hs

MOROCCO

THE 170,000-man Moroccan Army is the largest of the services in the Moroccan military, the Royal Armed Forces (Forces Armées Royales or FAR). Its mission of national defence is currently overshadowed by internal security: since 1975 the force has been engaged in a counter-insurgency (COIN) struggle in former Spanish Sahara (now named Western Sahara following Morocco's occupation in 1975), against the indigenous peoples there who man the Popular Front for the Liberation of Saguia el Hamra and Rio de Oro (Frente Popular para la Liberacion de Saguia el Hamra y Rio de Oro or POLISARIO). In their domestic security missions the army is assisted by the GR or Gendarmerie Royale.

Morocco's King Hassan II is commander-in-chief of FAR. He has a parallel line of authority over military HQs and units with the FAR General Staff (Etat-Major General or EMG), of which the King is chief of staff. Authority over the FAR is exercised directly from a Forward Headquarters (Etat-Major Avance). Administrative control over the EMG is through the National Defence

Administration. The King heads the National Defence Council, to which the General Office of Research and Documentation (Direction Generale des Etudes et Documentation or DGED), the national intelligence service, is directly subordinate.

Morocco is a former French protectorate, and its military organization still reflects this heritage with French remaining the language of administration. The Moroccan ground forces consist of units deployed in two commands nationwide, with 80 per cent of forces being located in the command which includes Western Sahara.

Major military units include: one mechanized and two motorized infantry brigades, a light-security brigade and two airborne brigades, six mechanized and two motorized infantry regiments (battalion-plus size), and independent units (11 artillery groups/battalions, an air-defence group, seven armoured squadron groups, 41 infantry battalions, three motorized/camel battalions, three recce cavalry battalions, a mountain infantry battalion, and five engineer battalions). The reserve is the 1,500 strong Garde Royale, which consists of a guard battalion and a armoured cavalry squadron.

The FAR increased threefold during the period 1975-85, and although in the past it had relied on voluntary enlistment, it implemented conscription for 18 months to ensure full manpower. Most enlisted personnel remain volunteers due to the employment opportunities the FAR offers, in an otherwise bleak economy.

The main aim of the FAR training programme is career development for professional officers and NCOs. The principal officer training institution is the Royal Military Academy at Dar al Bayda. Army graduates have the option of further specialized training followed by five years' field service. Some officers train abroad, especially in France and the United States. Advanced officer training is at the Headquarters Staff College at Kenitra. Enlisted training of an initial three months for conscripts is usually conducted at units to which personnel are assigned.

Above: A COIN unit mans a temporary desert outpost in the Western Sahara prior to a sweep in search of POLISARIO rebels. The FN's barrel cover protects it from sand.

The POLISARIO insurgency in the Western Sahara has resulted in commitments of resources and manpower to help the FAR meet the challenge posed by it. In the 1980s the army constructed a series of defensive berms to protect settled areas and mining installations. This was the highpoint of a relatively successful COIN effort. By 1990 Morocco had an experienced ground force, the largest in the Maghreb, expert in desert COIN operations but also able to defend the kingdom. Their expertise, together with King Hassan's pro-Western leanings, led to the decision to contribute a 1,000-plus Moroccan force to the allied coalition in the Gulf, a move not popular with domestic opinion which was in sympathy with Iraq.

Moroccan ground force equipment reflects the close ties the nation has historically had with France, its former colonial overlord, and, more recently, the United States. Some armoured vehicles useful in COIN operations have also come from South Africa.

EQUIPMENT

Armour:
M48 medium tank
AMX-13 light tanks
Steyr SK 105 tank destroyer
AMX-10RC, AML-60 & -90, Eland, & EBR-75 armoured cars
M113, Ratel -20 & -90, & UR-416 APCs
Anti-Armour:
106mm M40 RCL
Artillery:
105mm M101 & 155mm M114 Hs
155mm AMX-F3 & M109 SPHs
122mm BM-21 MRL
Air-Defence:
14.5mm ZPU-2 & -4 & 23mm ZU-23 AAGs
20mm M163 Vulcan SPAAG
Chaparral & SA-7 SAMs

OMAN

THE Sultan of Oman's Land Forces (SOLF) number 20,000 and are the largest element in the 25,500 strong Sultan of Oman's Armed Forces. The force has a territorial defence mission as well as an internal security role. The latter figured heavily in the 1960s and 1970s during the Dhofar rebellion, and as a result the force has considerable COIN experience. In addition there is a 3,500 strong tribal reserve force known as Firqat.

The SOLF consists of 14 battalion-sized regiments (one armoured, two artillery, one armoured/recce, eight infantry, one infantry/recce, and one airborne). One division and two brigade HQs exist to administer the forces as deployed, and two independent recce companies also exist. An independent company-sized infantry unit, called the Sultan's Special Force, is deployed in eastern Oman. The SOLF is supported by one regiment each of artillery, engineer, signals, and transport.

Terms of service in the force are strictly voluntary despite the difficulty in finding qualified personnel. The SOLF has a number of foreign military personnel, mostly British, seconded to its armed forces to provide needed military and administrative skills. The SOLF opened a staff college in 1986, supplementing existing SOLF schools for the combat branches as well as service support branches.

Omani ground force inventories reflect long ties with the West and much of the equipment is of British make. It has been carefully selected for the terrain and conditions of operation in the Arabian peninsula.

Units of Omani troops served with the 3,000 strong Gulf Cooperation Council force as part of the coalition forces which liberated Kuwait. They saw some tough combat in built-up terrain against Iraqi soldiers and performed creditably.

EQUIPMENT

Armour:
M60 & Qayid al-Ardh (Chieftain) MBTs
Scorpion & VBC-90 light tanks
Fahd, Saxon, & VAB APCs
Anti-Armour:
TOW & MILAN ATGWs
Artillery:
105mm Light & 130mm M46 guns
155mm FH-70 H
M109 SPH
Air-Defence:
20mm VAB, 23mm ZU-23-2, & 40mm Bofors L/60 AAGs
Blowpipe, Javelin, & SA-7 SAMs

Below: Omani troops deploy in the desert following their airlift by AB.205A-1 Iroquois of the Royal Air Force of Oman.

Above: Members of the Sultan's Special Force ride in a jeep favoured for this terrain. The unit is trained by Britain's SAS and rates as one of the best in the region. It recruits among the tribesmen of the Jebel area in the Dhofar region, a remote and hilly area.

QATAR

THE small Qatari Army numbers 6,000 and is for the most part a mechanized infantry force. It consists of six battalions/regiments (one Royal Guard, one tank, three mechanized, one field artillery), and an air-defence battery (Rapier). Following the 1990 Iraq-Kuwait crisis Qatar (a member of the GCC) has announced that it will replace its MBTs with US-made tanks, and probably increase its force size too. However, the small population size of Qatar makes it likely conscription will have to be introduced.

EQUIPMENT

Armour:
AMX-30 MBTs
Ferret armoured car
AMX-10P, VAB, & V150 Commando APCs
Artillery:
25-pdr (88mm) gun
155mm F3 SPH
Air-Defence:
Blowpipe, Rapier, & Stinger SAMs

Above: Qatari troops practise techniques for FIBUA. This was to pay dividends during the fight for the Saudi town of Khafji. Note that during this "house clearance" exercise the lead soldier carries no magazine in his rifle. This is an obvious security measure.

SAUDI ARABIA

DESPITE possessing state-of-the-art weaponry, the Saudi Arabian military is still structured and operated to take into account the maintenance of the internal balance of power in an almost-medieval monarchy. In addition to the 38,000-man Saudi Arabian Land Force (SALF, or the army proper), the Saudi monarchy has a 56,000-man National Guard (SANG) under a separate command structure. These are the largest forces in the Saudi military, which also includes the Air Force, Navy, Air-Defence, Frontier Force, Coast Guard, and a part-Saudi Peninsular Shield Force (composed of one understrength brigade drawn from all Gulf Cooperation Council states and one Saudi brigade) which is based in the north-east of the country.

The SALF is comprised of eight brigades (two armoured, four mechanized, one infantry, and one airborne/special forces). It is supplemented by a brigade-sized Royal Guard Regiment, five artillery battalions, and 18 ADA batteries. It is boosted by SANG which is built around two mechanized infantry brigades.

Despite its high-tech weaponry, the Saudi monarchy remains vulnerable due to its large size, extensive frontiers, and powerful neighbours such as Iraq and the newly-unified Yemen. The conquest of Kuwait by Iraq highlighted major defects in Saudi Arabia's capability to defend itself. As a result of such considerations, the Saudis announced in late-1990 that they would increase their armed forces to 120,000 personnel and introduce a divisional structure, consisting of five to seven divisions, each having 12,000 troops.

The Saudi ground inventory reflects the country's long-standing ties to the West. The Saudi government can afford the best military equipment available, and has purchased materiel for its ground forces methodically and carefully. Most recently it has been negotiating a major arms purchase agreement with the US.

With the hostilities against Iraq, the SALF was tested in battle for the first time against an external enemy. It seems to have performed well and this may result in expansion.

EQUIPMENT

Armour:
AMX-30, M60 & M1A1 (on order) MBTs
AML-60 & -90 armoured cars
AMX-10P, EE-11 Urutu, M3, M113
& V-150 Commando APCs
Anti-Armour:
84mm Carl Gustav & 106mm M40A1
RCLs
Dragon, HOT & TOW ATGWs
Artillery:
105mm M56 & M101, 155mm FH-70 &
M114 Hs
155mm M109 & GCT SPHs
107mm M30 & 127mm Astros II MRS
Air-Defence:
20mm M163 Vulcan & 30mm AMX-30 SA
SPAAGs
Shahine, Stinger, & Redeye SAMs

Below: Saudi Arabian M60s and crews train before their biggest test ever — the land offensive for the liberation of Kuwait.

SUDAN

SUDAN'S ground forces, with a total strength of 65,000, make up the bulk of the 73,000-man Sudanese People's Armed Forces (SPAF). The other services are all separate branches of the SPAF.

The SPAF has a Chief of Staff subordinate to whom is the Director of Military Intelligence (DMI), which, with the State Security Organisation (SSO), is heavily responsible for internal security. Subordinate to the General Staff are military districts, independent ground force units, and the functional corps. The ground forces have no separate general HQs, operating under direct command of the SPAF General Staff.

There are six military districts: Khartoum Regional Command (Khartoum), Eastern Command (Khashm al Qirbah), Western Command (Al Fashir), Northern Command (Shandi), Southern Command (Juba), and Red Sea Command (Port Sudan). The latter five military districts correspond with the SPAF's five infantry division HQs; the 7th Armoured Division is located at Khartoum and is a regular armoured division.

The bulk of SPAF's ground forces comprise 14 brigades (12 infantry, one mechanized, and one air-assault) distributed throughout the five military districts/infantry division HQs. The 7th Armoured Division consists of two armoured brigades (one light, one heavy) and a recce battalion. Subordinate to the Khartoum Regional

Command are the Khartoum Garrison, the Republican Guard Brigade, and an airborne brigade. Other major ground units include three field artillery regiments, two air-defence artillery regiments, and an engineer regiment.

Also subordinate to the General Staff are the SPAF's functional corps, which manage career development in specialized support areas; namely artillery, ordnance, engineers, transport and supply, signals, medical, maintenance, and chemical.

SPAF training is based largely on the British model, and closely follows the Egyptian structure and curriculum. Among the important schools are the Sudan Military College at Wadi Sayedna, the High Military Academy (formerly the Nimeiri High Military Academy) in Omdurman, and the Staff and Commander's College in Omdurman. These schools provide basic and advanced officer training; the High Military Academy is a war college modelled after Egypt's Nasser Military Academy. Non-commissioned officers are trained at the NCO School at Jubayt. Instruction in combat-arms is provided by the Infantry School at Karari and the Armour School at Ash Shaajara. Each of the functional corps has its own training school, with the most notable being the Artillery School at Atbara.

Service in the SPAF is voluntary, with the military regions each responsible for enlisting personnel for the force. Once recruited, every effort is made to ensure that enlistees are given extensive training for further professional development; retention is generally assumed, due to relatively high status and the comparatively good pay

that military service officers.

Sudan's large size and relatively undeveloped transportation infrastructure make logistics for offensive operations impractical; they would also pose significant problems for an invader coming from any direction other than the north. The south of the country contains much marsh and savanna, and it is in this region that Sudan's internal insurgent movements operate most effectively. The Sudanese People's Liberation Movement (SPLM) controls most of Sudan's southern Bahr al-Ghazal, Upper Nile, and Equatoria regions via its armed wing, the SPLA. The movement, dominated by the non-Muslim Dinka and Nuer peoples, comprises at least 30,000 personnel organized into battalion-sized units. The SPLA is a light-infantry force whose heavier weapons inventory includes captured or purchased SPAF field artillery, air-defence guns, and SA-7 SAMs.

EQUIPMENT

Armour:
T-54/55 & M60 MBTs
Type 62 light tank
AML-90, BRDM-1 & -2, Ferret, & Saladin
  armoured cars
BTR-50 & -152, OT-62, V-150 Commando &
  M113 APCs
Anti-Armour:
Swingfire ATGW
Artillery:
105mm M101, 122mm Type 54 & D-30, &
  155mm F3 SPHs
122mm Al Saqr-30 & BM-21 MRL
Air-Defence:
20mm M163 & M167 Vulcan SPAAG
23mm ZU-23-2 AAG
40mm Bofors L/60, 85mm KS-12 & 100mm
KS-19   AAGs

Below: Weidi Seidna air base in Sudan; a Sudanese Army officer inspects a selection of western arms with US Army colonels.

SYRIA

SYRIA, bordered by Iraq and faced by the challenge of Israel on its southern border, has developed a formidable land force. Syria's alignment with the USSR has resulted in ready access to a variety of the latest Soviet and Eastern bloc equipment. Although it has always been understood that the primary opponent is Israel, Syria has used its army to good effect in establishing its influence over Lebanon, and most recently it contributed a division to the international force in the Persian Gulf as part of the successful effort to contain Iraq.

Since 1948 Syria has been one of the principal opponents of Israel to the south. It has been a major member of Arab coalitions in wars against them in 1948, 1967, and 1973. In 1982 in the Lebanon the Syrian military faced the Israelis when the IDF invaded and occupied the southern half of the country. Despite high losses incurred by the Syrian Army in a series of defeats by the Israelis, Syrian forces are judged to have fought relatively well. Equipment losses were quickly made up by the USSR. Syria's interest in controlling Lebanon, which it regards as an unfinished agenda from the post-WWII settlement in the area, has been particularly active since 1974-75. Efforts by Syria to establish a military hegemony in the country and enforce an uneasy peace among the warring factions there appear to have been successful as of early-1991.

Currently, the Syrian Army is the largest of the country's armed forces. Numbering 300,000, it has, in addition to a core of career soldiers numbering 120,000, 130,000 conscripts and 50,000 reservists. President Hafiz al-Assad is commander-in-chief with a rank of lieutenant general. Reporting to him is the minister of defence and the chief of staff of the armed forces. Subordinate to the latter are the chiefs of staff of the individual services, including the army. At various times, however, individuals have held several posts simultaneously.

The Syrian Army consists of two corps HQs, to which are assigned five armoured divisions, three mechanized divisions, and a special forces (paracommando) division. Independent units include two mechanized brigades, two artillery brigades, seven independent special forces regiments, three surface-to-surface missile (SSM) brigades (FROG-7, Scud-B, SS-21), a coastal defence SSM brigade, and two coastal defence brigades. The regular forces are backed by reserves, which when mobilized can form nine mechanized and infantry brigades.

The Air-Defence Command, with 60,000 personnel comprises 95 SAM batteries all told. Eleven of the brigades are armed with SA-2 and SA-3 SAMs; 10 are armed with SA-6s and ADA. In addition there are two SAM regiments with SA-5s and SA-8s. A separate command, it has in the past been part of the army.

The Syrian Army is maintained by a conscription system that requires all able-bodied males to serve 30 months in the armed forces. Following conscription, a serviceman has the option of enlisting for five years of regular military service to fulfill his military obligations, or to become a reservist with a period of obligation lasting 18 years. Those who choose to enlist and demonstrate the skills to become an NCO during this period are, at the end of the five years, usually appointed to a career NCO billet if they opt to remain in the army. Even if an enlistee did not attain NCO status, he could re-enlist for up to 15 years' further service. Such a system maintains force size and encourages those who exhibit military skills to remain in the army.

Conditions of service for most military personnel, especially the enlisted, compare favourably with those of Syrian society in general. Great care has been taken to make military life attractive, and to ensure that benefits accrue to service thereby allowing the army to retain capable personnel as career soldiers. In addition, special skills, often lacking among many conscripts, are rewarded with additional technical pay. The end result has been to raise morale and encourage professionalism.

Below: Syrian commandos in Beirut. These shock troops have shown that they are highly-capable soldiers, as the IDF's finest have found out to their cost. A brigade served with the coalition in the Gulf.

While the enlisted are freely drawn from all sectors of society, the officer corps is heavy with members of the Druze and Alawite minorities. This ensures support for President Assad, himself an Alawite, and the highest staff positions, which are also heavily Alawite. Officer candidates must pass a mandatory entrance examination and be physically fit for service. Army officer candidates are trained at the Syrian Military Academy at Homs, while reserve officers are trained at the Reserve Officer School at Aleppo. These candidates are chosen from annual conscript intakes. Additional training has been available in France, Great Britain, the US, other Arab states, and especially the USSR. Due to the high standards established for Syrian Army officers, most such personnel are regarded as well-trained and very professional in attitude.

The Syrian Army is assisted in its mission by the paramilitary Republican Guard (primarily an internal security service), with about 10,000 personnel; the Frontier Force (Border Guard), with about 1,800; and the Gendarmerie (under the Ministry of the Interior), with 8,000 personnel.

The Syrian armed forces possess chemical weapons, and have the surface-to-surface missile assets to deliver chemical ordnance against their neighbours. Syrian chemical weapons are manufactured domestically. In line with Soviet CW doctrine, the force also possesses chemical defence units.

Syrian ground force equipment is almost entirely Soviet and Warsaw Pact. Syria's special status as the USSR's regional ally has allowed it to be the recipient of sizeable amounts of high-tech armament, especially in the realm of air-defence. However, the Syrians have a substantial amount of modern, although not state-of-the-art, equipment in other areas, such as armour and artillery. It is possible that recent developments in Europe may result in significant changes in Syrian access to Soviet equipment and training, namely in the form of restrictions.

EQUIPMENT

Armour:
T-54/55, T-62 & T-72 MBTs
BRDM-2 armoured car
BMP-1 IFV
BTR-60 & -152, & OT-64 APCs
Anti-Armour:
AT-3 Sagger & -4 Spigot, & MILAN
  ATGWs
Artillery:
122mm ISU-122, M1931/37, 130mm M46, &
  152mm ISU-152 guns
122mm M1938 & D-30 Hs
152mm M1937 & M1943 Hs
122mm 2S1, T-34/D-30, & 2S3 guns
122mm BM-21, 220mm BM-27, & 240mm
  BM-24 MRLs
Air-Defence:
23mm ZU-23-2 & 37mm M1939 AAGs
57mm S-60 & 100mm KS-19 AAGs
23mm ZSU-23-4 & 57mm ZSU-57-2
  SPAAGs
SA-7, -9, & -13 SAMs

TUNISIA

THE primary mission of the 30,000-man Tunisian Army, the smallest in the Maghreb, is national defence. In its secondary mission it trains the 3,500-man paramilitary Public Order Brigade (Ministry of the Interior) and supports the 10,000 strong Tunisian National Guard.

Major ground units include four brigades (two mechanized, one "Sahara" mobile infantry, and one paracommando) and six regiments (one armoured recce, one anti-tank, one field artillery, two air-defence under a brigade HQ, and one engineer). These units are deployed through four military regions: First at Bizerte, Second at Tunis, Third at Gabes, and Fourth at Beja.

Although enlistment is high enough to maintain unit fills, a selective conscription system of 12 months duration is also in effect. Major military and army training is conducted at the Academic Militaire, the Lycee Militaire, the Institut de la Defense Nationale, and the Staff College (Ecole d'etat major). Other, technically-based training is done at the NCO Academy in Bizerte, the Army Technical School, the Inter-Arms Training School at Boeicha, and the Anti-Air Training Centre.

Tunisian weaponry is usually French or US in origin, although army inventories also add Austrian, British, Brazilian, Italian, and other equipment.

EQUIPMENT

Armour:
M60 MBT
M48 medium tank
AMX-13 & M41 light tank
Steyr SK 105 tank destroyer
AML-90 & Saladin armoured cars
EE-11 Urutu, Fiat 6614, & M113 APCs
Anti-Armour:
TOW, MILAN, SS-11, & ACL STRIM-89 ATGWs
Artillery:
105mm M101 & 155mm M114 Hs
105mm M108 & 155mm M109 SPHs
Air-Defence:
20mm M163 Vulcan SPAAG
37mm M1939, Type 55,
  & 40mm M42 AAGs
Chaparral & RBS-70 SAMs

Above: Women too can serve with Tunisia's forces and receive firearms training.

YEMEN

DESPITE the recent union of North Yemen and South Yemen (People's Democratic Republic of Yemen), the armies of the two countries have not yet been merged. However, as Sana'a, former capital of North Yemen, is now the capital of the united Yemens, the armed forces HQs will also be there. The two nations currently have a total of 59,500 active ground force personnel (35,000 for North Yemen, 24,000 for South Yemen). Both nations have conscription: three years for the North and two years for the South. Some 43,000 personnel of the entire force are conscripts (25,000 in the North and 18,000 in the South).

Both Yemens have a brigade structure in which infantry units predominate. Both have armour, mechanized and artillery elements; while only North Yemen has airborne and commando/special forces capabilities. Both also have FROG-7 and Scud B missile brigades, reflecting the Warsaw Pact influence on their inventories.

Left: South Yemen's Young Communists show their support for the regime some years ago. The current situation is still a little unclear, but the military aspects of union do not seem to be under any immediate threat.

UNITED ARAB EMIRATES (UAE)

THE confederal nature of the UAE, which is composed of seven Sheikhdoms, is reflected in the current makeup of its 40,000 strong army which consists of seven "integrated" brigades (two infantry, one armoured, one mechanized, one Royal Guard, one artillery, and one air-defence) headquartered at the capital, Abu Dhabi. A non-integrated defence establishment built around an infantry brigade also exists at Dubai.

The turbulent events in the wake of the Iran-Iraq War have prompted the UAE to improve its ground forces. The UAE Army plans to modernize its artillery corps by acquiring a brigade's worth (about 76) of South African 155mm G-6 SP guns, and to upgrade its armour with 250 US M1A1 MBTs which have shown their quality.

EQUIPMENT

Armour:
AMX-30 & M1A1 (on order) MBTs
Scorpion light tank
AML-90, AMX-10P & VBC-40 armoured cars
EE-11 Urutu, M3, & VAB APCs
Anti-Armour:
84mm Carl Gustav & 120mm BAT L-4 RCLs
MILAN & HOT ATGWs
TOW, & Vigilant ATGWs
Artillery:
105mm Light gun
155mm F3 & G-6 SPHs
105mm M56 H
70mm LAU-98 & 122mm FIROS-25 MRLs
Air-Defence:
20mm M3VDA SPAAG
30mm GCF-BM2 AAG
Crotale, Rapier, & RBS-70 SAMs

EQUIPMENT

Armour:
T-34, T-54/55, T-62, & M60 MBTs
Saladin, BRDM-2 & Ferret armoured cars
BMP-1 IFV
BTR-60 & -152, & M113 APCs
Artillery:
76mm M1942 & 130mm M46 guns
105mm M101, 122mm M1938 & D-30, & 155mm M114 Hs
122mm BM-21 & 140mm BM-14 MRLs
Air-Defence:
23mm ZU-23 AAG
23mm ZSU-23-4 SPAAG
SA-6 & -9 SAMs

SUB-SAHARAN AFRICA

John W. Turner

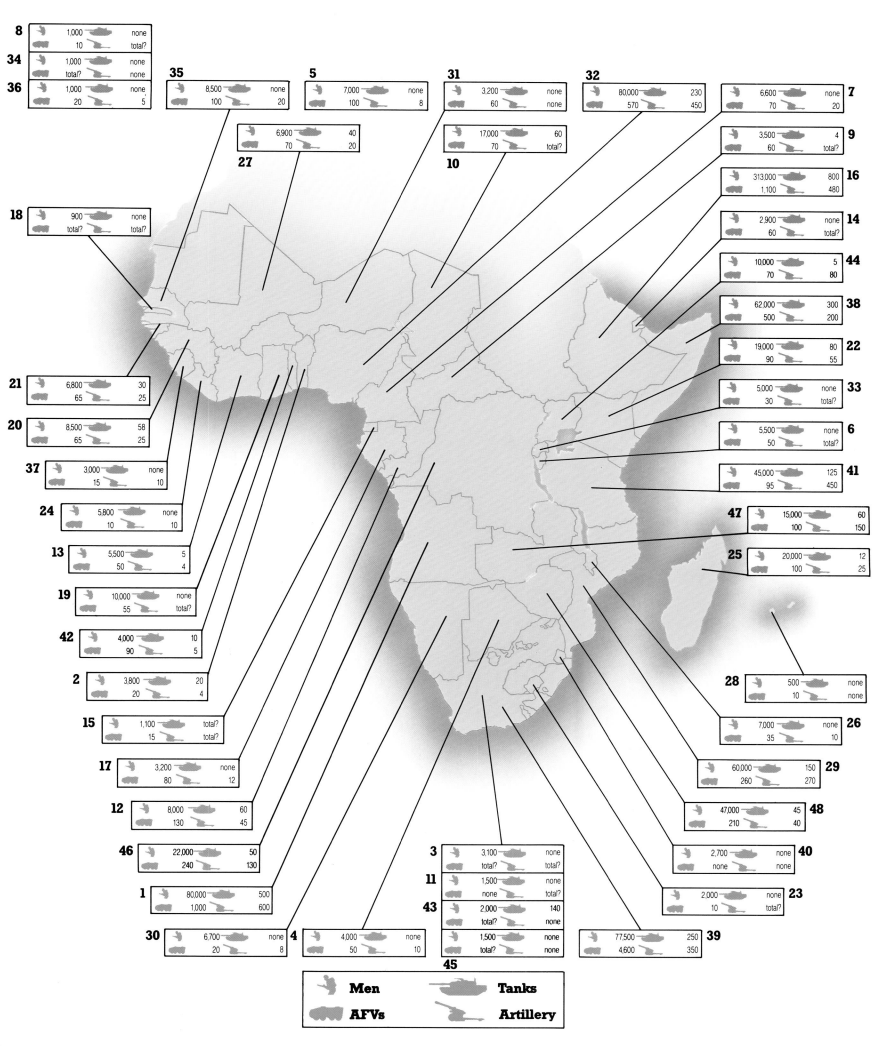

8
Men	1,000	Tanks none
AFVs	10	Artillery total?

34
Men	1,000	Tanks none
AFVs	total?	Artillery none

36
Men	1,000	Tanks none
AFVs	20	Artillery 5

35
Men	8,500	Tanks none
AFVs	100	Artillery 20

5
Men	7,000	Tanks none
AFVs	100	Artillery 8

31
Men	3,200	Tanks none
AFVs	60	Artillery none

32
Men	80,000	Tanks 230
AFVs	570	Artillery 450

7
Men	6,600	Tanks none
AFVs	70	Artillery 20

27
Men	6,900	Tanks 40
AFVs	70	Artillery 20

10
Men	17,000	Tanks 60
AFVs	70	Artillery total?

9
Men	3,500	Tanks 4
AFVs	60	Artillery total?

16
Men	313,000	Tanks 800
AFVs	1,100	Artillery 480

14
Men	2,900	Tanks none
AFVs	60	Artillery total?

44
Men	10,000	Tanks 5
AFVs	70	Artillery 80

38
Men	62,000	Tanks 300
AFVs	500	Artillery 200

22
Men	19,000	Tanks 80
AFVs	90	Artillery 55

33
Men	5,000	Tanks none
AFVs	30	Artillery total?

6
Men	5,500	Tanks none
AFVs	50	Artillery total?

41
Men	45,000	Tanks 125
AFVs	95	Artillery 450

18
Men	900	Tanks none
AFVs	total?	Artillery total?

21
Men	6,800	Tanks 30
AFVs	65	Artillery 25

20
Men	8,500	Tanks 58
AFVs	65	Artillery 25

37
Men	3,000	Tanks none
AFVs	15	Artillery 10

24
Men	5,800	Tanks none
AFVs	10	Artillery 10

13
Men	5,500	Tanks 5
AFVs	50	Artillery 4

19
Men	10,000	Tanks none
AFVs	55	Artillery total?

42
Men	4,000	Tanks 10
AFVs	90	Artillery 5

2
Men	3,800	Tanks 20
AFVs	20	Artillery 4

15
Men	1,100	Tanks total?
AFVs	15	Artillery total?

17
Men	3,200	Tanks none
AFVs	80	Artillery 12

12
Men	8,000	Tanks 60
AFVs	130	Artillery 45

46
Men	22,000	Tanks 50
AFVs	240	Artillery 130

1
Men	80,000	Tanks 500
AFVs	1,000	Artillery 600

30
Men	6,700	Tanks none
AFVs	20	Artillery 8

4
Men	4,000	Tanks none
AFVs	50	Artillery 10

3
Men	3,100	Tanks none
AFVs	total?	Artillery total?

11
Men	1,500	Tanks none
AFVs	none	Artillery total?

43
Men	2,000	Tanks 140
AFVs	total?	Artillery none

45
Men	1,500	Tanks none
AFVs	total?	Artillery none

47
Men	15,000	Tanks 60
AFVs	100	Artillery 150

25
Men	20,000	Tanks 12
AFVs	100	Artillery 25

28
Men	500	Tanks none
AFVs	10	Artillery none

26
Men	7,000	Tanks none
AFVs	35	Artillery 10

29
Men	60,000	Tanks 150
AFVs	260	Artillery 270

48
Men	47,000	Tanks 45
AFVs	210	Artillery 40

40
Men	2,700	Tanks none
AFVs	none	Artillery none

23
Men	2,000	Tanks none
AFVs	10	Artillery total?

39
Men	77,500	Tanks 250
AFVs	4,600	Artillery 350

Legend

- 🧎 Men
- 🚜 AFVs
- 🛡 Tanks
- 💥 Artillery

ANGOLA

THE Angolan Army is the principal service of the Angolan Armed Forces, more commonly referred to as the Popular Armed Forces for the Liberation of Angola or FAPLA. Its mission is territorial defence as well as the maintenance of internal security. The latter mission, the struggle against the National Union for the Total Liberation of Angola (UNITA), has dominated its agenda since the establishment of the Marxist Angolan government (MPLA) in 1975.

The FAPLA ground forces include the army together with Territorial Troops (TT), Border Guards, and the Militia or People's Defence Organization (ODP) which are essentially area-bound units that often support the army in local operations. The army itself comprises a staff, training centres, and field units, totalling about 80,000 personnel. Field units are controlled by the commanders of the five FAPLA political-military fronts into which Angola is divided.

The army underwent major restructuring in 1988 and 1989 as a result of such severe defeats by the UNITA and South African forces. The reorganization created new combat unit types that gave greater mobility and firepower. The principal units are the task force, a new formation, and the brigade. They are directly subordinate to the commander of the front in which they operate, for which they form operational groups, but can be moved throughout Angola as the military situation warrants.

In late 1990 there were at least a dozen of these task forces, many created from former infantry brigades. Each one has a command post (headquarters) and support units (armour, mechanized, artillery, air-defence, recce, signals, and logistics), with its main combat formations being several subordinate tactical groups. Designed for maximum manoeuvrability, each tactical group includes mechanized, optional armour, and artillery with organic support capability; personnel totals vary but are usually about 300.

Brigades were formerly the sole units in the manoeuvre role. Currently there are some 75 brigades (at least four mechanized, about 25 motorized and the rest light-infantry) with strength ranging from 1,100 to 1,300, although actual personnel levels vary considerably. The mechanized brigade consists of a tank and two mechanized (BMP-1) battalions, with an artillery battery. The motorized infantry brigade has an optional tank company, an artillery battery, an optional mechanized (BMP-1) battalion, and two (or three) motorized (BTR-60) battalions. The light-infantry brigade consists of a headquarters and three or more infantry battalions, each with organic support units.

Angolan Army units are trained and organized to fight a range of actions, from conventional to low-intensity conflict. Conventional employment is used against UNITA-controlled territory, most recently in the north-western part of Angola and enclaves in the north-east of Luanda. Light-infantry brigades and special counter-insurgency battalions conduct local counter-insurgency operations, working with the TT and ODP against UNITA units and base camps.

Despite extensive Soviet material support, the army has major logistical deficiencies. Furthermore, UNITA operates freely throughout Angola, leaving no secure rear area from which MPLA government forces can operate. These combined factors have led to the repeated failure of major military campaigns against UNITA. The latest major abortive offensive campaigns were in south-east Angola from December 1989 to May 1990, and in northern Angola from June to August 1990.

EQUIPMENT

Armour:
T-34, T-54/55 & T-62 MBTs
PT-76 light tank
BRDM-2 armoured car
BTR-60 & -152 APCs
Anti-Armour:
82mm B-10 RCL
AT-3 Sagger ATGW
Artillery:
122mm D-30 & M-46 Hs
122mm BM-21 MRLs
Air-Defence:
14.5mm ZPU-4, 23mm ZU-23 & 57mm S-60 AAGs
23mm ZSU-23-4 & 57mm ZSU-57-2 SPAAGs
SA-8, -7, -9, 13, -14 SAMs

BENIN

THE Army of Benin has five battalions (three infantry, one airborne commando, and one engineer), plus an armoured squadron (company-strength) and an artillery battery. There are 3,800 active personnel in the army, with selective conscription providing additions to the professional cadre.

The army is assisted in its internal security mission by several paramilitary forces, including the Gendarmerie (four mobile companies) and a People's Militia that between them have about 4,500 personnel. The Public Security Force brings the overall total to 12,000.

EQUIPMENT

Armour:
PT-76 light tank
BRDM-2 armoured car
Anti-Armour:
89mm RCL
Artillery:
105mm M101 H

BOPHUTATSWANA

THE Bophutatswana Defence Force is, primarily, a counter-insurgency infantry force of 3,100 (including an air wing) that has been organized and trained by South Africa since 1976. Its units, deployed through six military regions, include 1st Infantry Battalion, an airborne commando unit of less than company strength, three independent infantry groups of company size, a maintenance unit (supply and transport), a technical services unit, and at least two building and construction companies. An air wing, with four fixed-wing aircraft and five helicopters, supports the ground force. Plans exist to form a second infantry battalion.

EQUIPMENT

Armour:
Buffel APC

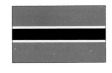

BOTSWANA

THE small Botswana Defence Force, totalling 4,500, is made up of two services, the army proper and the air force. Its primary mission is one of border defence, in which it is assisted by a paramilitary Police Mobile Unit of 1,000.

The army (ground force units) comprises eight companies (five infantry, one armoured car, one recce, and one engineer). It is armed with a mixture of equipment, and has received training from a variety of sources. Service is voluntary, with no conscription system reported.

EQUIPMENT

Armour:
V-150 Commando & Shorland armoured cars
BTR-60 APC
Artillery:
105mm M101 H
Air-Defence:
20mm M167 Vulcan SPAAG
SA-7 SAM

BURKINA FASO

THE Burkinabe Armed Forces total 8,700 personnel in all and includes an army, air force, and Gendarmerie. Their defence mission is supplemented by a People's Militia of some 45,000 men and women between 20 and 35 years of age trained part-time.

The 7,000-man army is the principal Burkinabe ground force. It consists of nine regiments or battalions (five infantry, one airborne, one armoured, one artillery, and one engineer) that average about 750 personnel each. Units are deployed throughout the country's six military regions. It is armed with a variety of weapons and equipment from French, British, Chinese, Soviet, Brazilian, and other sources.

EQUIPMENT

Armour:
AML-60/90, EE-9 Cascavel & Ferret armoured cars
M3 APC
Anti-Armour:
75mm Type 52 RCL
Artillery:
105mm M101 H
107mm Type 63 MRL
Air-Defence:
14.5mm AAG
SA-7 SAM

CAMEROUN

THE Army of Cameroun has 6,600 personnel deployed throughout three military regions with HQs at Yaounde, Douala, and Maroua that are in turn subdivided into a total of seven military sectors. Units include the 2,300-man Presidential Guard (one Guard, one armoured recce, and one infantry battalion with HQs in Yaounde, the capital) and regular combat formations. The latter consist of nine battalions (one airborne, five infantry, one engineer, one artillery, and one air-defence), of which one infantry battalion is a training unit. Both the artillery and air-defence battalions are oversized, with five and six component batteries respectively. It is well-officered and well-trained.

EQUIPMENT

Armour:
V-150 Commando & Ferret armoured cars
M3 & V-150 Commando APCs
Anti-Armour:
57mm Type 52 & 106mm M40A1 RCL
MILAN ATGW
Artillery:
75mm M116 & 105mm M101 Hs
Air-Defence:
14.5mm Type 58 & 37mm Type 63 AAGs
35mm Oerlikon GDF-002 SPAAG

Above: Crack troops from the airborne battalion parading in Yaounde. Their winged badges of qualification are visible on their right breasts.

Below: A gunner mans the 7.62mm turret MG of his V-150 Commando which has as its main armament a 90mm gun, either a Mecar or a Cockerill Mk III.

BURUNDI

BURUNDI'S military totals 7,200 personnel, and includes not only the army but also the air and naval forces as well as the 1,500-man Gendarmerie. Service throughout the Burundi military is strictly voluntary.

The army is 5,500 strong and includes four battalions (two infantry, one airborne, and one commando) augmented by an armoured car company. Its equipment comes from a number of sources that include France, the USSR, and China.

EQUIPMENT

Armour:
AML-60/-90 & Shorland armoured cars
M3, BTR-40 & Walid APCs
Anti-Armour:
75mm Type 52 RCL
83mm Blindicide
Air-Defence:
14.5mm ZPU-4 AAG

CAPE VERDE ISLANDS

THE Cape Verdean Army comprises 1,000 of the 1,200 total personnel of its armed forces. The army itself con-

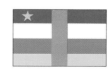

CENTRAL AFRICAN REPUBLIC

THE Army of the Central African Republic has 3,500 men and consists of the Presidential Guard Battalion plus four regiments (one Republican Guard, one Territorial Defence, one combined-arms, and one support/HQs). The Republican Guard has two battalions of infantry and the combined-arms regiment has a mechanized and an infantry battalion.

sists of four infantry companies of People's Militia kept at strength by selective conscription. A former Portuguese colony, Cape Verde receives military assistance from France, Portugal and the US.

EQUIPMENT

Armour:
BRDM-2 armoured car
Anti-Armour:
89mm RL

In addition to ground operations, the army makes riverine patrols.

France has about 1,200 ground force troops — an infantry battalion group, an armoured cavalry squadron, and an artillery battery — stationed in the Central African Republic. Elements of their Foreign Legion are often stationed in-country for training.

EQUIPMENT

Armour:
T-55 MBT
Ferret armoured car
BTR-152, ACMAT & VAB APCs
Anti-Armour:
106mm M40A1 RCL

CHAD

THE late 1980s saw Chad dissolve into chaos as the central government of President Habré came under assault from various insurgent groups, principally the Popular Salvation Movement, based in Sudan and Libya, which resulted in his overthrow.

The Chadean Army consists of approximately 17,000 troops. An accurate count is not possible as the force has been joined and deserted a number of times by groups of former rebels. The principal units comprise the élite Presidential Guard regiment, with the remainder consisting of an armoured battalion, three infantry battalions and 16 infantry companies, a recce squadron (company size) and two recce troops (platoon size), and two artillery batteries.

Ground forces are distributed through at least five military regions, of which one, with HQs at Faya Largeau in northern Chad, was responsible for successful operations against Libyan forces in the Aouzou Strip which they had occupied.

To assist Chad in warding off any Libyan threat, France has stationed about 1,100 ground force units in its former colony. These forces did not intervene to save Habré from the insurgents final, victorious offensive.

EQUIPMENT

Armour:
AML-60/-90, Panhard ERC-90 & V-150
  Commando armoured cars
Anti-Armour:
106mm M40A1 & 112mm Apilas RCLs
MILAN ATGW
Artillery:
105mm M101 H
Air-Defence:
20mm & 30mm AAGs
Stinger SAM

CISKEI

THE Ciskei Defence Force, formed from the South African Army's 141st Battalion in 1981, now comprises two infantry battalions and an airborne commando company, totalling 1,500 personnel in all. It is supported by an air wing of five fixed-wing aircraft and four helicopters.

While most training is provided by South Africa, some Israeli training personnel have been reported assisting the force. Most of the force's equipment is of light-infantry type, with no major ground force material.

CONGO

THE People's Republic of the Congo has an 8,000 strong army which consists of eight battalion-sized units (two armoured battalions, two infantry battalion groups, an artillery group, and one battalion each of infantry, engineer, and airborne commandos. The infantry battalion groups consist of an infantry battalion augmented with a light tank troop (PT-76 or PRC Type-62) and a 75mm or 76mm gun battery. The artillery group is a composite unit comprising 100mm and 122mm gun batteries, plus 122mm BM-21 MRL and 120mm mortar batteries.

There are approximately 500 Cuban troops stationed in the country. As part of its increasing interest in regional affairs, the Congo has contributed observers to the small UNAVM (UN) force currently overseeing Cuban troop withdrawal from Angola per implementation of United Nations Resolution 435. It has also begun to seek new military patrons.

EQUIPMENT

Armour:
T-54/55 & Type 59 MBTs
PT-76 & Type 62 light tanks
BRDM-1 & -2 armoured cars
M3 & BTR-50, -60, -152 APCs
Anti-Armour:
57mm M18 RCL
Artillery:
76mm M1942, 100mm M1944 & 122mm
  M1938 guns
75mm M116 Hs
122mm BM-21 MRL
Air-Defence:
14.5mm ZPU-2 & -4, & 57mm S-60 AAGs
23mm ZSU-23-4 SPAAG

COTE D'IVOIRE

THE army is 5,500 strong. It administers four military regions and fields four battalions (one armoured, three infantry) and a battalion-sized artillery group. They are supplemented by airborne, air-defence, and engineer companies. Augmenting the army are signficant paramilitary forces that total 7,800 in all. These include the 4,400-man National Gendarmerie, the 1,100 strong Presidential Guard, and a militia and military fire service (2,300 personnel in total).

EQUIPMENT

Armour:
AMX-13 light tank
AML-60/-90 & Panhard ERC-90
  armoured cars
M3 & VAB APCs
Anti-Armour:
106mm M40A1 RCL
Artillery:
105mm M1950 H
Air-Defence:
20mm M3 VDA SPAAG
40mm Bofors L/60 AAG

DJIBOUTI

THE small Djibouti Army of 2,870 is supplemented in its mission by 1,200 Gendarmes. The army consists of infantry, support, and border commando battalions plus company-sized armoured and airborne units.

The main missions of the Djibouti armed forces are territorial defence and maintenance of internal security; in the former it is assisted by France to protect it from its more powerful neighbours Somalia and Ethiopia. With the increase in unrest in neighbouring Somalia there have been border incidents with that nation, the most serious of which took place with an abortive raid by Somali soldiers in October 1990.

French forces deployed to Djibouti, which was once French Somaliland, in support of the régime include two ground units, the 5th Regiment Interarmes d'Outre Mer (naval infantry) and the 13th Demi-brigade de la Legion Etrangere (Foreign Legion), both battalion-plus size.

EQUIPMENT

Armour:
AML-60/-90 & BRDM-2 armoured cars
BTR-60 APC
Anti-Armour:
106mm M40 RCL
HOT ATGW
Artillery:
105mm M56 H
Air-Defence:
20mm M693 & 23mm ZSU-23-2 SPAAGs
40mm Bofors L/70 AAG

Right: Desert warfare offers the toughest conditions there are; the camel has proved itself a hardy animal and has been used in warfare for hundreds of years. These troops are operating against rebellious Somalis who are fighting a separatist war. They also guard the borders with more volatile neighbours, Somalia and Ethiopia where civil wars rage.

EQUATORIAL GUINEA

THE small 1,100-man army of this former Spanish colony has three infantry battalions armed with Soviet equipment. It is aided in its internal security mission by a 2,000-man paramilitary Civil Guard (Guardia Civil), organized in two companies.

Morocco is a major supporter of the current régime and a 360-man battalion of Moroccan Army infantry is stationed near Malabo, the capital.

EQUIPMENT

Armour:
T-34 & T-54/55 MBTs
PT-76 light tank
BRDM-2 armoured car
BTR-40 & -152 APCs
Artillery:
122mm Type 54 H

ETHIOPIA

ETHIOPIA has the largest ground force of any sub-Saharan African state, totalling at least 313,000 (with reserves) in 1990. Although ostensibly it has a national defence mission, this massive (by African standards) force is dedicated to propping up the current revolutionary régime of military strong-man Haile Mariam Mengistu in the face of a number of internal insurgent groups, the most important of which are the Eritrean People's Liberation Front (EPLF) and the Tigrean People's Liberation Front (TPLF). In the late 1980s the insurgent forces' improved capabilities posed a critical threat to the central government.

Currently, the Ethiopian Army is comprised of at least 30 infantry divisions, of which three are motorized, four are mountain, and three are light divisions. These are operationally subordinate to five field armies, of which the most important is the 2nd Army in Eritrea, or to regional commands. Details of unit make-up are sketchy, but may resemble Soviet models. Regular and motorized infantry divisions have tank battalions assigned to their theatre of operations and there are at least 32 tank battalions in all, equipped with a mix of Soviet and US tanks, of which some may be non-divisional. There are eight non-divisional airborne commando brigades, some with organic aviation assets. Supporting the field units are 37 artillery battalions and 12 air-defence battalions (three SA-2, three SA-3, and six other). The army also controls the 165,000 paramilitary troops that serve the Ethiopian Ministry of the Interior. There are also a number of foreign forces in Ethiopia; currently these include some 1,700 Soviet advisers, about 2,500 Cuban combat troops, and an unspecified number of Israeli military advisers.

The Ethiopian Army has an extensive training system, although it is overtaxed due to the need to train large numbers of new recruits. They receive 12 weeks' training, after which they are assigned to field units or sent for technical training.

Despite the large size of the army and the relatively small size of the insurgent forces opposing it, the difficult terrain and poor infrastructure throughout the country make it difficult to maintain an efficient logistics system. In addition, the diverse equipment, vulnerable supply lines, and poor logistics operations and planning cause major difficulties for the army in sustaining operations.

The militarily active insurgent movements number a dozen or so, but only two are of any real strength and significance. The EPLF or Sha'biyah is 30,000 strong and the TPLF or Weyane probably numbers 20,000. Despite the gravity of the internal threat posed by the EPLF and TPLF, the Ethiopian Army remains deficient in its ability to con-

Above: The largest army in southern Africa appears to be losing its civil war despite an abundance of Soviet military hardware.

duct effective counter-insurgency (COIN) operations. This appears in large part to be due to the wholesale adaptation of Soviet organization and doctrine in the 1970s that emphasized offensive capabilities at the expense of COIN and civil affairs operations.

A possible turnaround in the fortunes of the Ethiopian Army came in 1990 with a combination of Israeli military assistance and reorganization of the armed forces. As a result of the latter the country was divided into seven military commands, each under a "Revolutionary Campaign Centre Command." This may have helped to the army's to stabilize the insurgent situation, but things have since deteriorated.

EQUIPMENT

Armour:
T-34, T-54/55, T-62 & T-72 MBTs
M47 medium tank
M41 light tank
AML-60/90 & BRDM-2 armoured cars
BMP-1 IFV
BTR-40/-60/-152, V-150 Commando & M59
  APCs
Anti-Armour:
82mm B-10 RCL
AT-3 Sagger ATGW
Artillery:
75mm M116, 105mm M101, 122mm M1938
  & D-30 Hs
155mm M109 SPH
122mm BM-21 MRL
Air-Defence:
23mm ZU-23 & 37mm M1939 AAGS
23mm ZSU-23-4 & 57mm ZSU-57-2
  SPAAGs
SA-2, -3, & -7 SAMs
Aircraft:
Bell UH-1H Iroquois

GABON

THE small Gabonese Army (3,200 personnel) is supported in its ground mission by the paramilitary Gendarmerie (2,000 strong and organized into three brigades). Almost one-third of the army is formed into the Presidential Guard Battalion Group, directly under presidential control It comprises an armoured recce company, three infantry companies, and a battery each of field and air-defence artillery. The remainder of the army is organized into 10 companies (eight infantry, one airborne commando, and one engineer).

The army is bolstered in its mission by the presence of a French marine infantry regiment of approximately 550 personnel, and most foreign training and equipment is supplied by France. Recently, the US offered assistance and Brazilian purchases augmented the force.

EQUIPMENT
Armour:
Panhard AML-90, EE-3 Jararaca & EE-9 Cascavel armoured cars
M3, EE-11 Urutu & V-150 Commando APCs
Anti-Armour:
106mm M40 RCL
Artillery:
105mm M101 H
140mm MRL
Air-Defence:
23mm ZU-23 & 37mm M1939 AAGs

Above: Men of the Presidential Guard who protect the ruling regime from any opposition among Gabon's 40 tribes. The country retains strong links with France, as shown by the FAMAS assault rifle.

GAMBIA

THE small Gambian Army consists of an infantry company seconded to the Federal Armed Forces, plus an infantry battalion of four companies and an engineer squadron. The total army consists of about 900 personnel. It has no heavy equipment, only light infantry weapons.
Its federation with Senegal has ended.

GUINEA

GUINEA'S 8,500-man army consists of 11 battalions (one armoured, five infantry, one artillery, one engineer, one commando, one special forces, one air-defence) filled by conscripts. It is supplemented in its defence and internal security mission by a 1,000-man Gendarmerie and a 1,600-man Republican Guard.

EQUIPMENT
Armour:
T-34 & T-54 MBTs
PT-76 light tanks
BRDM-1 & -2 armoured cars
BTR-40, -50, -60 & -152 APCs
Anti-Armour:
82mm B-10 RCL
Artillery:
76mm M1942 & 85mm D-44 guns
122mm M1938 H
Air-Defence:
30mm M53 & 37mm M1939 AAGs
57mm S-60 & Type 59, & 100mm KS-19 AAGs
SA-7 SAM

GHANA

THE 10,000-man Ghanian Army is primarily an infantry force; it is supplemented in its task by a 5,000-man paramilitary People's Militia. The army's main units are two Command HQs based on infantry brigades with six battalions in total. The balance of the force comprises a two-squadron recce battalion, an airborne force built around a paracommando company, an independent infantry battalion, and artillery (mortar) and field engineer regiments (battalion size). Military service is voluntary.

EQUIPMENT
Armour:
Saladin & EE-9 Cascavel armoured cars
MOWAG Piranha APC
Anti-Armour:
84mm Carl Gustav RCL
Artillery:
25-pdr (88mm) & 105mm Light guns

Above: A Ghanian soldier in Liberia as part of the West African peace force.

GUINEA-BISSAU

THE army of Guinea-Bissau, with 6,800 personnel, is the largest of its armed forces. It consists of seven battalions or equivalent units (five infantry, one armoured, one artillery) plus a recce and an engineer company.

EQUIPMENT
Armour:
T-34 MBT
PT-76 light tank
BRDM-2 armoured car
Type 56, BTR-40, -60 & -152 APCs
Anti-Armour:
75mm Type 52 & 82mm B-10 RCLs
Artillery:
85mm D-44 gun
122mm D-30 & M1938 Hs
Air-Defence:
23mm ZU-23, 37mm M1939, & 57mm S-60 AAGs
SA-7 SAMs

KENYA

THE Kenyan Army, numbering 19,000, is small compared to most of its neighbours, but it is a quality force due to better training and support coordination. It is the largest of the elements in Kenya's armed forces and has a primary mission of territorial defence and a secondary internal security role. Terms of service are voluntary.

The major units consist of three brigades (one armoured and two infantry). The latter comprise two or three infantry battalions, an armoured recce battalion, and two artillery battalions each. Other units include eight battalions (five infantry, one air cavalry, one airborne, and one air-defence). Engineer support is prominent, with an engineer brigade and two engineer battalions filling out the order of battle. The Kenyans have received extensive military assistance in the form of equipment and training from the UK and the US.

EQUIPMENT

Armour:
Vickers Mk3 MBT
AML-60/90 & Shorland armoured cars
UR-416 & M3 APCs
Anti-Armour:
84mm Carl Gustav & 120mm Wombat RCLs
MILAN ATGW
Artillery:
105mm M101 H
Air-Defence:
20mm Ramta TCM-20 AAG

LESOTHO

THE land-locked nation of Lesotho, is surrounded by South Africa and the homeland of Transkei. The small Lesotho Army of 2,000 men, which staged a successful coup against the government in 1986, consists of seven infantry companies, a support company made up of recce, airborne, and 81mm mortar units, plus a small air squadron with five helicopters. The force receives military assistance from a number of sources.

EQUIPMENT

Armour:
Ramta armoured car
Aircraft:
MBB Bo-105

LIBERIA

AT the time of writing, the remnants of the Armed Forces of Liberia were based near the capital, Monrovia, after the intervention of the multi-national West African force that had landed in August 1990 to attempt a resolution of the bloody civil war in that country.

The intervention force consisted of troops from Nigeria, Ghana, Sierra Leone, and other West African nations. They were opposed by elements of the National Democratic Patriotic Front of Liberia (NDPFL), which had gained control of most of the country by July. A rival rebel faction, the Independent National Democratic Patriotic Front of Liberia (INDPFL), sought to ally itself with the West African force.

In the late 1980s the Liberian Army, the dominant force of the armed forces, was, primarily, an infantry force of 5,800 that consisted of the Executive Mansion Guard Battalion and six infantry battalions. It was augmented by artillery and engineer battalions and an armoured recce unit (squadron size). A small air wing was attached to the army as well. Most foreign military assistance came from the US.

EQUIPMENT

Armour:
MOWAG Piranha APC
Anti-Armour:
106mm M40 RCLs
Artillery:
75mm M116 H
122mm BM-21 MRL

MADAGASCAR

THE Malagasy Army comprises 20,000 personnel and is based upon two battalion groups plus three regiments (engineer, signals, services).

EQUIPMENT

Armour:
PT-76 light tank
BRDM-2 & Ferret armoured cars
M3 APC
Anti-Armour:
106mm M40 RCL
Artillery:
76mm ZIS-3 ATG
105mm M101 & 122mm D-30 Hs
Air-Defence:
14.5mm ZPU-4 & 37mm Type 55 AAGs

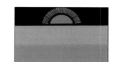

MALAWI

THE small but capable Malawi Army is for the most part an infantry force. Numbering 7,000 personnel, it is composed of three infantry battalions and a support battalion that includes a recce squadron. Terms of service are voluntary.

EQUIPMENT

Armour:
Fox, Ferret & Eland armoured cars
Anti-Armour:
57mm M18 RCL
Artillery:
105mm Light gun
Air-Defence:
Blowpipe SAM

MALI

THE army of Mali is a mixed force numbering 6,900. It is composed of 11 battalions (two armoured, four infantry, one paratroop, one engineer, and one special forces) and three air-defence batteries (two ADA, one SAM).

EQUIPMENT

Armour:
T-34 & T-54/55 MBTs
Type 62 light tank
BRDM-2 armoured car
BTR-40, -60, & -152 APCs
Artillery:
85mm D-44 & 100mm M1944 guns
122mm D-30 H
122mm BM-21 MRL
Air-Defence:
37mm M1939 & 57mm S-60 AAGs
SA-3 SAM

MAURITIUS

MAURITIUS, an island nation in the Indian Ocean, has no ground force. Its land security needs are met by a small paramilitary Special Mobile Force of battalion size. Its principal mission is one of counter-insurgency.

MOZAMBIQUE

DESPITE its large size (60,000), the Army of the Mozambican Armed Forces continues to have great difficulty in countering the rebellion by the National Resistance of Mozambique (RENAMO). Logistical difficulties and poor training prevent the force from performing effective counter-insurgency operations, despite the assistance of troops from neighbouring Zimbabwe, Malawi, and Tanzania, as well as British training at Nyanga in Zimbabwe.

Army units are usually under-strength. They are scattered among 10 regional commands throughout Mozambique, but the most important units are a tank brigade and seven infantry brigades. Each of the latter consist of nine battalions (one armour, three infantry, two motorized infantry, two artillery, and one air-defence). The tank brigade forms the Presidential Guard and is based in Maputo, the capital. In addition to the brigades, a number of small combat and combat-support battalions are scattered throughout government-held areas of the country, and six ADA battalions, assigned to urban centres, complete the tally.

RENAMO, the main opposition movement, holds much of the Mozambican countryside. However, control of some portions of the country by either side is often questionable, with anarchy and banditry reigning over much of Mozambique. RENAMO has at least 20,000 active troops formed into at least four active battalions in the central part of the country, as well as about 200 "special forces" troops. All of these are lightly-armed infantry. The resistance is armed with captured government weaponry, practically all of it Soviet or Communist origin.

EQUIPMENT

Armour:
T-34 & T-54/55 MBTs
BRDM-1 & -2 armoured cars
BMP-1 IFV
BTR-60, -152 APCs
Anti-Armour:
82mm B-10 & 107mm B-11 RCLs
AT-3 Sagger ATGW
Artillery:
85mm D-44 & 100mm M1944 guns
105mm M101, 122mm D-30 & M1938, & 152mm D-1 Hs
122mm BM-21 MRL
Air-Defence:
23mm ZU-23-2 & 37mm M1939 AAGs
57mm S-60 & ZSU-57-2 SPAAGs
SA-7 SAM

Above: A government soldier guards a train along the Beira corridor, a route often attacked by RENAMO and far harder to defend after the Zimbabwean withdrawal.

NAMIBIA

AFRICA'S newest nation has formed the Namibian Defence Force (NDF), consisting only of an army. It is controlled by the former guerrilla group who were elected following South Africa's withdrawal in 1989.

The NDF has six battalions: one each for logistics, recce, artillery, and engineer; plus the 3rd and 5th Infantry Battalions, each with 1,000 men. There are plans to increase this total to four infantry battalions. The border police, 1,500 strong, were placed under the army in 1990, making the total army strength about 6,700.

Despite SWAPO's former Eastern bloc ties they chose the UK to organize and train its new army. The current equipment formerly belonged to the People's Liberation Army of Namibia and consists of an odd assortment of old Soviet weaponry.

EQUIPMENT

Armour:
BTR-50 APCs
Artillery:
122mm BM-21 MRL
Air-Defence:
23mm ZSU-23-2 AAG

NIGER

APOOR land-locked country, Niger is mostly dry tropical desert. There was a coup in 1974 and the military retained power via a Supreme Military Council composed of army officers until very recently when matters were liberalized.

The small (3,200) Niger Army is deployed through three military districts, each built around an armoured recce squadron and two infantry companies.

The total force, which is filled by two-year tours of service per selective conscription, is composed of three armoured recce squadrons, six infantry companies, an airborne company, and an engineer company. The equipment inventory reflects continued post-independence ties with France.

EQUIPMENT

Armour:
AML-60/-90 armoured cars
M3 APC
Anti-Armour:
57mm M18 & 75mm M20 RCLs
Air-Defence:
20mm M3 VDA SPAAG

NIGERIA

NIGERIA'S army of 80,000 is the largest in West Africa and the second-largest standing army in sub-Saharan Africa after Ethiopia. It consists of four divisions which are assigned separate geographical areas of responsibility that correspond roughly to military regions. Each is built around a divisional HQ. They are: North-West, HQ Kaduna (1st Mechanized Division); South-West, HQ Ibadan (2nd Mechanized Division); North-East, HQ Jos (3rd Armoured Division); and South-East, HQ Enugu (82nd Composite Division).

Divisional organization for mechanized units consists of three mechanized brigades and one each of artillery and engineer brigades, plus a recce battalion. The 3rd Armoured Division has four armoured and one mechanized brigades, plus the support units for mechanized divisions. The 82nd Composite Division has a more complex organization, with its manoeuvre brigades consisting of one each of paratroop, air-portable (i.e., air-mobile), and amphibious brigades, plus artillery and engineer brigades and a recce battalion.

Terms of service are voluntary and the army's corps or arms of service follow the

British pattern: infantry, artillery, armour, engineers, signals, electrical/mechanical engineers, supply and transport, pay, and ordnance. The training system is also organized along British lines and Nigerian personnel have trained abroad in the UK, France, India, Ethiopia, Pakistan, Canada, and Australia.

EQUIPMENT

Armour:
T-55 & Vickers Mk3 MBTs
Scorpion light tank
AML-60/-90, Fox & Saladin armoured cars
Saracen & Steyr 4K 7FA APCs
Anti-Armour:
84mm Carl Gustav & 106mm M40A1 RCLs
Artillery:
105mm M56, 122mm D-30 & 155mm FH-77B Hs
155mm Palmaria SPH
Air-Defence:
40mm Bofors L/60 AAG
23mm ZSU-23-4 SPAAG
Blowpipe & Roland SAMs

RWANDA

THE Rwandan Army has 5,000 men and its role was emphasized in October 1990 when Tutsi exiles from Uganda had to be repulsed. It is composed of a commando battalion located near Kigali, the capital, and one recce, eight infantry, and one engineer companies.

EQUIPMENT

Armour:
AML-60 armoured car
M3 APC
Anti-Armour:
83mm Blindicide

SAO TOME & PRINCIPE

UNTIL 1985 Sao Tome and Principe had no military. Military agreements with the US in 1985 and Portugal in 1987 provided military training and equipment for a small army (about 1,000 personnel) that has since been established. The US and Portugal remain the major equipment and training suppliers.

A battalion (approximately 500) of FAPLA troops from Angola is stationed in-country.

SENEGAL

SENEGAL'S armed forces reflect continued close relations with France since independence. The army, a mostly conscript force of 8,500, consists of 10 complete battalions (one armoured, five infantry, one airborne, one commando, one artillery, and one engineer) and two infantry companies. A Presidential Guard horse detachment and three construction companies form the remainder of the force, which has a civil as well as a military mission. The force emphasizes professional standards for its personnel, with much training conducted in France.

EQUIPMENT

Armour:
AML-60/-90 & M20 armoured cars
M3 APC
Anti-Armour:
MILAN ATGW
Artillery:
75mm M116, 105mm M101, & 155mm 50 Hs
Air-Defence:
40mm Bofors L/60 AAG
20mm M693 SPAAG

SOMALIA

THE Somali Army is a largely conscript force of at least 62,000 personnel. The force consists of 57 brigades (four armoured, 45 mechanized and regular infantry, four commando, one SAM, and three field artillery), augmented with 30 field artillery battalions and one ADA battalion. These units are assigned to any one of 12 division headquarters throughout the country. There is also a Presidential Guard, otherwise known as the "Red Berets".

Despite its relatively large size the army has failed to carry out its mission of territorial defence or internal security. From April 1988 onwards a widespread rebellion afflicted the country, and human rights violations by the army drew the ire of Italy and the US who withdrew assistance.

Meantime, the insurgent activities of the Somali National Movement (SNM) and the United Somali Congress (USC) have proved successful with the régime of President Barre overthrown in early 1991. The army's future is open to question with the country having dissolved into chaos, with soldiers fleeing and anarchy reigning..

SEYCHELLES

THE island nation of the Seychelles has a small army of about 1,000 which has an internal security mission.

It consists of an infantry battalion, two artillery troops, and a support company. Its equipment is mostly from the Soviet Union, reflecting the current régime's political alignment.

SIERRA LEONE

THIS West African nation has a small but competent army of 3,000 troops consisting of two infantry battalions, two artillery battalions, and an engineer squadron (company-sized). Training in the UK and US, and high in-country personnel and training standards, have resulted in a competent force entirely capable of carrying out its mission of territorial defence. It recently sent troops to Liberia.

Above: A Somalian infantryman pictured during the exercise held with US forces and others in 1983 named "Bright Star".

EQUIPMENT

Armour:
T-34, T-54/55, & Centurion MBTs
M47 medium tank
M41 light tank
BRDM-2 & AML-90 armoured cars
BTR-152, BMR-600, & Fiat 6614 APCs
Anti-Armour:
106mm M40 RCL
Artillery:
100mm M1944, 105mm M56, 122mm M1938, & 155mm M198 Hs
Air-Defence:
57mm S-60, & 100mm KS-19 AAGs
23mm ZSU-23-4 SPAAG
SA-2, -3, & -7 SAMs

SOUTH AFRICA

THE South African Army (SAA) has the third largest standing force (77,500 personnel) on the continent. With reserves, however, it can mobilize the largest and best ground force in Africa, consisting of over 450,000 personnel. The SAA is the largest component of the South African Defence Force (SADF), the other services of which are the South African Air Force (SAAF), the South African Navy (SAN), and the South African Medical Service (SAMS). The military chain of command runs from the State President through the Minister of Defence and the Chief of the SADF, to whom the various services are subordinate.

The personnel system used to maintain the standing force combines a relatively small cadre of full-time servicemen (Permanent Force or PF personnel), numbering about 19,900, with conscripts (National Service Members or NSMs) serving mandatory one-year tours of duty and reservists (Citizen Force or CF personnel).

The three components of the SAA are the Conventional Forces, the Territorial Forces, and the Training Establishment (also known as "The Infrastructure") under the Chief of the Army Units, who also has some combat units directly available as a special reserve. The Conventional Forces consists of Formation HQs with attached combat and support units manned by reservists. The force includes the 7th and 8th Divisions, both consisting of a headquarters (HQs), divisional assets, and three attached brigades, while an attached SAMS medical battalion group provides ambulance and field hospital service. Division assets include a tank battalion, two artillery regiments, two air-defence regiments and combat service support elements. The brigades are mechanized, consisting of a HQs, three manoeuvre battalions (armoured, mechanized, and motorized), an armoured car (recce) regiment, a field artillery (155m SP) regiment, a field engineer regiment or squadron, a signals unit, a maintenance (supply and transport) unit, and a field workshop. Also attached to the Conventional Forces are the 60th Mechanized Brigade and the 44th Parachute Brigade. The personnel in Conventional Forces include PF and NSMs in Formation HQs and total CF manning in division and brigade manoeuvre and support units. Upon mobilization, a Conventional Forces division would consist of about 20,000 personnel and 4-5,000 vehicles.

The Territorial or Counter-Insurgency (COIN) Forces are organized into 10 Army Commands, plus the Walvis Bay Military Area (an enclave in Namibia). Each command is responsible for an internal security mission within its area and to effect this the SAA relies upon an organization of reserve forces called commandos. The latter, about 150 in total, are battalion-sized units subordinate to some 40 Commando Group HQs responsible for area security and which report to Army Command HQs. Commando Group HQs are assisted in their mission by COIN battalions. The Army Command, Commando Group, and Commando HQs are all manned by a small permanent force cadre which manages day-to-day unit operations. The remainder of the staffing is done by CF personnel or conscripts (NSMs).

The Chief of Army Units commands the Training Establishment proper as well as the rest of "The Infrastructure." The latter includes the Army Headquarters Unit and the Army Logistics Command. The Training Establishment consists of the many SAA schools plus the training battalions. These include combat or support speciality (e.g., infantry or armour) battalions as well as the coloured and black COIN battalions (some of the latter are attached to Army Territorial Commands). The core of the training unit system rests with eight infantry, two armour, and functional/support training battalions that are manned by PF cadre and have an active-duty unit status. Training is conducted in the training wing or group attached to each unit. In addition, there are two coloured and seven black COIN infantry battalions that have an active-duty defence/COIN mission as well as a training mission. A third type of unit, with a clearly operational mission, includes the 61st Mechanized Battalion Group at Walvis Bay as well as 31st and 32nd Battalions. These units or their personnel formerly served in Namibia (South West Africa).

Despite some force reductions in the SAA, the importance of the black COIN operational and training units continues to be recognized. Following the end of the war in Namibia the 32nd ("Buffalo") Infantry

Below: The Olifant MBT is the Centurion updated by ARMSCOR with a new powerpack and transmission. In Angola it was used successfully at Lomba River in 1987/88.

Battalion was moved to Pomfret in North Cape from its former base near Rundu. In addition, former members of Bushman units who fought in Namibia have been organized as 31st Battalion and located at Schmidtsdrift near Kimberley. With the ending of the apartheid system in South Africa, the number of black ethnic battalions should increase; an overall increase of black and coloured personnel in other SAA units is likely to take place as well. At present, 21st and 114th Battalion form two multi-ethnic units while the remainder are more wholly tribal in character: 111th Battalion (Swazi), 113th Battalion (Shangaan), 115th Battalion (Ndbele), 116th Battalion (North Soto), and 121st Battalion (Zulu).

The Training Establishment's operations support the military education of PF, CF, and NSMs in various combat and support areas. To do this, the SAA has established career progressions by corps (military speciality) with a school for each. The corps are infantry, armour, field artillery, air-defence artillery, engineer, signals, personnel services, ordnance services, technical services, military police, bandsmen, caterers', ammunition, intelligence, and womens'. Senior personnel attend SADF or advanced SAA schools in command, staff, strategic, or joint service areas. The most important among these are the SA Army College, Pretoria, as well as the Army Battle School at Lohatlha in the North Cape.

The schools are supported by an extensive network of training units, mostly battalions, that double an operational mission with one of training. The intention of this system is to ensure a high quality of operational training and place recruits with more experienced soldiers so that they learn by example as well as by participation. The end result is to produce soldiers of the highest quality who are not only well-prepared for national service duty but who continue to be trained as they progress through the reserve system. A rigorous system exists to select personnel for further advancement.

The Armaments Corporation of South

Above: Troops restore order to strife-torn Natal with Operation "*Iron Fist*" in 1990.

Right: The Ratel-90 fire-support vehicle caused havoc among Cuba's armoured units.

Africa (ARMSCOR) supervises and coordinates an extensive domestic armaments production programme that renders South Africa almost completely self-sufficient in military equipment. Transportation and supply is facilitated by the most extensively developed rail and road infrastructure on the continent.

At the SADF staff level, the Chief of Staff, Logistics, as well as the SADF Staff Logistics Directorate, coordinates armed forces

Below: The Rooikat is tailor-made for the African terrain. It has a 76mm cannon and its ground armour helps protect it from mines, a popular enemy weapon.

logistics. Tactical logistics is highly-organized and effective: supply and transport is done by maintenance units, while vehicle and equipment maintenance is done by field or base workshops. The tactical logistics system is fully able to support combat operational needs. SAA logistical vehicles are domestically produced.

The SAA is the most capable ground force on the continent. It has regional power-projection capabilities in addition to rapid local deployment ability and can conduct fully integrated operations with air and naval forces. Operational units have excellent combat-support and combat service support for operations. In the COIN mission

area, Territorial Force units form the basis for regional security management and conduct coordinated operations with local civil authorities to preserve internal order. Mobilization of both units and individuals as required is rapid and effective.

The end of the Cold War and economic difficulties have recently forced the SADF to undertake rationalization of the force. Some units will be reduced in force or re-assigned and it may be that reorganization will group the bulk of forces into three conventional and three counter-insurgency formations. Despite the recent shortening of compulsory national service from two years to one, it is expected that adjustments will be made in the reserve training system to ensure continued personnel quality. The number of PF personnel may even increase due to the need or desire to form more black COIN units.

EQUIPMENT

Armour:
Olifant, T-34 & T-54/55 MBTs
PT-76 light tank
Ratel tank destroyer
Eland, Rooikat & BRDM-2 armoured cars
Ratel IFV
Buffel, Bulldog, Casspir, Hippo, & Rhino
  APCs
Anti-Armour:
84mm & 106mm RCLs
ENTAC, ZT-3, & SS-11 ATGWs
Artillery:
25 pdr (88mm) G1 & 5.5in (140mm) G2
  guns
155mm G-5 & G-6 Hs
122mm Valkyrie MLR
Air-Defence:
35mm Oerlikon GDF-002 SPAAG
40mm Bofors L/70 AAG
20mm Ystervark 20-2 SPAAG
Cactus, Tigercat, SA-7, -8, -9, -13, & -14
  SAMs

SWAZILAND

THE small Umbufto Swaziland Defence Force (USDF), totalling 2,657, is a light-infantry force built around two army battalions; the force has an air wing, the Swaziland Air Force, whose mission supports the army proper. The force is also supported by a paramilitary contingent of 400 police.

TANZANIA

THE army of the United Republic of Tanzania is the principal force of the Tanzanian People's Defence Force (TPDF) and numbers 45,000, of which almost half are conscripts. It is supported in its mission by a Citizen's Militia of about 100,000. The army consists of nine brigades (one armoured, eight infantry) organized into three division HQs and supported by four artillery battalions (two field artillery, two mortar), three air-defence battalions (two ADA, one SAM), an anti-tank battalion, and two signals battalions.

EQUIPMENT

Armour:
T-62 & Type 59 MBTs
Scorpion & Type 62 light tanks
BRDM-2 armoured car
Type 56, BTR-40 & -152 APCs
Anti-Armour:
75mm Type 52 RCL
Artillery:
76mm ZIS-3 (M1942), 85mm Type 56, & 130mm Type 59 guns
122mm D-30 & Type 54 Hs
122mm BM-21 MRL
Air-Defence:
14.5mm ZPU-2 & -4 AAGs
SA-3, -6, & -7 SAMs

TOGO

TOGO's small (4,000 personnel) army is built around five regiments (two infantry, one Presidential Guard, one paracommando, and one support). The latter contains one field artillery and two ADA batteries, plus an engineer battalion. The two infantry regiments consist of a mix of armoured and mechanized units with motorized infantry. The Presidential Guard regiment has infantry and commando battalions and two combined-arms companies.

EQUIPMENT

Armour:
T-54/55 MBTs
Scorpion light tank
AML-60/-90, EE-9 Cascavel, & M20 armoured cars
UR-416 & M3 APCs
Anti-Armour:
75mm Type 52 & 56, 85mm Type 65 RCL
Artillery:
155mm M2 H
Air-Defence:
14.5mm ZPU-4 & 37mm M1939 AAGs

TRANSKEI

THE Transkei Defence Force (TDF) is the oldest of the four Homeland military forces organized and trained by South Africa. It was founded in 1975, with the first unit being 1st Transkei Battalion with 254 personnel. The current strength now exceeds 2,000, with a counter-insurgency infantry battalion, a special forces regiment, and support units. The special forces regiment consists of airborne, commando, mounted, and marine elements. Basic infantry training is provided by the TDF Infantry School, although advanced training is done in South Africa. The force is assisted by an air wing with two fixed-wing aircraft and two helicopters. The ground force equipment is all of South African make and it has been acquired to outfit a light-infantry COIN force.

UGANDA

THE Ugandan military is composed of a single ground service, the National Resistance Army (NRA), that has about 10,000 personnel. Uganda is still rebuilding its military, which suffered greatly during the troubled period of 1971-87. The NRA is still mostly a light-infantry force, with many younger personnel former insurgents who lack formal military as well as civil education.

The force is organized into six brigades and an unspecified number of independent battalions. While the NRA has an aviation wing, its 13 aircraft include only two combat helicopters and 26 support helicopters, limiting their use in the NRA's primary counter-insurgency mission against still-active insurgencies in the north. Extremely poor domestic economic conditions make military employment attractive and terms of service thus remain voluntary.

EQUIPMENT

Armour:
BTR-60 & OT-64 APCs
Anti-Armour:
AT-3 Sagger ATGW
Artillery:
76mm M1942 gun
122mm M1938 H
Air-Defence:
23mm ZU-23 & 40mm Bofors L/60 AAGs
SA-7 SAM

Below: The Amin years and the civil war killed thousands and created a generation of child soldiers such as this boy seen here.

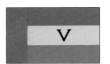

VENDA

THE Venda Defence Force (VDF) is the newest of the Homeland defence forces. It is a small (1,500) ground force that consists of infantry supported by an air wing of three helicopters. Major units include two infantry battalions, and an engineer troop. Personnel for the force, established in 1979, were drawn from the South African Army's 112th Battalion, which was eventually transferred in its entirety to Venda in 1981.

The VDF is trained and equipped by South Africa, and South African Army personnel are seconded as officers pending the training of qualified VDF officers. All VDF equipment is of South African manufacture, with the principal ground force item being a number of Buffel APCs.

ZAIRE

ZAMBIA

ZIMBABWE

THE Zairian Army consists of a general staff, schools, and field units. Army headquarters is in Kinshasa, the capital, with units deployed in nine military regions. Major field units include two divisions and seven brigades (three infantry, two airborne, one armoured, and one commando). Divisions include a regular infantry division, the Kamanyola Division, based at Kolwezi in Shaba Region, and the élite Special Presidential Division (DSP) based in Kinshasa with the mission of protecting the president and the régime. The rapid reaction force for the régime is the 31st Parachute Brigade, with units at Kinshasa as well as at Kamina Base (BAKI) in Shaba. Other important units are the 1st Armoured Brigade at Mbanza-Ngungu in Bas-Zaire and the 41st Commando Brigade located at Kisangani in Haut-Zaire. The army has approximately 22,000 personnel; about half of them are deployed in Shaba region.

Plagued by shortages of funds, Zaire relies on many nations for military support. Providers of equipment and training include the US, Belgium, France, China, and Israel. The army is also hampered by ineffective logistics, pervasive corruption, and political control. Morale is often poor and pay late and inadequate, with promotions and appointments subject to patronage. However, most personnel are well-trained by African standards and it has the potential, free from political manipulation, to be a professional and effective force.

Military doctrine and tactics generally reflect those of Belgium, France, and Israel, which provide the bulk of training input, and unit structures resemble NATO equivalents. Some units were deployed to Chad in the 1980s, and in 1984 and 1985 they successfully fought insurgent attacks at Moba, eastern Zaire. Two battalions of troops were sent to assist Rwandan government forces to repel an invasion by exiles in 1990.

EQUIPMENT

Armour:
Type 62 MBT
AML-60/-90 armoured cars
M113, YW-531, & M3 APCs
Anti-Armour:
57mm M18, 75mm M20, & 106mm M40
RCLs
Artillery:
85mm Type 56, 122mm Type 60, &
130mm Type 59 guns
75mm M116, 122mm M1938 & D-30 Hs
107mm Type 63 MRL
Air-Defence:
12.7mm, 14.5mm, & 40mm Bofors L/60
AAGs

Right: Troops in   old Mauser 98K rifles
Kinshasha armed with   hold back the crowds.

ZAMBIA'S relatively small army (15,000) has long been a client-state of the Eastern bloc and China.

The primary mission of the Zambian Army is territorial defence and internal security, especially in the often-troubled but economically vital Copperbelt area bordering Zaire. Terms of service are totally voluntary.

The Zambian Army is built around an armoured regiment that includes an armoured recce battalion, and six infantry battalions.

Three reserve infantry battalions back up the small force, and support is provided by three artillery battalions, two air-defence artillery batteries, and an engineer battalion.

Recent popular unrest due to social and economic conditions saw the army used to control order. Its loyalty was in doubt at one stage with rumours of a coup.

EQUIPMENT

Armour:
T-54/-55 & Type 59 MBTs
PT-76 light tanks
BRDM-1 & -2 armoured cars
BTR-60 APC
Anti-Armour:
75mm M20 & 84mm Carl Gustav RCLs
AT-3 Sagger ATGW
Artillery:
76mm M1942 & 130mm M46 guns
105mm M56 & 122mm D-30 Hs
122mm BM-21 MRL
Air-Defence:
20mm M55, 37mm M1939, 57mm S-60, &
85mm KS-12 AAGs

THE Zimbabwe National Army (ZNA) has 47,000 personnel. It is built around seven brigades, including a Presidential Guard Brigade and an armoured regiment. Other units include 26 manoeuvre battalions (three Presidential Guard, one mechanized, one commando, two paratroop, one mounted, and 18 infantry). Support units include an artillery regiment that includes two air-defence batteries, and an engineer support regiment. The force is maintained partly through conscription.

The ZNA is characterized by a number of quality units as well as an overall high-quality of personnel. This is due to an emphasis on training that reflects British military assistance in the 1980s, as well as the ZNA's once heavy involvement in Mozambique's insurgent war, maintaining the Beira rail and road corridor that is landlocked Zimbabwe's main trade lifeline.

EQUIPMENT

Armour:
T-54, Type 59 & 62 MBTs
Eland & EE-9 Cascavel armoured cars
UR-416, Crocodile, & YW-531 APCs
Anti-Armour:
107mm RCL
Artillery:
76mm M1942, 25-pdr (88mm), 105mm
Light & 122mm Type 60 guns
107mm Type 63 MRL
Air-Defence:
14.5 ZPU-1, -2, & -4, 23mm ZU-23-2, &
37mm M1939 AAGs
SA-7 SAM

Index

Abbreviations conform to those in the list on page 7. Illustrations are indexed in italics.